Also by Ruth Brandon

Singer and the Sewing Machine: A Capitalist Romance

The Dollar Princesses

The Dollar Princesses

Sagas of Upward Nobility, 1870-1914

Ruth Brandon

Alfred A. Knopf, Inc.
New York
1980

305. 52

B

This Is a Borzoi Book

Published by Alfred A. Knopf, Inc.

Library of Congress Cataloging in Publication Data

Brandon, Ruth.   The dollar princesses.

Bibliography: p.
1. Millionairesses—United States—Biography.
2. Upper classes—United States.
3. Wives—Biography. I. Title.
HQ1412.B73   1980   305.5'2   80-7627
ISBN 0-394-50403-8

Manufactured in the United States of America

First Edition

C, 2

Contents

Illustrations

Illustrations follow page 118.

Acknowledgements

Of the large number of people who helped me in the writing of this book, I should like most particularly to thank: Larry Borenstein, Christie Davies, Victoria Glendinning, Richard Kenin, Nigel Nicolson, Alain Ollivier, Frank Regas, Al and Diana Rose and Diana Vincent-Daviss. I am also most grateful to the helpful staffs of the New York Public Library, the New-York Historical Society Library, the Louisiana State Historical Society Library and the London Library.

'We are the dollar princesses'

'We are the dollar princesses' ran a line in a popular song of the Edwardian era. There was no need to explain who such ladies might be: everyone knew. The dollar princesses were a commonplace of European life. By the time the Great War broke out, scarcely a family existed in the high society of Europe which could not boast, or was not obliged to admit to, at least one American bride amid the branches of its family tree.

The 1915 edition of *Titled Americans*, a publication produced and revised annually in New York, listed no less than 454 American women who had married into the European aristocracy. 'The United States is very closely cemented to both England and France by international marriages, while Italy comes ahead of Germany in the American woman's preference,' it stated. There were by that time 42 American princesses, 17 American duchesses, 19 viscountesses, 33 marchionesses, 46 ladies, wives of knights or baronets, 64 baronesses and a positive glut of countesses – 136 of them. Most lived in either London or Paris, but among the farther-flung there were eight in Petrograd, three in Budapest, three in Madrid and two in Warsaw; we may imagine that these scattered sisters sought each other's company with a certain eagerness. No such comradely diversions were available to those who dwelt in splendid isolation in such cities as Palermo, Moscow, Tokyo and Belgrade, each of which boasted one lonely dollar princess.

This transatlantic traffic – the triumphant culmination, as it might be seen, of the story of those immigrants who had left Europe poor and unregarded in order to make a new start in the barbarous New World, and who now in the persons of their daughters, granddaughters or great-granddaughters so satisfactorily returned – was, by the end of the nineteenth century, no new thing. In 1825, for example, Mary Caton, granddaughter of Charles Carroll of Carrollton, then the last survivor of the signers of the Declaration of Independence, married the Marquis of Wellesley, Viceroy of Ireland. Thus on 4 July two weeks later Bishop England of South Carolina was enabled to toast Carroll in the following highly satisfactory words: 'To Charles Carroll of Carrollton: in the land from which his grandfather fled in terror his granddaughter now reigns a queen.'[1]

But a comparison of the marriage of this first American vicereine with that of the second, Mary Leiter, who married Lord Curzon seventy years later and went with him to rule over India, will show how much things had changed in the course of those seventy years. The society from which Mary Caton sprang was relatively simple and restricted, and in spite of the Declaration of Independence which her grandfather had signed, it was still very European in tone. Moreover, it was not associated with great riches. Life at Carrollton was a simple country life, very pleasant but not at all opulent. Mary Caton married Lord Wellesley because he fell in love with her, an event which flattered and delighted her and of which, being a widow (she had been Mrs Patterson) she was able to take advantage. They met by chance; it was not a marriage anyone had particularly sought after; and Mary Caton brought Lord Wellesley no special tangible benefits other than her beauty and her charming disposition.

How different was the affair of Mary Leiter and Lord Curzon! Miss Leiter's America was not that of the charming Caton sisters. The difference was epitomized in the career of her father, Levi Leiter. The Leiters, too, were old American stock, Mennonites who had emigrated from Switzerland to Pennsylvania in the early eighteenth century. Later on, Levi Leiter's branch of the family moved south to Leitersburg, Maryland, whence Levi, who could see no prospects in that sleepy country area, moved west to Ohio. Here he worked for a year in a store, and then moved on further, to Chicago, where he arrived in 1854.

If the East Coast was still half-European, Chicago was all-

American. It was the frontier: not twenty years earlier it had been
a settlement in a swamp, the settlers behind their stockade
periodically repulsing the marauding Potawatomies. But by 1850
the railroad had arrived – and the railroad made Chicago. It
became the trade and communications centre of a continent, and
that astute merchant Levi Leiter, in partnership with Marshall
Field, made his pile. And what a pile! Chicago fortunes were
the biggest – everything about Chicago, the fastest-expanding
city in the Union, was the biggest – and Levi Leiter's was one of
the biggest of all. His wife and three daughters took their place
in Chicago society, visiting and being visited by the wives and
daughters of other wealthy merchants in the elaborate dream
palaces that were now so rapidly rising from the swamp.

It was an unlikely setting for a future vicereine, and so the
Leiters thought. Accordingly they upped and went to Washington, a more suitable setting for the launch of the daughters. For
if they could not foresee nor stipulate an actual viceroy, they
certainly recognized—as did the Misses Leiter – that something
of the sort was not merely a possible but a likely match for girls
with the looks and fortune of Mary and her sisters. By now the
thing was so usual as almost to be the rule rather than the exception. 'There appeared to be a constant danger of marrying the
American girl; it was something one had to reckon with, like the
railway, the telegraph, the discovery of dynamite, the Chassepot
rifle, the Socialistic spirit; it was one of the complications of
modern life,' mused Henry James's Count Otto Vogelstein on
the boat to America.[2] Chance was not an especially large element
in the match between Mary Leiter and Lord Curzon.

The frequency with which such matches were now taking place
was formally recognized in the publication already referred to –
*Titled Americans: A list of American ladies who have married
foreigners of rank*, 'annually revised – issued quarterly. Illus-
trated with armorial bearings. Subscription price, $1.00 per year.'
This publication, besides giving all relevant details of those who
had already made their catch – 'Lady Wolseley – Miss Anita
Theresa Murphy, d. of late Daniel T. Murphy Esq. of San
Francisco, b. 1865, m. 1883 to Sir Charles Michael Wolseley,
Staffordshire, 9th Baronet, b. 1846, J.P.; Deputy Lieutenant for
Staffordshire; seat Wolseley Hall, Rugeley, Staffordshire;

creation of title, 1628; family traceable to 1281' (the family of
Lady Lister-Kaye, *née* Natica Yznaga del Valle, was alleged to be
descended from 'Sir Kaye, an ancient Briton, one of the Knights
of the Round Table') – also provided information perhaps of
more interest to ladies such as Mrs Leiter, with three daughters
to dispose of. It included: 'A carefully compiled List of Peers
Who are Supposed to be eager to lay their coronets and incidentally their hearts, at the feet of the all-conquering American Girl.'
The list in 1890 began with 'the Right Hon. John Abercrombie'
('Eldest son and heir to Lord Abercrombie; 48 years old;
educated at Harrow; formerly captain of the Rifle Brigade;
divorced from Baroness von Heidenstam of Sweden; has no
children; entailed estates amount to 16,000 acres yielding an
income of $75,000. Family seats: three castles in Scotland') and
ended with the Duc d'Uzès ('Is in his twentieth year, exceedingly
wealthy and holds the title of Premier Duke of France. The Duke
owns the whole of the town of Uzès in the valley of the Rhône.
His mother is the heiress of the celebrated Veuve Cliquot, of
champagne fame. Family seat: Chateau d'Uzès, Uzès, Rhône.')
More to the point, prospective fathers-in-law could ascertain
that 'the Earl of Ava's entailed estates do not, owing to
mortgages, yield their nominal income of $100,000.' For further
instruction in the arcana of rank, interested parties could turn
to the press. 'Dukes are the loftiest kind of noblemen in England,'
explained one New York newspaper in 1886. 'There are only
twenty-seven of them in the whole United Kingdom. Of these
there are only two available for matrimonial purposes. These
are the Dukes of Manchester and Roxburghe. The Duke of
Hamilton is already spoken for, the Duke of Norfolk is an old
widower, and the Duke of Leinster only eleven years old.'[3]

Cynical such listings and comments might be, but there is no
reason to suppose that their authors' tongues reached very far
into their cheeks. They merely exhibit that curious and almost
endearing lack of reticence with which the American press commented on social life. Nothing was tacit; Americans did not go
in for the unspoken. If an American father was to sink his daughter
and a large slice of his capital into some scion of the nobility, he
wished to know what he was getting in return. The com-
mentators were merely realistic: as it happened, both the Duke

of Manchester and the Duke of Roxburghe married American girls.

The principle underlying these transatlantic unions was clear to all. When the Duke of Sutherland visited New York *The World* carolled: 'Attention, heiresses, what will you bid?'[4] The union between Lord Curzon and Mary Leiter later became one of impassioned mutual devotion, but it is inconceivable that it would have taken place had Mr Leiter not possessed the means and the willingness to underwrite Lord Curzon's vaulting political ambitions.

Both sides were almost distressingly open about the financial basis of such affairs. In February 1901, an advertisement appeared in the *Daily Telegraph* addressed to the lawyers or business representatives of heiresses:

An English Peer of very old title is desirous of marrying at once a very wealthy lady; her age and looks are immaterial, but her character must be irreproachable; she must be a widow or spinster – not a divorcee. If among your clients you know such a lady, who is willing to purchase the rank of a peeress for £25,000 sterling, paid in cash to her future husband, and who has sufficient wealth besides to keep up the rank of a peeress, I shall be pleased if you will communicate with me in the first instance by letter when a meeting can be arranged in your office. I beg you to keep this confidential. The peer will pay handsomely for the introduction when it is arranged.

In neat complement, a broker giving a New Orleans address advertised: 'Will any dukes, marquesses, earls or other noblemen desirous of meeting, for the purpose of marriage, young beautiful *and* rich American heiresses communicate with.... Absolute discretion guaranteed.' Belles at White Sulphur Springs, Virginia, Cleveland, Ohio and Newport, Rhode Island, persuaded their indulgent papas that fair exchange was no robbery: if a fabulous title was to be had for the underpinning of a fabulously broke estate, was this not an excellent way of disposing of a spare hundred thousand or two? The sons-in-law also recognized the benefits of the arrangement. 'Love to Orme and Dick, yours affectionately, Mungo,' wrote the Honourable Michael Herbert to Richard T. Wilson. 'P.S. Will you send us another letter of credit for £2,000 made out to Hon. Michael Herbert and Mrs L.B. Herbert.' But even such a prospect could not reconcile the

Duke of Manchester to his fate when his son and heir, the scoundrelly Viscount Mandeville, proposed to marry the young and beautiful Consuelo Yznaga. The Duke was said to have been almost heartbroken at the thought of 'a little American savage' becoming his daughter-in-law. (This was in 1874, and this Viscount Mandeville was to be the father of the Duke of Manchester referred to in *Titled Americans*.)

'For a Bostonian nymph to reject an English duke is an adventure only less stirring, I should say, than for an English duke to be rejected by a Boston nymph,' wrote Henry James, the literary chronicler (with Edith Wharton) of such adventures. It is doubtful if such a scenario was often played out in real life: even if the girl was unwilling she had usually (as we shall see) to reckon with her mother's ambition as well as her own. And if she rejected the duke, it was usually because there was a convenient prince in the offing. Nevertheless the adventure was there: how could it not be when such disparate worlds, such different hopes and expectations, such crude ambitions, were brought together in abrupt and awkward union?

2

Artificial High Societies

MISS BOSTON: Good manners are everything.
MISS CHICAGO: That's what I tell pa, but he will persist in using his fingers, instead of a knife, to eat his pie with.
Town Topics, July 1895

Such was the East Coast opinion of the rude Midwest; and the consuming nightmare of those who were immersed in polite East Coast society was that all – from the European point of view, the standpoint of established social mores – might be tarred with the Chicago brush. For what, to the European, could be more *outré* than the notion of America, that broad, wild continent, repository for the dregs of the Old World, filled with copper, railroads, and howling savages? 'Here is a wild Indian – a Shoshone – just riding up to the door of my tent and silently watching me ...' wrote Henry Adams from Wyoming Territory, confirming this view. 'There are quantities about here, but luckily a friendly tribe. Among the Sioux I should not feel quite so comfortable.... Out here the Indians are still a real thing and take scalps when they get a chance. The whites are afraid of them and hate them with a bitter hatred, but the government tries to maintain the peace....'[1] As late as 1893 Paul Bourget, latest in a long line of curious Europeans, felt the place strange enough to undertake a voyage of discovery in order to try and explain it and its denizens to himself and his fellow Old-Worlders. 'How it draws me – that New World,' he said; and he called his book *Outre-Mer*, a title redolent of the strange and the unknown.

Such a place might have many advantages – gold and freedom

being only two – but they were not social advantages. Considering who peopled America – to say nothing of the fact that the principle upon which the place was founded was that 'all men are created equal' – the notion that snobberies and social distinctions might be found there was laughable.

So the European might reason. But such reasoning did not take into account some of the most essential differences in social attitudes between the Old World and the New. Europeans were used to an organic, encrusted society in which the accretions of ages were occasionally displaced by a more or less convulsive upheaval, but where – like the layers of ash settling over Pompeii – the centre of disturbance was usually neutralized by the simple process of being embedded amid the re-grouped components of the *status quo ante*. They could naturally not see how there could be any social differences amid the generalized raw newness of America.

But this was to reckon without American enterprise. Americans had formed a new society, unlike anything which had existed before. Why should they not, then, form societies within that society, if they felt so inclined? For of course, American society was not uniform, any more than that of Europe. It was a heap; and those who were at the top of the heap, for whatever reason, were naturally anxious that others should be aware of this. They were also anxious to make it clear that the heap was strictly pyramidal in shape. It was not easy to get where they had got, and the opportunity was not one which might be afforded to just anyone. And because these stratifications were more or less artificially imposed – insisted upon from the top, as it were, rather than supported upon a firm base of assorted retainers – they were stressed with a lack of subtlety which might have seemed not so much extraordinary as unnecessary to a European.

Take, for example, one of the oldest-established of these stratifications – that of New Orleans, the Creole city famous for its beauty, its food, its cultural traditions – and for the culmination of its social year: the carnival of Mardi Gras.

What festivity could be more spontaneous, more freely participated in, more for and of the people than Mardi Gras? On this day of all days, all are equal. Behind the disguise of the mask and the fancy dress, what can it matter who is who? So might reason the European, used to the social discretions, the un-spoken usages, the countless gauze curtains which so indistinctly and gradually reveal nuances of relationships and obligations in the Old World.

But such reasoning did not do here. For in America *things were what they seemed* – however much they might smack of artifice. Those kings and queens, those dukes, maskers and maids of honour, were not – in their own eyes – mere puppet royalty; their finery was not – for them – any mere mockery, assumed for a day, forgotten for the rest of the year. On the contrary, such positions were deeply coveted, grimly and insistently fought for. To be king or queen of the right float – that is, the float of one of the more exclusive 'krewes' or secret societies – was, and is, to be acknowledged as one of the social leaders of New Orleans. And in April, almost as soon as the processions and rejoicing are finished, each krewe will get down to the organiza-tion of next year's carnival, the selection of a theme, the designing of the float and the costumes – and the choosing of the royalty, who will receive the eagerly awaited accolade in the form of a scroll of parchment brought to the house on Christmas Day.

The 'krewes' of New Orleans are closed clubs, and member-ship rarely exceeds 200: in some, membership is actually willed to a relative or friend. Each krewe represents a particular social group in the city, and some are and were more exclusive and sought-after than others. It is through the krewes – Rex, Comus, Momus, Proteus and the fancifully titled rest – that social distinc-tions became elaborated and enshrined in the carnival.

If the carnival, with its frivolity, its maskers, disguises, trinkets, floats, flambeaux and balls seems somehow un-American – more the kind of thing one might expect to find in the West Indies or Latin America – that is because its origins are of course not American, or at any rate not WASP. New Orleans was a French Catholic city, and Mardi Gras was a Creole festival – the Creoles being the descendants of the original French and Spanish settlers. In its early days, while the city was still a French possession before the Louisiana Purchase of 1803, Mardi Gras was not elaborately organized. With the coming of the Americans, the first traces of organized exclusivity began, because the Creoles, conscious of their cultural heritage and their often aristocratic descent, bitterly resented the intruding Americans. The Americans, of course, in their turn disliked the licence and frivolity of Mardi Gras, and took the opportunity, after Aaron Burr's ill-fated attempt on the city, to ban the whole affair as offering too much opportunity to potentially subversive elements. It was restarted only in 1827; and now the Americans, too, joined in, hiding their guilt behind their masks. The Creoles shrank more and more into their own community. Everyone could join in the gaieties of the processions, but invitations to the balls which followed them were harder to obtain. There were, of course, non-exclusive balls which might, like the quadroon balls, be infinitely more entertaining than the select ones; but, human nature being what it is, people wanted to go to those balls to which they were ostentatiously *not* invited. Americans were not invited to Creole balls. They therefore took the obvious step, and began to organize their own processions and their own balls. If the Creoles could be exclusive, so could they. If the Creoles could set themselves up as an aristocracy, so too could they. Even if they had no particle to their names, they could be kings, queens, dukes, just as well as the Creoles. Kings and queens of what? Why, kings and queens of the krewes, of course.

So the titles of king, queen, and maid-of-honour in the more sought-after krewes became badges of social acceptance. A complicated etiquette developed for the balls, a kind of 'mock revival of monarchic rule'. (Not always so mock, in the eyes of participants: the Duke and Duchess of Windsor, visiting the Carnival, deferred to Rex and his queen). At each ball, the king and queen of the particular krewe are the most important persons present; then come the dukes and maids of honour; then the 'nobles of the city' – the maskers on the float – and last of all the spectators at the ball, who represent the king's 'subjects'. An invitation to a ball is by no means a guarantee that you will dance once you get there. Most balls begin with a tableau; this is followed by the grand march of the king, queen and their court. Then come the 'call-outs'. At each ball, the season's debutantes, and other young women considered worthy of the honour, will have received 'call-out cards' with their invitations, and they are called out by the maskers for dancing. Then there may be some general dancing; and at midnight the court will depart to continue their party elsewhere.

When 'Kingfish' Huey Long came to power in Louisiana he disapproved heartily of Mardi Gras. His slogan, 'Every Man a King', was patently contradicted by the Carnival. For by then the snobberies which had developed were immense. King of the Carnival is Rex, of the krewe of that name, and his queen is queen of Carnival, a position which money cannot buy. The other most exclusive krewe is Comus. These two courts meet at the Comus ball. Robert Tallant tells the story of how a very powerful and influential businessman, a member of Rex, decided that his daughter was to be queen of Carnival. If she was not, he warned the selection committee that he would do his best to break every man who stood in his way – a threat which he was in a position to enforce. What was to be done? The girl's family background was not considered worthy of this honour, and she was not among those who were in the running for queen, but her father was undeniably powerful. Rex bowed to *force majeure*. Comus, however, did not. When the news reached Comus's queen, she flatly refused to meet the unworthy queen of Rex. A fine form of retribution was worked out. Comus's queen withdrew, and 'emissaries went into a department store and located a salesgirl of "good family" but no money, who consented to be the queen of Comus. It was she the mate of Rex met at the Comus Ball, and ever since New Orleans society has recited with great glee the story of when the young woman who was Queen of the Carnival had to bow to a "shopgirl".'[2]

It may be thought that the deep South presented a particularly ripe seedbed for the creation and development of snobbish forms. After all, many of its original inhabitants had been genuine aristocrats – though more than one commoner tried to pass himself off as a member of a grander family than his own. It is said that Bienville himself, founder of New Orleans, was the son of an ambitious father who had his children christened with the titles of great families as part of their names, as a social boost. But such claims generally had to be proved. In the early days of the colony, the authorities were so particular about such matters that 'it became a routine thing for families to bring to French America with them their family records'.[3] Those who had thus proved themselves naturally discouraged attempts at familiarity by lesser mortals. Then too the slavery system preserved a leisured class throughout the South, who had time to think about these things. At the same time the existence of slave labour discouraged the influx of those vulgar and pushing poor European immigrants which threatened to overwhelm the better families in the North (or so the pitying southerners considered).

But in fact such snobberies were by no means confined to the South. On the contrary, by the last quarter of the nineteenth century, the United States was as riddled with the consciousness of petty social distinctions as any European nation. Such considerations had penetrated even to Chicago, that legendary centre of social savagery. 'There are social jealousies ... as keen between pork-butchers and hotel-keepers as between dukes and princes of the blood,' reported W.T. Stead, who visited Chicago in 1894, adding (no doubt to the fury of such Chicago social luminaries as Mrs Potter Palmer, the hotel-keeper's wife, and Mrs Ogden Armour, the pork-butcher's): 'It is sad to see the same snobbery and "tuft-hunting" which have been the laughing-stock of all sensible men in aristocratic Europe reproducing themselves in a new society, where the distinction between those who are in the first file and those who are in the last is almost indistinguishable to the uninstructed eye of the casual observer.'[4]

What was true of Chicago was true of virtually every other city in the Union. In each the criterion for entry into the inner circle was slightly different. In Chicago, none other being available, it was purely and simply cash. 'When you have got money and plenty of it you have arrived, and you cannot get any higher except by getting more money,' said Stead; adding that: 'if you have no taste for piling up a monstrous pedestal of dollars, there is singularly little to excite interest.' Those who required more complex criteria, with the more complex life that went with them, might try their luck elsewhere. In Boston it was a question of whom you knew; in New York, not just of how much you were worth, but how long you had had it; in Philadelphia, of who your parents were.[5]

But despite this evidently ineradicable predisposition of people all over America not to be equal if they could possibly avoid it – that is, if they possessed the means in some way to establish themselves on top of the social heap – it is perhaps no accident that the determined organizer of the most rigid of these, so to speak, artificial aristocracies, Ward McAllister, came originally from the South. Observed one southerner: 'When the aristocracy of the North East and the Middle West came to a realization of what a powerful group this new immigrant element formed, and that politics were being taken out of the hands – not partially but completely – of the better element, who had controlled the welfare of the country since colonial days, they ... felt that family prestige at least could be preserved by exclusiveness....'[6] It was McAllister, whose family came from Georgia, who formulated the rules by which this exclusiveness was to be maintained.

By no means all members of the McAllister family were as concerned with social matters as Ward: his brother Hall, who went to San Francisco during the Gold Rush in 1849 and set up as a lawyer there, had a motto: 'Ten millions or nothing.' But young Ward travelled widely in Europe in his youth, and this experience of the civilization of the Old World left a profound impression upon him. 'It was [at the Grand Duke of Tuscany's, in the Pitti Palace] that I first learned what a ball supper should be,' he later wistfully recounted; and one gets the impression that he fully shared the opinion of the then American Minister in Rome: 'I have the greatest admiration for my countrymen; they are enterprising, money getting, in fact a wonderful nation, but there is not a gentleman among them.'[7] It was not that he was, like many Americans who were domiciled in Europe, so pro-European as to be anti-American. On the contrary, he was American enough to reply to the Austrian Minister at Florence, who wanted to know what was the decoration worn by a fellow American: 'Sir, my country is a Republic; if it had been a Monarchy, I would have been the Duke of Pennsylvania. The Order I wear is that of the Cincinnati.' The minister was deeply impressed.[8] Nevertheless, he determined on his return to repair the omission noted by the American Minister in Rome: he would make gentlemen out of his countrymen – some of them.

On his return to America McAllister accumulated a substantial fortune. He was then free to take up what he considered to be his life's work. He came to New York determined to create a society – or at any rate to take in hand such as existed. For something that took itself to be society did exist in New York. Its doyen had once been old Isaac Brown, sexton of Grace Church, who knew everything about everybody. He would stand in a ballroom muttering comments: 'Old family, good old stock,' or, 'He's a new man; he had better mind his p's and q's or I will trip him up. Ah, here comes a young fellow who intends to dance his way into society. Here comes a handsome boy, the ladies are crazy about him', and so forth.[9]

But one old man does not constitute society – not to McAllister's way of thinking. He had his own very definite notions as to what, ideally, society should be. Its first attribute, as he saw it, was exclusiveness; and the first necessity, in a place like New York, to devise rules which would dictate who was to be kept out. Mrs Potter Palmer, with typical Chicago directness, kept people out in the simplest possible way: there were no handles on the outside of her doors, so that admission might only be obtained at the discretion of those within. New York, however, needed a slightly subtler principle.

In Europe, and in French New Orleans, such a principle existed naturally. 'Society' was a cousinship; everyone knew everyone else and almost all were in some way related. To some extent this also applied in New York. There were the old Dutch families, the patroons, whose distinction lay in the fact that they had been there longest; but they were not particularly distinguished in any other way, and were a plodding lot compared with the stylish and civilized Creoles. 'Fashionable parties,' wrote Washington Irving of them, 'were generally confined to the higher classes, or noblesse, that is to say, such as kept their own cows, and drove their own wagons. The company commonly assembled at three o'clock and went away about six, unless it was in winter time, when the fashionable hours were a little earlier, that the ladies might get home before dark.'[10] Then there was money; old money, chiefly acquired as a result of the enormous increase in New York real estate values; and new money, made in some form of business. If it was obvious that society – the society to be – could not be confined to the patroons, it was equally apparent that not all the money could be included. Cash might provide an automatic open sesame in Chicago, but Chicago was not New York – and New York must be seen to be more exigent than Chicago.

McAllister solved his problem by dividing potential socialites into two groups: nobs and swells. Nobs were those who had, so to speak, been born with the spoon of social desirability in their mouth; swells had to buy it. 'A nob can be a swell if he chooses, that is to say if he will spend the money; but for his social existence this is unnecessary. A nob is like a poet – *nascitur, non fit*; not so a swell – he creates himself.'[11]

Having established his categories, McAllister set about creating a social framework from which all those who did not qualify might be excluded. He did this by creating, in 1872, the Patriarchs – 'the leading representative men of the city, who had the right to create and lead society'. In order to make his selection, McAllister formed an executive committee of three 'who could make the best analysis of men; who knew their past as well as their present, and could foresee their future'. The committee met daily at McAllister's house, and got down to the serious task of making a list of suitable names.

The Patriarchs were to be limited to twenty-five in number, and they and only they would have the right to issue invitations to the Patriarchs' balls – the guest list of which could thus be taken to define who was included in society. Each Patriarch could invite four ladies and five gentlemen (including himself) to each ball; guests would also include any distinguished strangers who happened to be in town, up to fifty in number. 'The object we had in view,' wrote McAllister, 'was to make these balls thoroughly representative; to embrace the old Colonial New Yorkers, our adopted citizens, and men whose ability and integrity had won the esteem of the community, and who formed an important element in Society. We wanted the money power, but not in any way to be controlled by it. Patriarchs were chosen solely for their fitness; on each of them promising to invite to each ball only such people as would do credit to the ball.' He added: 'We knew ... that the whole secret of the success of these Patriarch Balls lay in ... making it extremely difficult to obtain an invitation to them, and to make such invitations of great value.'[12]

The Patriarchs' balls were a wild success. All aspired; few

were chosen. Everyone was as aware of who had been omitted from the guest list as of who had achieved an invitation. If the ruse employed by two of Edith Wharton's 'buccaneers' to capture the coveted invitation – passing themselves off as the sisters of an English lord just engaged to a friend of theirs – was never actually practised in real life there were many who would not have hesitated to do such a thing had the opportunity presented itself. But had it all become too exclusive? The strict limits on numbers at the balls meant that it was impossible to invite all the daughters of even the most desirable people. What was to be done? Rather than bend his original rules, McAllister decided to introduce the Junior Patriarchs – otherwise known as the Family Circle Dancing Classes, or FCDCs. Immediately, he found himself besieged by anxious mothers eager to have their daughters attend the dancing classes. They could perhaps accept that they themselves might never make it into society, but why should they submit to the same fate on behalf of their daughters? Besides, once a daughter was accepted, might she not pave a way in for her mamma? A single generation, after all, meant a lot in the New World. 'How many of the swellest of the swell were anything at all twenty years ago – fifteen years even?' asked *Town Topics* in 1877. 'Where were the Vanderbilts, socially, even five years ago? The Astors had just fifteen years the social start.'

McAllister was entirely sympathetic to these anguished parents. Naturally everyone would wish to enter the society he was so assiduously nurturing, and who but he held the key – who else should be the arbiter? He devoted his mornings to the reception of aspiring mothers. Women entirely unknown to him would visit his house, their sole words of introduction being, 'Kind sir, I have a daughter'. At which 'cabalistic' formula McAllister would spring up, bow to the ground, and say: 'My dear madam, say no more, you have my sympathy; we are in accord; no introduction is necessary; you have a daughter, and want her to go to the FCDCs. I will do all in my power to accomplish this for you; but my dear lady, please understand that in all matters concerning these little dances I must consult the powers that be. I am their humble servant; I must take orders from them.' At which he would stand back in delighted recognition of how false these words were – for he and he alone held the power of admission.

He noted that 'the family always went back to King John, or in some cases to William the Conqueror' – an assertion which he met with the lofty reply that in his opinion four generations of gentlemen make as good and true a gentleman as forty; it did not do to start counting generations too closely in New York. Even when the FCDC list was full, this still did not stop the daily stream of imploring mammas. They were probably the same ones who, when the Tuxedo Club was opened in 1884 on the same consciously exclusive and selective lines by the 'cold and exacting' Pierre Lorillard, 'pulled every string they could muster in order to be included. Failing, they wept bitterly. Men almost broke their necks in an attempt to get an entering wedge into what was tantamount to a closed circle.'[13]

What – one may wonder – was the fatal attraction exercised by these social arrangements? What was it about the policy of deliberate exclusion that produced this pavlovian effect upon the excluded? What was so much better about the Patriarchs' balls than any other balls, the Tuxedo Club than any other? What was so desirable about the life of McAllister's chosen few?

It seems that the pleasure was almost purely that of being included – of which no small part was the consciousness of excluding others. Any other pleasure appears to have been decidedly incidental to the main point of the proceedings. For example, McAllister recounts that he organized a series of little informal luncheon parties at the fashionable summer resort of Newport, Rhode Island. And what is the first thing he says about them? That they were 'the stepping-stones to our best New York society'.[14] That was why people clamoured to come to them – not because they were fun. Fun? That rigid protocol, that stern consciousness of being of the elect – social equivalents of New England Calvinism – were not conducive to fun. Indeed, while outsiders fought for an entry, members of the elect – some of the younger ones, at least – were chafing at their fate. 'To take a meal with them was to look dullness squarely in the eye – oh, the barbaric insularity of their clannish dialogue, their oafish jokes and silences!' wrote Blanche Oelrichs, a daughter of one of society's leaders, Mrs Herman Oelrichs, of lunch parties with her contemporaries. Discussion in those circles centred mainly upon such topics as whether the cotillion favours at Mrs Stuyvesant Fish's next ball were to be of silver or gold.[15] Young Cornelius Vanderbilt, son of Grace Wilson Vanderbilt, *the* Mrs Vanderbilt of her day, could never understand 'why we should spend every glorious summer afternoon at Newport showering the colony with our calling cards when we had already nodded and spoken to our friends several times since breakfast.... How vividly I can recall the tedium of those occasions when, proceeding at a snail's pace in a shiny black victoria and clutching our hateful card cases in spotless white gloves, we accompanied Mother on this sacred ritual.'[16]

No; fun was not in question. The fact of being included in the party was enough in itself. Once one had conferred the supreme accolade of sending an invitation card, what more was needed? 'Nothing was done for the guests' entertainment beyond providing them with a vast amount of elaborate food, often served on silver or silver-gilt plates, and with many varieties of wine.... One was rarely amused by one's neighbour.... After dinner the men retired to the smoking-room in true Anglo-Saxon style, and stayed there till it was time to go home,' grumbled Margaret Terry Chanler, who had been brought up in the altogether more light-hearted atmosphere of Italy.[17] Mrs Chanler was distressed not only by the tedium but by the extraordinary rigidity of American society, exemplified for her one evening in Rome by the refusal of a young man from Boston to be introduced to two young ladies from the same city who happened to find themselves at the reception because 'they did not move in the same society in their native Boston'. Certainly the company was not enlivened by the distinguished writers, painters and actors who graced the most distinguished gatherings in Europe. 'My Uncle and Aunt, with all their fondness for the theatre, would never invite actors to their house. Some of the most distinguished brought letters, but not even the high standing of the Bartletts, McCreadys and Kembles would induce them to relax their rule,' recalled one Philadelphia lady.[18] It was the rigidity of insecurity, the necessity of sticking to rules arbitrarily superimposed; but that did not make it more amusing.

Not all socialites were content with this stuffiness and lack of spontaneity. Mrs Stuyvesant Fish was one of New York's leading matrons, one of the arbiters, with Mrs Oelrichs and Mrs Astor, of who was 'in' and who never would be; but Mrs Fish, a woman of spirit, nevertheless found herself intolerably bored. She therefore decided to try a little reform from within. Henceforth no dinner at Mrs Fish's was to last longer than fifty minutes. The number of courses was not altered, but their duration was. Woe betide the guest who let his fork rest on his plate before he had finished: instantly the dish was whipped from in front of him, to be replaced by another. Occasionally Mrs Fish, aided by her court jester Harry Lehr, organized outrageous stunts. A lavish tea party would be thrown for her friends' dogs; an ape dressed in uniform would be seated in the place of honour at the dinner table; Lehr in disguise would be passed off as the Tsar of Russia and introduced to the awed assembly in regal style. Staider elements looked upon these exploits with horror and dismissed them as 'the kind of thing which brings society into disrepute'; they were considered to offer altogether too much easy ammunition to the dreaded socialists, to the bomb-wielding anarchists whose dread deeds figured almost daily in the press. But Mrs Fish's protests were strictly confined. Her fifty-minute dinners were as rigidly framed as the Patriarchs' balls; her invitation lists remained as restricted as those of Proteus, Momus or Rex.

And every detail – every movement of each one of those four hundred chosen souls who could be fitted into Mrs Astor's ballroom and who were thus popularly considered to constitute society – was revealed and recorded by the press: Mrs and Miss Harriman are giving a tea party; Mrs Fish will remove to Garrison-on-the-Hudson on Thursday; Mrs W.K. Vanderbilt has gone to Hot Springs for rest and recuperation. One sheet, *Town Topics*, was wholly concerned with such doings; and every newspaper in every town ran its social column. 'A fashionable woman of title from England remarked to me that we were a hundred years behind London, for our best society was so small, every one in it had an individuality,' complacently recorded McAllister. This individuality 'was accorded only to the highest titled people in all England, while here any one in society would have every moment chronicled.... There is no spot in the world where people are more *en évidence*,' he concluded.[19]

This passion for publication was uniquely American, as were the ambiguities connected with it. For was not America the home of democracy, the annihilator of the concept of the nobility? – and yet was there any press in the world more obsessively concerned with the smallest doings of the rich and the titled than the American? 'During my adolescence, *Town Topics* ... played an enormous part in everyone's life,' recalled Blanche Oelrichs. 'Climbing matrons were driven to despair by its jibes; indiscreet young married couples went in terror of its insinuations; hardy financiers whose pile concealed a more than ordinary toll of ruined persons hastened to try and buy off the editor....'[20] Meanwhile, social aspirants could rack their brains over *Town Topics*' weekly social puzzles.

Miss R., of Boston, is visiting young Mrs G. in New York. Mr H., who knows Miss R., and whom Mrs G. has informed that Miss R. is staying with her, having organized a theatre-party with following supper at Delmonico's, writes to Mrs G. asking her husband and herself to chaperone the party, and stating that he cannot invite her friend Miss R., as he had arranged the party in effect before her arrival. Mr H. is a strong business friend of Mr G. What shall Mrs G. do? A: Explain the matter frankly to Miss R., laying especial stress on the point that the party had been arranged before knowledge of her coming. If Miss R. is a sensible girl she will, of course, understand it. Mrs G. should then go to the party.

The public lapped it up – and not only the public. If a barb in *Town Topics* or *The World* drove many a climbing matron to despair, the despair was not such as might have been occasioned by omission of her name from the columns of these publications. If one's social goal was to force an entry into the most exclusive circles, half the satisfaction of achievement would have been lost if one's erstwhile acquaintances had not been able to read all about it. Thus the boundaries of 'society' – whatever society one might be concerned with, in whatever town one happened to live – were kept clearly and rigidly defined, and the doings of the elect were continually and tantalizingly dangled before the noses of those who might wish to join that hallowed group, but had not yet contrived to do so.

Although on the surface it might seem that these intricacies, plots, exclusions and self-consciousnesses, which so much more than scalp-hung Indians characterized, by the last quarter of the nineteenth century, what Europeans viewed (in Henry James's words) as 'the grey American dawn of the situation', in fact contradicted all that America stood for, a closer look will show that this was not at all the case. The rigidly imposed etiquettes of Ward McAllister, posed in characteristic stance at the door of Delmonico's salon on the evening of a grand dinner, instructing each gentleman as he entered which lady he was to take in, the social strivings of Mrs Potter Palmer (who *never* received callers without prior arrangement) and Mrs Ogden Armour, the refusal of Cincinnati merchants to mix with a 'mechanic' whose shop was as large as theirs but who 'assists in making the articles he sells' (as encountered by Mrs Frances Trollope) – all these might seem absurd and pathetic reflections of just those aspects of Europe which Americans repudiated. In fact, however, they were American to the core – as American as the big business which financed them. For were not both deeply imbued with the same essential characteristics – the spirit of competition and the spirit of upward mobility? If the European aristocracies – those grand dukes of Tuscany upon whom Ward McAllister so hopefully modelled his ball suppers – were occasionally disposed to admit hitherto undesirable strangers into their midst, it was in an attempt to salvage as much as possible of the *status quo*. European societies were static and their aristocracies dedicated to keeping them so. But the proudest boast of the New World was its freedom from this dead hand. There was no *status quo*, and the deeply competitive spirit of the denizens of the United States was based upon this assumption.

This competitiveness, this determination always to be on the move upward, was not absent from what might be considered – what certainly was considered by those concerned – the very top. If one was a Vanderbilt, where was there left to go? Yet Cornelius Vanderbilt, great-grandson of the original Commodore, remembered an occasion when his grandmother, during a family dinner, turned to her daughter-in-law Gloria, wife of her son Reggie, with the words: 'When I am gone, my dear Gloria, *you* will be Mrs Vanderbilt.' At which her other daughter-in-law Grace crisply retorted: 'Nonsense, Neily [her husband] is older than Reggie. When that day comes, then *I* shall be Mrs Vanderbilt.' Grace, one of the daughters of the fabulously wealthy Richard T. Wilson – a man whose initials were not known to Ward

McAllister when he compiled the 1890 edition of *Titled Americans* in which he appears as '– Wilson' – was under no illusions as to her status. 'Dear poor Marie Antoinette, I feel so sorry for her,' she once said. 'If the revolution ever came to this country, I would be the first to go.'[21]

So, true to the spirit of competition and adaptability, American wives and daughters educated and re-educated their tastes to fit their changing social condition; like Edith Wharton's Mrs St George, who had at one time regarded the ballroom of the Grand Union Hotel at Saratoga Springs as 'her idea of a throne-room in a palace, but since her husband had taken her to a ball at the Seventh Regiment Armoury in New York her standards had changed, and she regarded the splendours of the Grand Union almost as contemptuously as the arrogant Mrs Eglinton of New York, who had arrived there the previous summer on her way to Lake George, and after being shown into the yellow damask "bridal suite" by the obsequious landlord, had said she supposed it would do well enough for one night.'[22] And behind Mrs St George, queuing up to learn what their new standards should be, were those endless lines of others whose husbands had made fortunes in Cleveland, Ohio, Chicago, Illinois, Butte, Montana, St Paul, Minnesota, San Francisco, California – for the further west, the more money there was to be made, or so it sometimes seemed; and by the most undesirable people! And the one aim in life of the wives and daughters of such people was to become desirable, as quickly as possible.

3

Young Men on the Make

The young Britishers who are *on the make*, as they call their search for rich wives, do not come to Washington....
Henry Adams to Charles Milnes Gaskell, 1878

If European example had its effect on the conduct of certain aspects of American social life, America, even in the nineteenth century, was not without its effect on Europe. Mrs Ogden Armour, wife of the Chicago meat-packer, might emulate, or at least outspend, duchesses; her husband certainly affected the spending power of the dukes. 'Lady Henry Somerset lamented the other day that Armour was rendering it difficult for the small farmers on her Gloucestershire estates to obtain paying prices for their cattle,'[1] reported W.T. Stead in 1894. Such international knock-on effects are today so commonplace as to be scarcely worthy of comment, but at that time this was regarded as annoying interference from a hitherto unconsidered source. It was true that some financiers were beginning to notice that events on one side of the Atlantic strongly influenced what might happen on the other. The narrowly averted collapse of Baring Brothers Bank in 1890, and the subsequent efforts by the Bank of England to draw gold into London – gold which was only too readily sold by the United States – was a major factor in the catastrophic panic which engulfed the States in 1893. This train of events was gloomily noted by the astute Jacob Schiff of Kuhn, Loeb in New York, in his correspondence with Sir Ernest Cassel in London, but it apparently went unnoticed and unsuspected everywhere else, including in the United States Treasury.

However, despite the occasional setback there could be no denying that the wealth of America, and of many Americans, was apparently bottomless. Enormous fortunes, of a volume unprecedented in Europe, were apparently being made there every day by the most unlikely people. At the same time that large portion of the European aristocracy whose fortunes were founded in agricultural landholdings saw their incomes decline while the cost of keeping up their enormous establishments rose.

Such fortunes as remained were, in England, carefully kept together by means of primogeniture. 'One man born two years before another comes in for title, wealth, position and opportunity; the second son comes in for a beggarly income, grudgingly given, while the grandchildren of the eldest son and the grandchildren of the second son may be poles apart in wealth and status,' recorded a faintly shocked American observer of the British; in the States all a wealthy man's children, including his daughters, might expect a fair share of the fortune. 'An Englishman with $500,000 gives his daughters $25,000 on marriage and is called very generous, while an American father, worth the same amount, would think $100,000 none too much to bestow upon his daughter,' observed Chauncey M. Depew. However, it had to be admitted that here was a Hobson's choice: 'It is hard domestic doctrine, this, of all to the eldest and little or nothing to the younger ones, but when one looks about and sees the seedy, out-at-elbows *noblesse* of France, Italy, Germany, Russia, without leadership, without wealth, without power, and often merely the anaemic transmitters of foolish faces, the system appears to have something to be said in its favour.'[2]

However, the same observer noted that just because there was less money around in Europe than America, this did not mean that Europeans cared less about money than Americans did. On the contrary: they would stoop as no independent American would allow himself to stoop in order to get the stuff, by any possible means. Everybody, 'from the Prime Minister to whom an earldom is given ... down to the railway porter content with twopence' took tips. 'There are few Americans of a certain standing who cannot tell extraordinary tales of the humiliating proceedings of needy aristocrats from England; from the men who are out-and-out blacklegs to the women who exploit their

American hosts for the purpose of gambling on the stock-market.'³ He concluded that the preoccupation with money in Europe where (it was presumed in America) nobody deigned to mention anything so vulgar was much greater than in America where (it was assumed in Europe) nobody ever thought about anything else.

The reason for this singleminded obsession was not far to seek. America, utilitarian and nonconformist in tone, had never made a cult of pleasure. The marble palaces of Newport, the imposing mansions of Fifth Avenue, were grandiose monuments to business success rather than comfortable houses. Henry James, visiting George Vanderbilt's carefully planned estate in North Carolina, found echoing, draughty spaces, insufficiently servanted, towering around too few guests. Indeed, servants were hard to find – white ones at any rate – because no one wished to be anything so un-American. A girl would far rather work in a factory than be a maid, not because she earned more – she probably saved less – but because the notion of service was distasteful. Then the house once built and staffed, people had little idea of how to pass their leisure hours. (Men had few leisure hours, anyway.) Artists carried a vague aura of sin about them so that (as we have seen) they were never received in 'good company', however illustrious they might be. Besides, who could sit back and relax, in that atmosphere of pulsing competitiveness? And how is pleasure possible without relaxation?

In what contrast to that jockeying for position which was the main preoccupation from New Orleans to New York, is Lady Warwick's description of English country-house life. 'Entertainment among the elite was undoubtedly an art,' she wrote. 'The enchantment lay in setting us at ease in a luxury that was exquisite, without thought of cost. Here, in an atmosphere of beauty, men and women reposed; even statesmen lost their stateliness, and surrendered to delicate suggestion. Petticoat influence!' How decadent! How un-American! How infinitely beguiling! Such entertainments even had the added attraction of a sense of purpose amid the delights. Lady Warwick points out that because the gossip-writers of the press did not concern themselves with these private parties, but only with 'the most ornate happenings', it was possible for public opponents to conduct privately friendly

discussions in a way that might otherwise have proved very difficult. 'It can be said that matters of high importance to the State
were constantly decided between Liberals and Conservatives in
the country houses of England.'[4] No wonder the American
observer recorded that: 'To have been somebody and to become
nobody, to have had and not to have, are more appalling
changes here than with us.'

But to provide such entertainment 'without thought of cost',
to be able to reciprocate such hospitality (as was essential if one
was not to become known as a sponger) – to participate in the
very expensive delights of life on this level, it was necessary to
be rich, exceedingly rich. And if the ancestral estates no longer
produced what they once had, or if what they produced no longer
went far enough, then there was only one thing for it: to marry
money.

Such a necessity was not self-evident to some future fathers-
in-law of noble but impoverished sprigs. Leonard Jerome, a self-
made man of considerable wealth and culture all three of whose
daughters married into the British aristocracy, thoroughly disapproved (says his granddaughter) 'of the European aristocrat's
habit of looking for heiresses instead of opportunities to earn'.[5]
Such an attitude certainly would not have gone down well in his
circles. But, seen from the aristocrat's point of view, what was
to be done? Certainly money was to be made in business – but
to go into trade was unthinkable (as well as risky). All the acceptable professions for younger sons – politics, diplomacy, the
church, the army, the navy – required rather than provided
money. One could make do with a good family background and
a small income, but one certainly could not set up an establishment on such flimsy foundations. Certainly one could not offer
oneself, in such circumstances, to the kind of girl one was most
likely to meet – the sister of one's friends, 'reared in a great
mansion and accustomed to the grand style'. Rather than set up
impoverished house together, both parties might prefer to remain
single.

Or the young men might marry heiresses; in which case
American heiresses were often infinitely preferable to the home-
grown variety. For in class-conscious Europe there were so many
ways in which a wife from the wrong stratum might shame one

– not least by insisting that her parents be produced on public occasions; and even if she decently detached herself from her family, everyone would know exactly who they were and where the money came from. But the same was not true of an exotic import from America. Who knew what went on in the grey American dawn of things? So many thousands of miles were almost equal to a sufficiency of generations as far as the provenance of the money went. As to class, in the New World the concept was without meaning. All Americans were more or less equally unacceptable. One might therefore pick the richest without compunction. Then there was far less question of undesirable relatives. These would probably visit only at infrequent intervals, and when they did their curious manners could be attributed to their foreign origins. An additional advantage, as far as the British aristocracy was concerned, was that an American bride, though foreign, could speak English.

A certain tradition of European aristocrats marrying American girls had already been established. Mention has already been made of Mary Caton; and she by her first marriage was related to Betsy Patterson, who in 1798 married Jerome Bonaparte. Not all these early transatlantic marriages turned out well, the American brides sometimes turning out to be an unfortunate advertisement for their compatriots. In the early years of the nineteenth century Maria Bingham of Philadelphia (whose sister Anne Louisa had married Alexander Baring, later Lord Ashburton) ran off, at the age of fifteen, with the Comte de Tilly. Her frantic parents instituted a search and the couple were found in bed at the milliner's, having been married in the meantime by one Mr Jones, a Universalist minister. The marriage did not last. Maria divorced Tilly and married Henry Baring, by whom in turn she was divorced on account of one Captain Webster. Maria then married, not Webster, but the Marquis de Blaizel – a union which must be assumed to have been a love-match, since Baring kept most of her fortune when he divorced her.

Perhaps the most violent of these early unions was that of Micaela Almonester, from New Orleans, and Joseph Celestin Delfau de Pontalba, who married in 1811 (Creole girls possessing the same linguistic advantages relative to the French aristocracy as other Americans to the British). At the time of their marriage Micaela and Celestin were sixteen and twenty respectively, a time of life when a certain amount of tender emotion may be hoped to enter into the most businesslike mating; but whatever their intentions, the motives of the groom's parents were never in doubt. They were interested in the bride's fortune – but in Micaela they had met their match. When the couple married, Micaela's mother, Mme Castillon, settled $130,000 on her daughter – a very large sum in those days. However, the settlement was made only on condition that the Baron de Pontalba settle a similar amount on his son. The Baron, seeing little alternative if the match was not to fall through, was forced to comply; but later made his son sign a secret declaration that he, Celestin, would never hold his father to this obligation. Micaela, when one day she came upon this document, was furious; she had already been made to sign, just before she entered her first childbed (she bore her husband three sons), a 'project of testament', in case she died in childbirth. Micaela alleged that the Pontalbas were trying to get their hands on her fortune, but in this they were thwarted by Mme Castillon; when this lady died in 1826 it was found that she had removed her son-in-law's participation in her daughter's inheritance.

It was not only money which came between the Pontalbas. She liked the gay life of Paris, while he preferred the quiet of the family château, Mont l'Eveque, near Senlis in northern France. Twice they separated, and finally parted in 1831. Micaela was to supervise the upbringing of the children. But the eldest boy, Celestin, who had been placed in a military academy, was headstrong and unmanageable. He ran away from the academy and took refuge in his mother's house in Paris – for which exploit he was cut out of his grandfather's will: his brothers were not even named in this document. Finally he became too much for Micaela, who in 1834 resolved that his father's family must take over responsibility for him. With this in mind she drove to Mont l'Eveque. What happened next was described in a letter dictated by Micaela and sent to a friend in New Orleans:

Madam,
It is in Mme de Pontalba's name, and from her bedside, that I am writing to inform you of the dreadful misfortune that has just befallen her....

Mme de Pontalba, having attempted in vain through friends to find a way to reconcile her son M. Celestin with the Pontalba family, who no longer wished to see him since the young man had gone to live with his mother ... decided to try by her own efforts to break down her husband's inflexible attitude; and with this end in view, she betakes herself, three weeks ago, to the Château of Mont l'Eveque.... She had a long conference with her husband, whom she had wished to see by himself, so as to avoid her father-in-law's making a scene, as she was very much afraid of him.

The next forenoon, she was preparing to return to Paris when M. de Pontalba Sr, who had been watching her since morning, takes advantage of a moment when she was alone.... He goes up to the room, locks the door on the inside, and, with two double-barrelled pistols in his hands, he informs Mme de Pontalba that the only recourse she has left is to commend herself to God, as she is going to die.

'You will never dare fire on me,' she tells him; and for reply, she receives in her chest a shot from a pistol loaded with three balls. She cries out, begs for mercy from this madman who answers: 'It is too late now,' and he fires two more shots at her, point-blank. The fourth shot, aimed at her forehead and her throat, misfires twice, and while the assassin was busy priming the weapon, Mme de Pontalba, with supernatural courage, shakes herself loose from him, runs to the door, which she manages to open, and takes flight to an antechamber on the floor just below where she falls. There she receives assistance from her maid, who had heard everything at the door without being able to enter.

Mme de Pontalba had four wounds in the chest above the heart, two of them slight and the other two deep, from which the blood gushed forth in torrents. The first finger of her left hand was shot away, and the third horribly shattered. By a very special protection of Providence, none of the wounds turned out to be fatal....

As for the father, he punished himself by his own hands for what he had done. After the crime, he went and closed himself up in his study, and there he fired two pistol shots into his heart. He died instantly.[6]

After this, Micaela returned to Paris, where she lived – reconciled with her husband, although her mother-in-law always shunned her – to the age of seventy-eight.

Would all American brides prove so provoking, and all such marriages end in similar disaster? The young men who in ever-increasing numbers crossed the Atlantic in search of suitable heiresses sincerely hoped not. These young men became a well-known and cynically accepted feature of the New York social scene. *Town Topics* frequently published paragraphs on the subject, of which the following is typical: 'Ward McAllister who claims the distinction of having engineered the marriage of the widow Hammersley to the Duke of Marlborough has a Polish prince on hand who is anxious to wed an American with a ten million dollar dot. He is Prince Poniatowski and a Polish prince is about as marketable a commodity as last year's hat. I strongly advise Ward to bring on additional Dukes.' (In fact Poniatowski was more successful than *Town Topics* gave him credit for, since in 1893 he became engaged to Miss Maud Burke of California. She was much in love with him, but apparently the charms which were later to ensnare George Moore and Sir Thomas Beecham, to say nothing of her considerable fortune, were not enough: he jilted her and she rebounded across the Atlantic and into the unlikely arms of Sir Bache Cunard, a foxhunting squire from Leicestershire. It is not recorded whether, contemplating her subsequent career, Poniatowski felt he had made a great mistake in not hanging on to the future Lady Cunard, or whether, on the contrary, he felt profound relief.)

Certainly not all the young scions of the impoverished nobility who spent their last pennies on the ocean voyage were so concerned with the question of compatibility as to pass up a good prospect merely on account of possible shoals ahead. Viscount Mandeville, the dissolute son of the Duke of Manchester, trawling likely waters, was introduced to the seventeen-year-old Consuelo Yznaga at one of the weekly balls of the United States Hotel at Saratoga Springs in 1875. He willingly accepted an invitation to visit the Yznagas, and while at their house contracted typhoid fever, from which he took a long time to recover. His convalescence gave him an opportunity to fall in love with Consuelo – and she with him; and to the dismay of his parents, he proposed and was accepted.

The dismay should have been all on the bride's side. Consuelo was described by her goddaughter, Consuelo Vanderbilt, as 'beautiful, witty, gay and gifted, with the ability to play by ear any melody she had heard.'[7] The qualities of her new husband proved less amiable. Soon the details of her misery were being gleefully publicized. *Town Topics* wrote:

Lady Mandeville has Spanish blood in her veins; she shows Bohemianism in her character and the style of dress she chooses.... She is married to the elder son of the celebrated Duchess of Manchester, Viscount Mandeville, whose taste for gallant adventures marriage does not seem to have cured.

Occasionally he leaves London to give himself up all the more freely to his pranks and betakes himself to Ireland, where he loves to stay and where his society is loved in turn. Sometimes he wings his flight towards the sources of the Gulf Stream to put the Atlantic between his *chères amies* and his wife. Viscount Mandeville has a seat in Parliament as a Conservative, but the stenographers have never noticed his presence there as far as I can learn. I do not believe he is intelligent, notwithstanding his evident efforts to play smart. He is fond of politics, but he was intended rather for manual than for intellectual labor....

The son of this marriage, Lord Kimbolton (or Kim, as he was familiarly known), pursued a similar amatory career with even more brazen abandon, and apparently untrammelled by his mother. Kim knew the States well. He and his mother had often taken refuge there among her friends and family from her appalling husband. In 1883, when Kim was seven, he and Consuelo, by now Duchess of Manchester, spent the winter with the W.K. Vanderbilts. The postman, delivering a letter for Viscount Mandeville, remarked: 'How I would like to see a real life lord,' only to be surprised by the sight of little Kim approaching with the words, 'Then look at me.'[8]

The years did not improve him. He knew what he wanted from the beginning, becoming notorious for the remark that he would have either to marry an Astor or a Vanderbilt or throw in the sponge. Unfortunately, no Astors or Vanderbilts would look at him twice. His absolute penury was common knowledge; the fact that he could not pay his livery bills made headlines. At one point he was in pursuit of Miss May Goelet. 'ENGLAND'S POOREST DUKE AFTER OUR RICHEST HEIRESS,' screamed the press. 'The quest of an American heiress by a British Duke is one of the few picturesque features of fashionable American life. But for such incidents it would be hopelessly dull. It is reported that he is going to Newport and that *The Duke and the Ducats*, a romance of Newport in the summer of 1898, will probably be a suitable title for a story to be published in about six months' time.'⁹ Miss Goelet subsequently married the Duke of Roxburghe, a much better bet.

Kim possessed other disadvantages. He was not only poor, he was a libertine, and the example of his father gave little reason to suppose he would be reformed by mere marriage. When in 1899 – by then having succeeded to the dukedom in his turn – he joined the staff of the *New York Journal* for the summer ('The Duke of Manchester – one of the most promising peers in England – joins the *Journal* staff') he was at some pains to deny the rumours:

Cléo de Mérode? I saw her once. I was not infatuated. Ethel Barrymore, Edna May, Gertrude Elliot, Mrs Potter, Lily Hanbury, and Jessie Mackay, that is the litany of my love affairs of the footlights, according to the newspapers. It is foolish. Some of these actresses I have never met. Some young society women are also mentioned. I have seen Miss Pauline Astor and Miss Gould, but do not know them personally. It is but right that I should say I was never engaged to Miss Muriel Wilson. I was engaged to her cousin, Miss Jones-Wilson, but that was broken off. Lots of this talk about me is mere idle gossip.¹⁰

It was the sort of interview which immediately sparks off more gossip.

In the end the Duke's reputation was such that he had to take a chance on an unknown – and moreover, had to marry her before any settlement was arranged in the hope that her father would, in the event, make the best of the inevitable. On 20 November 1900, the *New York Times* reported that: 'An inspection of the register of the Marylebone Parish Church shows that the report of the marriage of the Duke of Manchester to Miss Helena Zimmerman of Cincinnati is true.' The Dowager Duchess – that Consuelo whose mother-in-law had been 'deeply grieved' at her own marriage – would not believe the marriage had taken place and 'evinced extreme displeasure at the idea of her son's marrying Miss Zimmerman'. Again, it is hard to see why the bridegroom's, rather than the bride's family, should have been so displeased. Not long before the wedding, the Duke had been declared bankrupt with liabilities of $135,500. It was devoutly to be hoped that his new father-in-law was not only very rich but would come up to scratch. Mr Eugene Zimmerman showed remarkable dignity in the circumstances. 'I have never disapproved of the match – all stories to the contrary notwithstanding, I believe it is a love affair, pure and simple,' he manfully told the press, which now hastened to find out who he could be. He was, said *The World*, 'until the marriage of his daughter to a duke, decidedly what is known as an obscure millionaire. Indeed, many people who knew him as the Vice President of the Cincinnati, Hamilton and Dayton Railroad and owner of a modest house in Cincinnati did not even believe that he was a plain millionaire. After the somewhat spectacular marriage of his daughter, however, the fact became evident that he was a multimillionaire of handsome proportions.' Mr Zimmerman, it turned out, was not only Vice President of the Cincinnati Railroad but was also a director of several other railroads, a considerable stockholder in Standard Oil, and one of the largest owners of coal and iron lands in the West. The Duke of Manchester had fallen on his feet.

The Marquis Boni de Castellane, on the trail of one of the largest fortunes of all in the person of Miss Anna Gould, was altogether more devious. Nothing could be further from the super-refined Boni than that crudeness which so unashamedly manifested itself in the Manchesters, father and son. Their cheerful cynicism was replaced in his case by a self-absorption so supreme that it was almost poetic. His *Confessions*, published after Anna had divorced him and married his cousin, the Prince de Sagan, are an exercise in self-justification so blatant as to acquire a certain charm:

> In justice to myself, I can honestly affirm that Miss Gould's fortune played a secondary part in her attraction for me. She was, in many respects, unusual – and the unusual has always fascinated me! I was never a fortune-hunter, and although I shall probably be given the lie, I can only repeat, and urge in my defence, what is perfectly true, that during the twelve years of my married life I never attempted to feather my nest at the expense of my wife. True, I spent her millions, but, as I shall endeavour to prove, I have actually represented a more than profitable investment for her.[11]

From the beginning, Anna's friends and relatives were suspicious of the exquisite Castellane – a circumstance which merely 'aroused his fighting spirit'. European society, and especially those American girls already established within it, watched his manoeuvres with fascination. The pair first met in Paris where, aware of the disapproval of Miss Gould's chaperones, Boni set siege. 'I passed under her windows on horseback, I wrote to her several times, I sent her Persian lilac. The first roses bloomed for her.' Then, in the conviction that, given this overture, absence would do its proverbial work, he took himself off to London, convinced that Anna would not stay in Paris long without him. With satisfaction he watched her departure for America. His intentions were already the talk of London and Paris. Said Minna, Marchioness of Anglesey (formerly Miss King, of Georgia): 'I can read you, Boni, as easily as an open book. You look so self-satisfied that you must be excessively pleased with yourself. Come, own up! Have you decided to marry Anna Gould?' She then proceeded to warn him off, thereby merely strengthening his intention – a process which was given the final touch by a conversation he overheard at a dinner given by Mrs Paget, *née* Miss Minnie Stevens and now an intimate of the Prince of Wales. At the next table he heard a couple discussing him, ignorant that the subject of their conversation was listening avidly. They assured each other that he was a profligate and a ne'er-do-well.

'And,' resumed the first speaker, 'it is almost certain that he will eventually marry Anna Gould.'

'My dear lady,' said a gentleman of the party ... 'take it from me, that girl will never be silly enough to accept a man who is foolish enough to *want* to marry her.'[12]

His appetite finally whetted, Boni set sail for New York, where he arrived so devoid of cash that his cab-fare from the landing-stage was charged to his account at the Waldorf-Astoria.

Boni was not impressed with America. New York did not at first sight appeal to him 'and the horrible Statue of Liberty might have justified Mme Roland's historic exclamation: "Oh, Liberty, what crimes are committed in thy name!"'[13] (He conveniently forgot that the statue was a present from the French

people.) The press besieged him, and let him know that the
fortunes of the Goulds were founded upon a patent mousetrap,
a piece of information which much pleased Boni. He moved on
to Newport, where he was overwhelmed by hospitality, hostesses
vying for his presence. However, he found the quality of the
entertainment wanting; he did not like the perpetual terrapin,
clam broth and oyster crabs which constituted fashionable
cuisine, and, like Margaret Chanler, found the dinners dull: 'If
spending money to excess constitutes a claim to success, many
Americans can lay claim to it, and if a lavish display of gold and
silver plate makes for happiness, many American hostesses must
exist in a perpetual Utopia.' He visited the George Goulds
(Anna's eldest brother and his wife) at home, 'let me confess it,
intensely curious to sample the *mise en scène* which must
insensibly have influenced Miss Anna Gould's outlook on life,'
and found it sumptuous and bizarre. He took a trip to Florida,
conducted a flirtation with a lady, visited Mrs Potter Palmer in
Chicago and visited an Indian reservation. ('The Redskins and I
had nothing in common; I hardly spoke during the expedition,
but during the day I occasionally bathed with the naked savages.')
Then he set out to hunt big game. The expedition had armed
guides and took plentiful provisions. 'We encamped in the snow,
five days' distance from any human habitation. Our horses fed
on roots, and we lunched and dined off our kills.' Boni had
previously poured scorn on American 'foxhunting', which was
more usually drag hunting, as a feeble pretence; but he found this
genuine sport no more appealing. 'To speak frankly, I was dis-
appointed with everything and everybody, and the scenery left me
metaphorically and physically cold,' he grumbled disarmingly.
But his aim was achieved. One day on the way back to the camp
the sound of a horn was heard, to be followed by the sight of an
Indian runner on the horizon – 'a bronze Mercury traversing
the eternal snows'. It was a telegram from Miss Gould announcing her arrival in New York. Since she had taken such immense
trouble to convey this piece of news, Boni could hardly refuse
to join her. His manoeuvres had succeeded. Anna had succumbed.

Anna was staying with her sister Helen, an austere woman
who – as Anna predicted – did not take to Boni. Given the
characters of the religious and abstemious Helen and the

licentious and precious Boni this was not surprising, but Boni's explanation gives more of an idea of the lines along which his mind was running: 'The dominant idea of the Gould Family was to keep the Gould Fortune in America; it was nothing short of an obsession with them, and it was responsible for much of the injustice and bitterness which I was destined to experience later at their hands.'[14]

Boni and Anna now conducted some curious conversations. 'I will never marry you,' she remarked one day.

'My dear lady, you forget that I have not asked you to marry me,' coldly replied Boni; to which she rejoined: 'Frenchmen are dangerous – everyone says that they are born liars and unfaithful husbands.' To which Boni, giving a first-hand demonstration of the underhand qualities complained of, responded: 'Precisely so, and this is the reason why you must not dream of marrying *me*.'[15]

Anna's fate was sealed: after playing on her jealousy by flirting with some other girls, Boni went on a winter journey with the George Goulds and a party which included Anna. On this journey, in Quebec, Boni proposed and Anna accepted. Boni begged her 'to make me doubly blest by adopting my religion' but at that Anna balked. Unhesitatingly she replied: 'I will never become a Catholic, because if I were to do so, I should not be able to divorce you, and if I were not happy I would not remain your wife a moment longer than was necessary.' On this supremely un-European and un-aristocratic note, Anna affirmed that her fate was not necessarily sealed.

4

American Beauties

> She was not fast, nor emancipated, nor crude, nor loud, and there wasn't in her, of necessity at least, a grain of the stuff of which the adventuress is made. She was simply very successful, and her success was entirely personal. She hadn't been born with the silver spoon of social opportunity; she had grasped it by honest exertion.
>
> Henry James, *Pandora*

Expect what they might when they first set out across the Atlantic in search of a fortune, it is probably true to say that the one thing for which the questing European aristocrats were not prepared was the American girl. There she stands, enshrined in the pages of Henry James, her chief chronicler: fresh and dainty, each of her multifarious frills laundered and pressed, squarely facing the realities of the world; Isabel Archer, Daisy Miller, Pandora Day, Milly Theale – a formidable phalanx. And to the European, the American girl was formidable. In Europe, the married women were the ones to be reckoned with and the girls, until they married, had no real place in society. In America, quite the converse was true. 'With us,' wrote Paul Bourget, 'the passage from girlhood to wifehood is an event. Here it is quite the other thing: it is a resignation.'[1] He quotes a telling remark made to him by a young lady: 'I should like, above all things, to be a widow. I have always thought how nice it would be to lose my husband on my wedding-day. I should have less reason to mourn as I should know him less. I should like to see him struck with lightning as we come out of the church. It is so nice to be a young widow.'[2]

Such an attitude would have seemed totally incomprehensible in Europe. There, the unmarried girl had no freedom; the married woman, provided she was discreet, every freedom. Socially, the mother was all, the unmarried daughter nothing, except as a potentially interesting prospect. The notion that the unmarried daughter might be the socially dominant figure of the family would have been unthinkable; yet that was, as often as not, the way things worked in this curious new land. Remarked a contemporary of Miss Mary Leiter, the future Lady Curzon: 'When her father built his own home (in Washington) . . . it was minutely described in the press of the country, particular emphasis being given to the apartments appropriated to Miss Leiter's use, so undoubtedly was she the social genius of her family and the figure who held the interest of the public.'[3] It was usual for the family to bring out its daughters, but this process was reversed in the case of the Leiters. They simply did not exist, socially, until the daughter, as it were, presented them and vouched for them. 'Comparatively little was heard of her family socially till after her debut . . . and their present social prominence in the United States is due to the remarkable impression she everywhere created.'[4] Such was Miss Leiter's presence, beauty and social poise that she was even able to carry with her her faintly ridiculous mother, so prone to malapropisms – 'Mr Leiter is going to the fancy ball in the garbage of a monk'; 'What a pity dear Sally Loring is so obscene' (obese); 'Yes, we were invited to the ball at Devonshire House and Mary danced in the Duchess's own caviar' – and so conscious of her extreme wealth and the advantages it bestowed: 'Now help yourself well, Mr Roosevelt, you don't get anything like this at home'; 'Let my third footman take your coat, Mr Lodge.'[5] But Mrs Leiter followed obligingly and obediently enough in the wake of her phenomenal daughter.

The relations between headstrong American belles and their bemused and complaisant parents must have presented an extraordinary social puzzle to those European young men, so conscious of their own all-powerful mammas and *mamans* at home, and so very interested in the younger – but not the older – generation. How often they must have wondered 'that the human belongings of a person . . . should not be a little more distinguished', and how often must the proud parents have reacted as Mr and Mrs

P.W. Day reacted to the attentions of their lovely daughter Pandora – those parents 'whom she seemed to regard as a care, but not as an interest': 'When their daughter drew near them Mr and Mrs Day closed their eyes after the fashion of a pair of household dogs who expect to be scratched.'[6]

If Mary Leiter was particularly successful, she was by no means unique. The 'beauty' was a recognized feature of American life, and one particularly remarkable to European visitors unaccustomed to any respectable Old World equivalent. 'There are two or three in every city,' wrote Paul Bourget, 'and their supremacy is so well recognized that you are continually receiving such invitations as "Pray come to tea tomorrow afternoon, to meet Miss –, the Richmond beauty."' Bourget's description of the beauty perfectly fits Mary Leiter: 'She must be very tall, very well formed, the lines of her face and figure must lend themselves to that sort of reproduction of which the newspapers and their readers are so fond. She must also know how to dress with magnificence, which here is inseparable from elegance.'[7] It was the type immortalized by Charles Dana Gibson as the 'Gibson Girl' – personified most absolutely in his wife, Irene Langhorne Gibson, the sister of the future Nancy Astor. Mary Leiter also posed for Mr Gibson.

The beauty had a definite social role, a generally acknowledged niche:

> Once recognized, though she may not be more than twenty years old, she enters upon a sort of official, almost a civic, existence. In the newspaper columns devoted to 'Social Gossip', the types spontaneously form her name, so often have the compositors set it up. She is as necessary a part of every grand dinner and ball as the roses at a dollar apiece.... She would not be fulfilling her mission if she did not represent [her own] city in New York, Washington, Newport, at the races, the regattas, all the events where, as on a stage, American society displays itself.[8]

To the bemused European the independent operations of the American belle, though fascinating, were *outré*. They merely represented yet another of the barbaric social phenomena which abounded in this strange land, where nothing was ever quite what one might have expected it to be. But in fact, within her own society, the position of the belle was entirely logical – the natural result of the social conditions into which she was born.

The first of these – and the one which had perhaps the most influence on social attitudes – was that the America of the last quarter of the nineteenth century was, most strongly, an immigrant society. Of course not all families were recent immigrants – and we have seen the effect this had on the organization of 'good' society throughout the States, length of settlement, indeed, being the chief definition of social acceptability. But most people were more recent arrivals; and it is a characteristic of immigrants that they focus their social ambitions on their children. The first generation gains a foothold; the second generation (maybe) makes money; the third generation gains social acceptance.

In these circumstances, the presence of parents or surrogate parents, so essential as a mark of respectability in Europe, might be a positive social disadvantage in the States. Nobody wanted to know the appalling Jay Gould, but all social doors were open to his children. Everyone knew how their father had come by his millions – by swindling shareholders, ruining investors, printing stock certificates on his own printing machine, hiring private armies of thugs to secure control of disputed sections of railroad. The presence of Mr Gould (even had he been well enough – which he usually was not) would have been no social asset to any of his children. But his millions were undeniable and heritable, and they were an asset whose provenance everyone was happy to forget. As Thorstein Veblen observed, 'It is a matter of common notoriety and byword that in offenses which result in a large accession of property to the offender he does not ordinarily incur the extreme penalty or the extreme obloquy with which his offenses could be visited on the ground of the naïve moral code alone.'[9]

It was not that people were not aware who the father of the pretty miss driving along so smartly in her phaeton might be. On the contrary, they were precisely aware; for this was not a large society, nor one drawn from an infinity of backgrounds. Paul Bourget remarked on 'the almost total absence of adventurers and adventuresses in a place like Newport' and attributed this to the fact that 'it is easy to deceive a composite society but not a society of businessmen' where everyone knew exactly what his neighbour was worth. The names which appeared in the gossip columns were household names – not on account of their social activities, or at least not primarily so, but because behind every social name stood a successful businessman, whose business or businesses were in active and constant operation. J.P. Morgan was better known than his daughter Anne; E.H. Harriman, than his daughter-in-law Mrs Borden Harriman.

But these essential backers of the social scene did not often appear on it. The job of the men was to earn the money; the job of the women, to spend it. That separation and segregation of peer groups which is still such a marked feature of American life, with its singles apartments and towns for the elderly, was early established. The belles spent much of their time with their contemporaries, driving, picnicking or indulging in other forms of mild amusement with other girls and young men of their own age, on terms of comradely freedom unimaginable amid the more stilted etiquettes of Europe. Their mothers led a life of indolence and their fathers worked. Even within the same city – New York – the separation was marked physically as well as occupationally. The men were downtown, the women uptown. Henry James recalled how 'at the very moderate altitude of Twenty-Fifth Street, he felt himself day by day alone in the scale of the balance; alone, I mean, as the music-masters and French pastry-cooks, the ladies and children – immensely present and immensely numerous, these, but testifying with a collective voice to the extraordinary absence ... of a serious male interest.'[10] James wistfully noted that he would very much have liked to be able to observe the downtown business life, 'the major key', instead of being confined to the uptown world of women, which he saw as 'the minor key'. But between the two there was no bridge. One was of one or the other. 'Families live side by side rather than with one another,' said Bourget,[11] and within this loose-knit structure, each member knew his or her business.

The father's business, socially speaking, was clear cut. Almost every year, Richard T. Wilson would receive an anguished cable from Paris, where his daughter Grace (the future Mrs Cornelius Vanderbilt) was gathering her wardrobe for the next year. 'Father, what shall I do? I'm supposed to sail on the *Teutonic*, and Worth doesn't have my dresses ready.' On receipt of this,

Mr Wilson would say to his brother-in-law, who worked in the Wilson bank, 'What are we going to do about Grace?' and his obliging relative would reply, 'Well, Major, I guess I better go bail her out again. When do you want me to leave?' 'This afternoon at three,' would be the typical response, and Grace's uncle would go straight over to Paris and make Worth's life a misery until the dresses were ready on time. Father was there to make sure his daughter got everything she wanted, when she wanted it. He provided the money and smoothed the paths.

And what did she do for him? To begin with, she adored him. Paul Bourget, product of a demonstrative Latin civilization, found Anglo-Saxon family life a cold affair, and assumed that this apparent chilliness must reflect the real state of relations between parents and children. But the evidence is that all the belles dearly loved their daddies. Mary Leiter displayed the greatest devotion to her father, and wrote of her father-in-law: 'He wished me to call him Papa, but I have never brought my lips to it, for anyone less like my own beloved Papa I cannot imagine.'[12] When Consuelo Vanderbilt separated from the Duke of Marlborough, her father, now divorced from her mother, often played host to his daughter's hostess; he bought her a house in Paris, where she hoped he would spend a great deal of time with her.

But these pretty, bejewelled daughters also played an important symbolic role *vis-à-vis* their all-providing papas. They were the living proof of their parent's success. For, kept constantly at work earning the money, the American man needed his wife and daughters to display it for him. The details of this role formed the basis of Thorstein Veblen's immortal analysis *The Theory of the Leisure Class*, published in 1893 when the whole process was at its height. Veblen examined such phenomena as 'conspicuous consumption', 'conspicuous waste', 'vicarious leisure', 'pecuniary canons of taste', 'dress as an expression of the pecuniary culture', and so on. He was continually being fired from the universities funded by those prominent and successful predators and exponents of the pecuniary culture who so fascinated him; and a glance at his writings shows why. On dress: 'It is true, the corset impairs the personal attractions of the wearer, but the loss suffered on that score is offset by the gain in reputability which comes of her visibly increased expensiveness and infirmity.' On the occupations of wives and offspring: 'Ostensibly purposeless leisure has come to be deprecated, especially among that large portion of the leisure class whose plebeian origin acts to set them at variance with the tradition of the *otium cum dignitate*. But that canon of reputability which discountenances all employment that is of the nature of productive effort is still at hand, and will permit nothing beyond the most transient vogue to any employment that is substantially useful or productive.' On the wife's principal occupation: 'Throughout the entire evolution of conspicuous expenditure, whether of goods or of services or human life, runs the obvious implication that in order to effectually mend the consumer's good name it must be an expenditure of superfluities. No merit would accrue from the consumption of the bare necessaries of life....' So the labouring plutocrat could confidently leave his wife and daughters to display his wealth before a critical public, bedecking themselves with jewels and elaborate clothes before setting out on the most mundane of occasions – a morning drive, or an afternoon's shopping; hiring extra footmen for grand dinner parties simply in order to have them stand at symmetrical intervals up the staircase between the torchères; building pleasure palaces of marble and porphyry, filled with priceless works of art, in which the provider rarely set foot – for Newport and such resorts were feminine preserves, the men being fully occupied 'downtown'. Among the men, only gigolos and adventurers such as Harry Lehr, the ineffable protégé of Mrs Stuyvesant Fish, or the sick, frequented midweek Newport. Thus Blanche Oelrichs would be regularly saddened by the sight of Mr Ogden Goelet, leaning on the arm of his nurse as he walked slowly through his massive iron gates and up his drive to his immense house, a copy of one of the Loire châteaux. People would say, 'Poor Mr Goelet, he's unable to digest anything but hothouse grapes.' And, 'Goelet has worked himself to death.' But he had achieved his château, and his daughter would marry a duke.

Having made the required mark at home, the belles and their mammas set out *en masse* for abroad.

Abroad had its place in the fixed American social calendar.

43

One went there in the early summer, after New York and before Newport, in order to buy one's wardrobe in Paris and view, and if possible participate in, the social scene there and in London.

In this last respect, the 'best' section of society took yet another opportunity to dissociate itself from less desirable elements. They went abroad just as much as anyone else, but, wrote Edith Wharton, cousin of Rhinelanders and Schermerhorns and born into the nobbiest of nob circles, they 'did not, perhaps, profit much by the artistic and intellectual advantages of European travel, and to social opportunities they were half-resentfully indifferent. It was thought vulgar and snobbish to try to make the acquaintance, in London, Paris or Rome, of people of the class corresponding to our own.'[13] The best people thus confined themselves to 'public ceremonials, ecclesiastical or royal', and had only distant glimpses of these, since 'it would have been snobbish to ask, through one's legation, for reserved seats or invitations'. Others were less inhibited by good form, and no doubt enjoyed themselves far more.

For what, after all, was the purpose of coming to Europe? What did abroad have that at home did not? It had historic relics and ruins and art galleries and the best *couturiers* – but with a certain effort and enough expenditure, such things could be uprooted and imported. However, it also had aristocracy – aristocracy and the ceremonial that went with it. This, of course, was something that Americans had formally renounced. But distance and the desirability of pleasures abjured imbued it with glamour. American ambassadors in London were besieged by mothers who, having none of the reservations of Edith Wharton's group, were anxious above all things to get their daughters presented at court. What else was an ambassador – or, more particularly, an ambassadress – there for? Heaving a sigh, ambassadors pointed out that the number of presentations in their gift was strictly limited; but they were unable to pretend that the pinnacle was altogether impossible of achievement. 'Your letter with account of your audience with the Queen was most interesting and, after the children and I had thoroughly enjoyed it, we posted it to Mamma last evening,' wrote Mrs May Goelet from Fifth Avenue to her younger sister, seventeen-year-old Belle

Wilson, in London. 'The titles which always attend such ceremonials must have given you a few moments of discomfort. I mean your description of the interview is quite what I imagined such a function to be – a great fluttering about the heart and an unnatural voice as though one's very life depended upon the effect of the visit – a feeling of intense relief when it is over. I think you are enjoying yourself more than at Newport,' she added enviously.[14]

Even in America, Americans liked their aristocrats to behave like aristocrats – which, given the country's reputation, was not always realized by the aristocrats in question and could lead to confusion. When the Grand Duke Alexis of Russia visited New Orleans for Mardi Gras, New Orleanians fell over themselves to welcome him in the correct manner. In front of City Hall a special dais had been erected, giving the best possible view of the processions with a red and gold canopy and the most throne-like possible chair for the Grand Duke to sit on. The streets were crowded with maskers, torn between their interest in the processions and the fascination of this actual royalty amid the imitations. But – calamity! – when he had been welcomed by the mayor and received by the governor, Alexis refused to take his place upon the throne. The city fathers pleaded, but the Grand Duke was adamant. No, 'he preferred to stand with the others. He did not really understand this at all. He appreciated their intention, but was not this a democratic country? He was amazed at this reverence for a title in a nation that had rejected titles. Had not their own Mr Thomas Paine said something on the subject – something about titles being only nicknames at best? He was here, the honored gentlemen must understand, only as a lieutenant in the Imperial Russian Navy, and he preferred to be treated as such.'[15] But snobbery does not disappear merely because it is officially abolished in the name of democracy.

This combination of a democratic upbringing and a fascination with aristocracy was apt to produce a curious effect. When Frances Trollope asked an American woman of her acquaintance how she would like to go back and live in England, the lady replied, 'Why, you know I would not affront you for anything; but the fact is, we in America know rather more than you think; and certainly, if I was in England, I should not think of associating

45

with anything but lords. I have always been amongst the first here, and if I travelled I should do the same. I don't mean, I am sure, that I would not come to see you, but you know you are not lords, and therefore I know very well how you are treated in your own country.'[16]

Secure in such expectations, confident of their status as belles, liberally endowed with that quality which Americans called 'snap', used to the high level of activity endemic in social life at home, Yankee girls making their debut amid the subdued pleasantries of the European social scene were unmistakable. They took their place in *Punch*'s portrait gallery:

ENGLISHMAN to fair New Yorker: May I have the pleasure of dancing with you?
DARLING: I guess you may – for I calc'late that if I sit much longer here I shall be taking root!
Two young ladies stand together in a ballroom: a gentleman approaches.
'Here, Maria, hold my cloak while I have a fling with a stranger.'

Of course, the quality of standing out, as American girls undoubtedly did in Europe, could be seen as a good or a bad thing – depending on what side of the Atlantic the viewpoint originated. Remarks Henry James's old Lady Davenant – a character based upon a formidable London dowager of his acquaintance – to the young American girl Laura Wing:

'You are uncommonly dressy, you know.'
'I'm sorry I seem so. That's just the way I don't want to look.'
'You Americans can't help it; you "wear" your very features and your eyes look as if they had just been sent home.'[17]

But *Town Topics*, remarking the same quality, sees it quite differently. 'At a dinner dance given recently by the Marchioness of Granby, in honor of Princess Ena ... it was easy to pick out the American girls. They dress so well and know exactly how to put on their clothes.'[18]

And to Price Collier, that keen observer of things English, the boot was quite on the other foot: it was the English women who were dowdy. 'What hats, what clothes, what shoes, what colours, what amorphous figures! Who permits that nice-looking girl to wear a white flannel skirt, a purple jacket, and a fur hat with a bunch of small feathers sticking out of it at right angles? ... The grotesque costumes of the women could make one stop to stare, were it not that they are so common one ceases at last to notice them.'[19] 'Fashion was not fashionable in London until the Americans and the Jews were let loose,' said Henry Adams.[20]

Yes, certainly they had 'snap', these daughters of the New World who, fortified with the certainty of cushioning banks of dollars back home, came to 'affront their destinies' in the Old. There were those who felt that when an American beauty married a European peer, the gain was all Europe's. 'The American girl comes along, prettier than her English sister, full of dash, and snap, and go, and she is a revelation to the Englishman,' wrote the financier, politician and man-about-town Chauncey M. Depew. 'She gives him more pleasure in one hour, at a dinner or ball, than he thought the universe could produce in a whole life-time. Speedily he comes to the conclusion that he must marry her or die. He knows nothing of business, and to support his estate requires an increased income. The American girl whom he gets acquainted with has that income, so in marrying her he goes to heaven and gets – the earth.'[21]

That of course was only one view, and perhaps a rather one-sided one; but it could reasonably be asked – and rarely was in Europe, such was the assumption of superiority – what, really, was in it for the girls?

5

Getting Married

'Is she black his anguished mother Selina Brightlingsea'[1]

W.T. Stead, that fervent campaigner against the exploitation of women, was horrified by the increasingly usual practice among rich Americans of marrying their daughters to members of the aristocracy. 'What do you think of your women if they allow themselves to be disposed of in this fashion?' he demanded of a Chicago audience in 1894 – many of the members of which probably wished nothing better for their own daughters. 'In feudal times when an estate was made over to a purchaser the contract was not complete until at the same time the seller took a handful of dirt from the estate and gave it to the purchaser. Your American beauties and American heiresses are no more than that handful of dirt which marks and accompanies the transfer of their fortunes to our stone-broke nobles.'[2]

Stead was not alone in his condemnation of such marriages. Many of the 'best' people on either side of the Atlantic disapproved of these unions in which (it seemed) the best *partis* on both sides were irrevocably lost to their compatriots. When Percy Wyndham, the son of George Wyndham, the noted and much respected statesman and wit, announced his engagement to Lord Ribblesdale's daughter, Diana Lister, in 1913, his father's immediate response seems to have been, more than anything else, relief. 'Percy has done all I ever asked,' he wrote to his niece, Lady Cynthia Asquith. 'I told him *not* to marry an American, or a Jewess, or an heiress, but just an English young lady. So he has conformed.'[3] (But Percy died in 1914, and the next Lady Ribbles-

dale was herself an American – the erstwhile Ava Astor.) Likewise, when Gertrude Vanderbilt married Harry Whitney in 1896,
the *New York Journal*'s comment was that this was 'from an
American standpoint, the greatest wedding this country has ever
known. Money will marry money next Tuesday. Broad acres will
be wed to broad acres. Railroads will be linked to railroads. But
it will be an American wedding. There will be no foreign
noblemen in this – no purchase of titles. The millions all belong
in America and they will all remain here. . . . An American boy,
an American girl, an American courtship.'[4]

Even Ward McAllister, only begetter of so many of these transatlantic alliances, joined in the chorus – though his intention was
to build up the social confidence, not just the social competence,
of his countrymen. 'The wealthy men of America should be
ambitious to build up families composed entirely of native stock
instead of importing, from time to time, various broken-down
titled individuals from abroad,' he wrote. 'There is no reason why
an American should not be as proud of a lineage which dates
back a hundred years as a European is of one that dates back a
thousand. And it should be borne in mind that in this shorter
period there is not so much opportunity for scandal.'

Certainly the popular press seemed to be in agreement with
Stead as to the utterly cynical motivation which lay behind these
transatlantic marriages. They were excellent news fodder, providing pages of copy – the preparations, the presents, the decora-
tions, the clothes, the guests, the food, the future position of the
bride; but no proper American ought to view them with approval.
Typical was the response to the announcement of the engagement between Isabelle Singer, heiress to the sewing-machine
fortune, and the young Duc Elie Decazes, an ornament of
Parisian society. Commented *The World*: 'What the original cost
of the Duke was does not appear, but it is evident already that
French noblemen properly married, decorated, appointed,
housed and fed are very costly commodities for an American
heiress to deal in.' The *New York Tribune*'s headline was: 'SHE
PAYS ALL THE BILLS – HE THINKS HIMSELF CHEAP AT THE
PRICE.'[5]

Was such cynicism justified? The motives of the young men in
question have already been examined; but on the American side

too, it did not necessarily overstate the case. All the participants in the transatlantic drama were perfectly aware of the rules, and of the fact that adherence to them might be quite unconnected with any question of personal preference. Blanche Oelrichs, for example, was a close observer of this particular social scene. Her elder sister was a friend of Consuelo Vanderbilt and Miss May Goelet – two participants of whom we shall hear more. But insofar as she herself was concerned, Blanche knew that because she was not rich, she was not in the running for a lord. Two of her close friends were Michael and Sidney Herbert, the sons of Belle Wilson – whom we last met being breathlessly presented to Queen Victoria – and the Hon. Michael Herbert, a younger brother of Lord Pembroke, who, having married Belle and with the liberal aid of Mr Wilson's well-stuffed bankbook, pursued a most distinguished diplomatic career, ending up as a highly successful and popular British Ambassador in Washington. Blanche knew the Herbert boys as 'the absolutely fascinating nephews of Mrs Ogden Goelet and Mrs Cornelius Vanderbilt' (*nées* May and Grace Wilson). She was much taken by them:

Michael and Sidney were Eton boys and had a nonchalant humor and self-confidence entirely lacking even in the football captains of Groton and St Marks, whom I now numbered among my timid beaux. How conversationally gauche and stricken these victorious athletes were in comparison with the lissome, marvellously-groomed Herberts! . . . There were parties at Aunty Grace's, and Aunty May's, and wandering about the royally clipped and smooth parterres of Mrs Goelet's great garden, Michael and Sidney would propose to me by turn, in the starlight, and next day scratch with a pin on the walls of our dingy summer house . . . 'Blanche Herbert'. . . . And yet I knew very well that over and beyond our being all children, marriage with penniless Blanche Oelrichs would never have been permitted Michael and Sidney by any of their strong clan.[6]

Blanche was well aware of what things would have been like if she had had money. On a family holiday in Austria the Austrian Ambassadress to Washington, who chanced to be there at the same time, and who laboured under the misapprehension that Blanche was an heiress, spread the word among likely suitors. As a result Blanche noticed various young and not-so-young gentlemen dogging her footsteps from Vienna to Carlsbad. The

father of one of them asked Mr Oelrichs for her hand, informing him (while Blanche listened riveted at the keyhole) that the
young couple would of course have to live in Krakow while his
son finished his military service. 'And what would be your
daughter's dot?' he then inquired. 'Not a cent!' returned Mr
Oelrichs, quick as a flash. Next day the young man wrote to
Blanche 'with creditable despair and passion', telling her that
his father had ordered him back to his regiment at Krakow for
an indefinite period. Others begged her to elope with them.
When Mr Oelrichs found out the Ambassadress's mistake, he
roared with laughter and told the discomfited lady: 'So, that
accounts for all this attention to the Baby!... But, my dear
Baroness, I am not the rich Oelrichs! That's my brother, and he
only married a rich wife!'[7] 'At this point,' writes Blanche, 'life
seemed to hold nothing whatever but despair plus humiliation.'

But, even though she was poor, Blanche Oelrichs did not lack
for American proposals of marriage. There were plenty who,
though they were rich enough, still could not acquire the dot she
carried with her – that of her family connections; the Oelrichs
were related to almost everybody, which made Blanche a priceless asset for the rich sprig of a climbing family, whose wealth
could not disguise the fact that they knew nobody. The year before
her debut, she records, she received an offer of marriage from a
very rich young man:

His family in the last twenty-five years have achieved the 'social
top', wherever that may be. But at the time of his proposal, he was
somewhat in need of that nebulous absurdity I was thought to possess –
'social position'; so he proposed in the lounge room of his steam
yacht, both amusing and alarming me by bolting the door for action
first! After expressing his desires, he cried out: 'And my father says
he will give me an extra million if you accept.'

Blanche nevertheless turned down the proposal, at which her
sister burst out angrily, 'Don't you realize how dreadfully difficult things are for Papa, and what do you expect?'[8]

What the elder Miss Oelrichs expected was that Blanche
should, like so many of their set, regard marriage as a form of
currency. Blanche herself expected to follow her inclinations –
and was in fact to do so, though this did not make her

particularly happy. But at least she had the satisfaction of knowing that she had made her own mistakes. Others were not so fortunate. One such was Consuelo Vanderbilt.

The story of how Consuelo Vanderbilt was married to the Duke of Marlborough is a history of true love thwarted, bullying parents, ancient lineage, wealth, titles, position and misery that would not have been out of place in a triple-decker bestseller. Consuelo was the daughter of W.K. Vanderbilt and his socially ambitious wife Alva, who had smashed her way to the head of New York society in 1883 with a spectacular fancy-dress ball given in honour of Lady Mandeville, the former Consuelo Yznaga and the godmother of the future Duchess of Marlborough. Miss Vanderbilt, beautiful, intelligent and endowed with one of the world's fabulous fortunes, was evidently going to be the catch of the century. Her mother was determined that such potential should not be wasted. Consuelo was a match for the most exalted: no other suitors would be permitted. The exact identity of those who might be considered was narrowed down, when Consuelo was just seventeen, to two. It was during a journey to India made on the Vanderbilt yacht in 1893 that Mrs Vanderbilt arrived at her decision. During the course of that voyage the Vanderbilts spent a week as guests of the Viceroy and Vicereine, Lord and Lady Lansdowne, at Government House in Calcutta. This, Mrs Vanderbilt decided, was the scale of life for Consuelo. There were thus only two possible husbands for her: Lord Lansdowne's heir, or his cousin, the young Duke of Marlborough. When Carolus Duran painted Consuelo's portrait that year, Mrs Vanderbilt persuaded him to abandon his usual background of a red curtain in favour of a classic landscape, so that the picture could in the future fittingly take its place among those of other duchesses in the palatial setting for which its subject was irrevocably destined.

The Vanderbilts left India and made their way via Paris to London. While in Paris Mrs Vanderbilt received five requests for the hand of 'la belle Mlle. Vanderbilt au long cou'; but only one of them, Prince Francis Joseph of Battenberg, was seriously considered. At the time it seemed as if he might become the next King of Bulgaria, and the prospect of an actual crown glittered tantalizingly before the eyes of Mrs Vanderbilt, just as the prospect of the Vanderbilt millions constituted an enticing lure for the Prince. But Consuelo 'felt aversion rather than attraction' for Francis Joseph; and Mrs Vanderbilt, having had time to think again about the shaky state of Balkan crowns – even if acquired rather than potential – raised no objections to the refusal. (As it turned out, Francis Joseph's royal aspirations came to nothing.) The Vanderbilts went on to London, where Consuelo was duly introduced to 'Sunny', the young Duke of Marlborough. 'He had a small aristocratic face with a large nose and rather prominent blue eyes. His hands, which he used in a fastidious manner, were well shaped and he seemed inordinately proud of them.'⁹ They did the London season, during which Consuelo received several more proposals from 'uninteresting Englishmen' drawn to her wealth like wasps to jam. These were duly rejected; and in the autumn, the Vanderbilts returned to America.

Here Consuelo fell in love. The object of her affections, which were eagerly reciprocated, was one Winthrop Rutherfurd. The Rutherfurds were members of the very best society, rich, intelligent, and extremely handsome; but Winthrop did not measure up to Mrs Vanderbilt's idea of a husband for Consuelo, being neither the future Lord Lansdowne nor the Duke of Marlborough. Mrs Vanderbilt set herself to break up the affair. 'During the following months I was to suffer a perpetual denial of friendships and pleasures, since my mother resented my seeing anyone whose loyalties were not completely hers,' recalled Consuelo – and this of course included anyone who sympathized with Rutherfurd. As soon as possible, Mrs Vanderbilt planned to sweep Consuelo back off to Europe. Meanwhile, however, it was impossible to keep her entirely isolated. On the day before the departure, which happened to be Consuelo's eighteenth birthday, while cycling on Riverside Drive, Rutherfurd and Consuelo managed to ride ahead of the other cyclists, and Rutherfurd proposed and was accepted. They agreed to keep the engagement secret; Rutherfurd promised to follow Consuelo to Europe and see her there; when they returned to America, they could plan an elopement. There was no time to arrange anything more definite before Mrs Vanderbilt, pedalling furiously, caught up with them.

Consuelo did not tell her mother what had happened, but Alva did not need to be told. During the five months they spent in Europe Consuelo heard nothing of Winthrop. It later transpired that her mother had refused him admittance when he called upon them in Paris, and had intercepted all his letters – and all Consuelo's to him. In Paris, Consuelo 'like an automaton' tried on clothes, went to concerts, museums, churches, dances, and endured her mother's sarcasm at her martyred air. Then they went on to London, where 'I felt I was being steered into a vortex that would engulf me.'

The visit to England was a short one, and the outstanding event in it was a visit to Blenheim Palace, seat of the Marlboroughs. Consuelo and the Duke had already renewed acquaintance at a ball; now she was to see his home. It was huge and monumental. The small party, consisting of Consuelo and her mother, the Duke and his two sisters, and two or three young men, 'seemed lost in so big a house'. They listened to music and the Duke showed Consuelo round the estates. 'When I left Blenheim after that weekend I firmly decided that I would not marry Marlborough,' wrote Consuelo. She dreamed of Winthrop and the life they would lead together in their own country. It would mean a battle with her mother, but it would be worth it.

But Consuelo had underestimated the formidable Alva. There was to be no possibility of unlicensed dalliance at Newport, since Consuelo was, quite simply, never allowed out. She led the life of a prisoner in the marble cage of the Vanderbilt 'cottage'; the porter had orders never to let her out unaccompanied. She met Rutherfurd once at a ball, but Alva noticed them dancing together and dragged her away. On the way home, Consuelo resolved to have it out. She informed her mother that she was going to marry Rutherfurd, and added that she considered she had a right to choose her own husband.

She had known there would be a storm; but what a storm, she could never have imagined. Alva raged. There was nothing too bad for her to say about Rutherfurd. He was a well-known flirt, he was carrying on a blatant affair with a married woman; he wanted to marry an heiress. There was madness in the family, and it would be impossible for Consuelo to bear his children. Consuelo said nothing, but was evidently not prepared to give way. 'There was a terrible scene in which she told me that if I succeeded in escaping, she would shoot my sweetheart, and she would, therefore, be imprisoned and hanged, and I would be responsible.'[10] Mrs Vanderbilt was not used to being defied, and even the prospect of such an occurrence was too much for her. Later, she sent her friend Mrs Jay to visit the recalcitrant Consuelo in her room.

Condemning my behaviour, she informed me that my mother had had a heart attack brought about by my callous indifference to her feelings. She confirmed my mother's intentions of never consenting to my plans for marriage, and her resolve to shoot X. [Rutherfurd] should I decide to run away with him. I asked her if I could see my mother and whether in her opinion she would ever relent. I still remember the terrible answer. 'Your mother will never relent and I warn you there will be a catastrophe if you persist. The doctor has said that another scene may easily bring on a heart attack and he will not be responsible for the result. You can ask the doctor yourself if you do not believe me!' . . . In utter misery I asked Mrs Jay to let X. know that I could not marry him.[11]

If the situation was an agonizing one for Consuelo, it was hardly less so for the Duke. To begin with, neither his parents nor Consuelo's offered a very enticing picture of what marriage might entail. In those days, when divorce was a scandal to be avoided at all costs, both Consuelo and Sunny Marlborough were the offspring of marriages so intolerably awful that divorce had been the only way out. The Vanderbilt divorce was not made easier by Alva's insistence on its being legalized in New York State, where adultery was the only permitted ground. The last years of the Vanderbilt marriage had been deeply unhappy, punctuated by dreadful scenes that, said Consuelo, 'made of marriage a horrible mockery'. The Marlborough family history was no happier. Sunny's father, who had been clever and eccentric, had also been a compulsive womanizer. Among the Prince of Wales's set, to which he and his paramours belonged, the guiding rule was the eleventh commandment. Nobody was expected to be faithful to his or her spouse (although the woman was expected to provide some male offspring of unimpeachable paternity before seeking extra-nuptial solace) but these affairs must never be made public. The aristocracy must set an example and maintain its position; above all, no scandal must ever touch the Prince of Wales, the heir to the throne.

After seven years of marriage Sunny's father, who was then still Lord Blandford, the title held by the heir to the dukedom, had broken all these rules. He was having an affair with Lady Aylesford (who had produced three daughters, but no sons, for her husband), and while her husband 'Sporting Joe' Aylesford was off on a tour of India with the Prince of Wales, the two decided to elope. Aylesford received a letter to this effect while the party was encamped during a big game hunt. Enraged, he returned to England determined to shoot Lord Blandford and then divorce his wife.

Society was fascinated and appalled. What would happen next? Lord Blandford began to get cold feet. Lady Aylesford, who was expecting Blandford's baby and was by now in a state of panic, then gave her lover – for what reason it is hard to imagine – a packet of admiring letters she had once received from the Prince of Wales. Perhaps she was trying to make him jealous, or hoped he would realize what a prize he had in her. At any rate, Blandford's brother, Lord Randolph Churchill, seized on these letters as a way out of the impasse. He went to see the Princess of Wales and told her that 'being aware of peculiar and most grave matters affecting the case, he was anxious that His Royal Highness should give such advice to Lord Aylesford as to induce him not to proceed against his wife'.[12] As a result of this blackmailing manoeuvre, relations between the royal family and the Churchills were broken off. The Prince announced that he would not visit any house in England which remained open to the Churchills. Lord Aylesford let it be known that 'in order to avoid great public mischief' he would not go on with his divorce. Lady Blandford left Lord Blandford, and when some years later he succeeded to the dukedom she refused to take the title of duchess, preferring to remain Lady Blandford. She finally divorced the Duke and he, visiting America in 1888, met Mrs Lily Hammersley, a rich widow (so rich that she had changed her name from Lilian to avoid the obvious lampoonist's rhyme with 'million') and determined to marry her. Leonard Jerome, whose daughter Jennie was married to the Duke's brother, Lord Randolph Churchill, wrote to his wife: 'I rather think he will marry the

Hammersley. Don't you fear any responsibility on my part. Mrs H. is quite capable of deciding for herself. Besides I have never laid eyes on the lady but once. At the same time I hope the marriage comes off as there is no doubt that she has lots of tin.'[13] Yes; she had lots and lots of tin; and when she got to Blenheim, there to find a great many pictures of the Duke's current paramour prominently on display, the new Duchess gritted her teeth and did what was expected of her. Blenheim's fourteen acres of roofs were re-leaded, central heating was installed, a boathouse was built. And, after all, she was Duchess of Marlborough, and her husband was not without charm, and was certainly not a bore. A close acquaintance described him thus: 'I have known one or two first-class minds whose achievements have been nil. Take George, eighth Duke of Marlborough, an almost incomparable mind, indeed in receptivity, range and versatility, hardly to be matched....'[14]

That had been in 1888; and now it was 1896, and the roof would soon need seeing to again. And where was the money to come from this time? There was only one answer: America. Sunny, the ninth Duke, resigned himself to the inevitable. Not surprisingly, considering the miserable circumstances of his childhood, he was not a happy young man. He, too, had a girl with whom he was in love; but she was not rich, and his whole upbringing had taught him that a dukedom carried responsibilities which transcend the personal. As he was continually to impress upon Consuelo after they were married, he felt that he was only a link in a chain, and it was up to him to make the best possible provision for the links to come. He renounced his love and came over to America to do his duty.

So the two sad young people were pushed into each other's company at Newport. As soon as the Duke arrived, Consuelo was released from her isolation and thrown into the midst of the season's gaieties. Alva began by throwing a ball to outdo all other balls at Marble House. Then there were endless parties, lunches on board yachts, visits to the casino, drives and dinners. Finally, Marlborough proposed, during an evening at home in Marble House 'in the Gothic Room whose atmosphere was so propitious to sacrifice'.[15] It was unkindly rumoured that Marlborough had first proposed to Consuelo's cousin Gertrude, daughter of Mrs

57

Alice Vanderbilt – *the* Mrs Vanderbilt of her day – whose 'cottage', The Breakers, had been completed at just about the same time as Marble House – but that Gertrude had turned him down, when he returned to the slightly less wealthy Consuelo. The two Mrs Vanderbilts did not speak; everyone was scandalized that Alva should have divorced her husband – and in New York State!

Be that as it may, Alva had her way, and the troth was now plighted. When Consuelo told her young brothers about it, one of them, Harold, said: 'He is only marrying you for your money' – at which the poor girl could put a good face on it no longer and burst into tears.

All the obstacles were not yet surmounted. To begin with, there was the question of marriage settlement. Nobody was denying the fact that 'he was only marrying her for her money,' but the question remained – how should the money which the bride would undoubtedly be bringing with her be apportioned? Such questions arose even when the couple concerned were the most passionate of lovers, let alone in a case like this one. The betrothal of Jennie Jerome and Lord Randolph Churchill had nearly foundered over the problem of settlements – the difficulties again arising not from arguments about the amount of money (though Leonard Jerome was not able to provide quite as much as Randolph's family might have hoped, owing to recent reverses on Wall Street) but about its apportionment. American fathers, having made their way in the world, had not done so in order that their sons-in-law should eventually control those large portions of their estate which they assigned to their daughters. In America, the money a girl brought to the marriage remained her own; in Europe, it was expected to be assigned to the husband to be spent as he thought best. He would, it was to be hoped, prove generous to his wife.

Such feudal arrangements stuck in the gullet of American parents. Visiting the Jeromes in Paris while the details of his and Jennie's marriage settlement were being worked out, Randolph wrote: 'Mr and Mrs Jerome and myself are barely on speaking terms, and I don't quite see what is to be the end of it. I think both his conduct and Mrs J.'s perfectly disgraceful and I am bound to say that Jennie entirely agrees with me.'[16]

But in the end a compromise was reached. Mr Jerome wrote to Randolph's father:

> In explanation of my own action in respect to it [the settlement] I beg to assure you that I have been governed purely by what I conceived to be for the best interests of both parties. It is quite wrong to suppose I entertain any distrust of Randolph. On the contrary, I firmly hope and believe there is no young man in the world safer, still I can but think your English custom of making the wife so utterly dependent upon the husband most unwise.
>
> In the settlement as finally arranged I have ignored American customs and waived all my American prejudices and have conceded to your views and English custom on every point – save one. That is simply – a somewhat unusual allowance of her money to the wife. Possibly this principle may be wrong but you may be very certain my action upon it in this instance by no means arises from any distrust of Randolph.[17]

He finally settled £3000 a year on the pair; the Duke, with five daughters to dower and marry off and the vast upkeep of Blenheim to finance, paid Randolph's debts of £2000 and increased his allowance to £1100 a year.[18] It is probable that both sides felt aggrieved, but the Duke, at any rate, had pushed things as far as he safely could: any more pressure and the goose might well have flown with all the golden eggs.

In Consuelo's case, too, the marriage settlements 'gave rise to considerable discussion'. The Marlboroughs sent across their family solicitor whose avowed intention was that of 'profiting the illustrious family' whose interests he was engaged to further. To this end he devoted considerable persistence. 'Finally,' says Consuelo, 'the settlements were apportioned in equal shares at my request.'[19] Whatever their distrust of such equality, the Marlboroughs cannot have been dissatisfied with the end result of their lawyer's labours. Sunny received $2,500,000 in 50,000 shares of capital stock of the Beech Creek Railway Co., on which an annual payment of 4 per cent was guaranteed by Vanderbilt's New York Central Railway Company. This income was for his life: it continued even when his marriage to Consuelo ended.

Eventually all the arrangements were agreed. The wedding date was fixed for 6 November; it had originally been 5

November, but (Marlborough pointed out) that was Guy Fawkes Day and 'it would not be suitable for him to be married on the day that an attempt had been made to blow up the House of Lords'. Mystified, Consuelo concurred. But if her lot seemed inevitable, she was not resigned to it. How little she was resigned to it is shown by the later evidence of her aunt who said that 'her mother, fearing that she might, at the last moment, change her mind and retract her consent to marry Marlborough, placed a guard on the door of her room on the day of her wedding so that nobody could speak to her or even approach her.'[20]

Consuelo's own description of her wedding morning is appalling.

I spent the morning of my wedding day in tears and alone; no one came near me. A footman had been posted at the door of my apartment and not even my governess was admitted. Like an automaton I donned the lovely lingerie with its real lace and the white silk stockings and shoes. My maid helped me into the beautiful dress, its tiers of Brussels lace cascading over white satin. It had a high collar and long tight sleeves. The court train, embroidered with seed pearls and silver, fell from my shoulders in folds of billowing whiteness. My maid fitted the tulle veil to my head with a wreath of orange blossoms; it fell over my face to my knees. A bouquet of orchids that was to come from Blenheim did not arrive in time. I felt cold and numb as I went down to meet my father and the bridesmaids who were waiting for me. My mother had decreed that my father should accompany me to the church to give me away. After that he was to disappear. We were twenty minutes late, for my eyes, swollen with the tears I had wept, required copious sponging before I could face the curious stares that always greet a bride. To my mother, who had preceded us to the church, the wait appeared interminable and she wondered whether at the last moment her plans would miscarry.[21]

Throughout this whole episode the behaviour of Alva Vanderbilt must appear, by any standards, extraordinary. There was never the slightest pretence that the marriage was organized for anyone's benefit but her own (and, incidentally, the Malborough family's). Hers was the pleasure of ordering the trousseau: Consuelo was not consulted on the grounds that she had no taste, anyway. When the wedding was arranged, Consuelo realized that her mother must have ordered the bridal gown during their last visit to Paris – while Consuelo had still been

hoping to marry Winthrop Rutherfurd, and before even Marlborough had made up his mind. Alva, not Consuelo, chose the
bridesmaids: they were all daughters of her own friends. She
even used the occasion of the wedding to further her feud with
the Vanderbilt clan. Consuelo was not allowed to accept any
presents from her Vanderbilt relatives, and had to have them sent
back without so much as a letter of explanation or apology.

Why did she behave in this way – with such cruelty to a
daughter whom, as their later relations seem to affirm, she did
genuinely love?

Part of the clue must lie in her own experience. She herself
had made a loveless but advantageous marriage; why should
Consuelo expect anything different? One could not expect to
follow one's inclinations from the first. After Consuelo's marriage, Alva herself remarried – her husband this time being Oliver
H.P. Belmont; and this union, during its short length – Belmont
died not long after – was very happy. In this, too, Consuelo
followed her mother's pattern, contracting a happy second marriage with an old admirer, Jacques Balsan. Then, 'history records
many marriages of convenience,' said Consuelo, talking of the
affair. So it does – alliances between princely or aristocratic or
business houses. In forcing through this marriage, Alva was simply
giving logical expression to her view – shared, as already noted,
by Mrs Grace Vanderbilt – that the Vanderbilts had achieved
quasi-royal status. Consuelo's choice of suitable consorts was
thus as narrow as that of any royal princess.

It was perhaps unfortunate for Alva – and certainly unfortunate for poor Consuelo – that the latter was so utterly out of
sympathy with this view of her position. There were many of
her friends, more worldly and less intellectual, who might have
been far less distressed by the whole affair – might, indeed,
merrily have joined in the pantomime. But Consuelo had had the
education which befitted a good American girl – and it was not
the education which befitted a duchess. When Marlborough first
showed Consuelo round his estates, some months before he proposed marriage but (she later conjectured) on the day when he
finally made up his mind that, for the sake of those same estates,
he must marry her, her first thoughts as she viewed the neat
cottages and cap-doffing villagers were of Gladstone and John

Bright, political economy and the theory of the rights of man. Such were not usual nor particularly comfortable notions for a future duchess in that epoch to entertain; 'so much deference ... seemed to me both snobbish and ridiculous, for after all we were only two very young people. But in time I learned that snobbishness was an enthroned fetish which spreads its tentacles into every stratum of British national life.'[22]

Most of the American mothers who scoured the European aristocracy for suitable husbands for their daughters, did so with rather different motives from Mrs Vanderbilt's. For what, in the end, had Alva achieved when once she had married her daughter to the Duke? The personal satisfaction of having, as usual, imposed her will and got her own way; the social satisfaction of seeing Consuelo suitably connected. But the standing of her family and herself was in no way changed by the marriage. When one has reached the top, where is there left to go?

In the view of many mothers, this was sadly to waste the potential advantage marriage to a duke might confer. No Vanderbilt needed the social boost of such a marriage. What, on the other hand, might it not do for those who had not yet quite made it socially? 'The Americans who forced their way into good society in Europe were said to be those who were shut out from it at home,' observed Edith Wharton. '... And as for the American women who had themselves presented at the English court – well, one had only to see with whom they associated at home!' What had such ladies to lose in turning to Europe? Faced with a choice between snubs from the narrow-minded matrons back home whose sole pleasure lay in proving their exclusiveness by excluding, and acceptance – for whatever reason – by the no less amusing and desirable circles of Old World society, why should they hesitate? And when they returned as Lady This, the Duchess of That, the Countess of the Other – who would dare exclude them then? American socialites might fume. 'Sometimes ... we cannot help laughing to see the names of women figuring among your "*haute noblesse*" who would never get inside a decent house anywhere in the States,' remarked one. 'But more often we are sorry that your social "leaders" are so easily taken in.'[23] But they could do nothing about it. Upper-class Europeans *would not* recognize American social distinctions. To them

Americans were rich or poor, amusing or dull; the first categories being sought after, the others, not. To carp, as Marie Corelli did, that 'one may presume that there is some cogent reason why an American citizen of the greatest Republic in the World, should elect to desert his native land and "settle down" under "rotten old monarchies". . . . Surrounded as we are today socially by American Bounders of every description . . . the one straight and simple fact remains – namely, that all the best Americans still live in America'[24] – was simply to prove that one was irretrievably middle class. For socially speaking, did not all Americans bound?

In this context a girl's success in Paris, London or Rome might have a double importance. It might secure acceptance for herself; it might also perform that service for her family back home.

Who, for example, would dare ignore Miss Jennie Chamberlain in New York after two years in Europe that had seen her on the most familiar terms with no less a figure than the Prince of Wales? *Town Topics* reported that: 'she will return to her native country with princely honors heaped upon her, and known by name the world over as the young lady who braved the lion in his den and called him Jumbo [sic].'[25] Miss Chamberlain and her mother had left for Europe armed with nothing more than letters of introduction from 'a prominent lady living in Fifth Avenue' (and possibly down on her luck), and had tenaciously worked their way up the ladder of London society until Jennie achieved the very top rung – when, without waiting to be dropped she returned to her native shores to capitalize upon her success. 'When she was with us she created no furore, and was known simply as the pretty Miss Chamberlain from the West. Now she will come back to us in quite a different light, and the belle of London Society,' artlessly admitted *Town Topics*, a transmogrification which could never have been far from Miss Chamberlain's mind.

A more notable case in question was that of Mrs Paran Stevens and her daughter Minnie. Paran Stevens was a rich hotel-owner from Boston, and rumour had it that Mrs Stevens, his second wife (his first had died), was, when they first met, a chambermaid at one of his hotels. Mrs Stevens was born Marietta Reed, the daughter of a country storekeeper 'or in plain words a grocer', says one account; but then what was John Jacob Astor but a fur trapper? By the time the Stevenses hit New York, however, that item of ancestry had receded into the mists of the past, while the hotels were still much in evidence. Naturally, a pushing, thrusting hotel-keeper's wife was not considered acceptable.

Mr and Mrs Stevens married in 1850, when she was nineteen and he was in his forties. They moved to New York from Boston, setting up house at 244 Fifth Avenue, in the early 1860s. By so doing, they were enabled to keep a close eye on Mr Stevens's most important venture – the Fifth Avenue Hotel, of which he had been part owner since its construction in 1858. If the old New Yorkers ostracized Mrs Stevens, she could comfort herself that through the sumptuous amenities of the hotel, she was able to become acquainted with the world's princes – including the Prince of Wales – who stayed there whenever they came to visit New York. So Mr Stevens pursued his business and horse-racing interests, and Mrs Stevens bided her time.

In 1872 Mr Stevens died, and now the forceful Marietta felt free to act. She might not move in the circles she considered she merited in New York, but (thanks to the Fifth Avenue Hotel) she had the most exalted acquaintances abroad, where the question of ancestry was not thought applicable to Americans; all that was required of them being that they be rich and entertaining – which Mrs Stevens and her daughter undoubtedly were.

So Marietta and the glamorous Minnie, tall, green-eyed and as ambitious as her mamma, set off on their travels. Minnie was now nineteen – just the right age to be launched socially. The first thing the ladies did on their arrival in England was to pursue their old acquaintance with the Prince of Wales. The Prince was always delighted to be amused by pretty ladies. They were invited to Sandringham and Marlborough House. They were on their way.

This was really the beginning of the epoch of the dollar princesses. As we have seen, there had, over the past hundred years or so, been a number of transatlantic matches; but it was the 1870s that saw the establishment of this occasional phenomenon as a recognized habit. In the forefront of the contingent were Minnie Stevens and her friends. In 1874 Jennie Jerome, daughter of a business and horseracing acquaintance of Mr

Stevens, married Lord Randolph Churchill; and in 1876 Consuelo Yznaga, with whom Minnie had grown up, married Lord Mandeville, the Duke of Manchester's heir.

This marriage both set an example for Minnie Stevens to follow and bid fair to help her on her way. If Consuelo could marry a future duke, why should not she? And who could be better placed to introduce her to such? Far from needing to be coerced by her mother, as that other Consuelo was to be, Minnie Stevens needed no encouraging. She was set on an aristocratic marriage; nothing else would do.

Of course, it was not necessary for the duke (it was naturally preferable to marry a duke if possible: one might as well aim for the top) to be British. There were perfectly good dukes in France, and by 1877 – she was by now twenty-four – Miss Stevens had found one. Minnie's duke was the subject of a correspondence between Frances, Lady Waldegrave and Mrs John Adair of Rathdaire, *née* Cornelia Wadsworth of Geneseo, New York. 'Dearest Lady Waldegrave,' wrote Mrs Adair, '. . . . Did you hear of the Duc de Grammont having a man of business in New York go thoroughly through her [Miss Stevens's] affairs, and finding out she has really only £5000 a year which he did not consider sufficient for the Duc de Guiche? How galling for a girl to be put in such a position! I do hope she will marry Lord Rossmore. Her Mother must have mismanaged her property dreadfully to have reduced it so much.' Lady Waldegrave wrote in her turn to Lady Strachey: 'I must say I think this business very cruel, but at the same time I can't help thinking she deserved a snubbing as she told me she had £20,000 a year and would have more, and she told me that sum in dollars as well, so there is no mistaking the amount.' Lady Waldegrave felt particularly sore on this point, possibly because Minnie had been relying on her for suitable introductions and sponsorship, and she must have been afraid that people might think her party to the deceit.

Unabashed, Minnie continued her campaign. Certainly she had plenty of that supremely American quality, snap. Wrote Mrs Adair to Lady Waldegrave:

We have just been staying at Tandaragee (the Manchesters' place in Ireland) with Lord and Lady Mandeville – poor little thing, she is so delicate – so utterly helpless – and *most* charming. . . . She cannot endure a country life, and is quite miserable at Tandaragee, although she has Miss Stevens with her who is the brightest cheeriest companion, the more I see of her the more I like her. I hope she will marry an Englishman – she is suited to life in this country which poor little Consuelo Mandeville is not. She has two Irish admirers – Lord Rossmore and Lord Newry. I think the first means business, but the second only amusement.

But neither Lord Rossmore nor Lord Newry came to anything. There were, however, plenty more fish in the sea. Lady Waldegrave seems, despite the disappointment over the money, to have continued her good offices. In December she wrote to tell Lady Strachey that: 'I had a line this morning from Lord William Hay proposing to run down here ... he says he wants a good chat with me. I wonder if it is about Miss Stevens as her Duke has thrown her over.' Wrote Minnie to Lady Waldegrave: 'The matrimonial fever is raging so very much that I hope it will attack me' – but it failed to do so in the person of Lord William (although a year later Minnie told Lady Waldegrave that she had refused him more than once).

Though the matrimonial fever might attack others, it was becoming clear that neither dukes nor even lords were being fatally smitten with it in the vicinity of Miss Stevens. It was by now 1878; Minnie was twenty-five, and she had been around and known to be in the market for a husband since she was nineteen. Always a realist, she made up her mind to take what was going. This turned out to be Arthur Paget, who was undeniably charming, but was neither a lord nor even a knight – so Minnie would not be a ladyship unless a blameless career in the Brigade of Guards garnered him a knighthood in the fullness of time (it did). But he was definitely aristocratic – the grandson of the first Marquis of Anglesey – and, what with his connections and hers, Minnie would be well established in society. On 27 July 1878, they were married in St Peter's Church, Eaton Square. The Prince of Wales personally 'evinced extraordinary condescension' and paid a visit to the bride's mother the day before the wedding. The wedding presents were gorgeous: the Prince of Wales contributed a Louis XIV clock and candelabra which he had bought at the Paris Exhibition; the Princess of Wales gave a serpent bracelet of gold set with sapphires, diamonds and rubies. A year later, when Minnie did her duty and produced a son, the Prince was godfather when he was christened Albert Edward Sidney Louis Paget. Minnie had made it.[26]

And so had Mrs Stevens. One morning in the late 1870s, after Minnie's marriage, Mrs August Belmont, one of New York's undoubted social leaders, drove up conspicuously one morning to pay a call at 244 Fifth Avenue. All New York noticed. Of course, old New York was not what it had been. The distinction had been drawn between nobs and swells – but not even Ward McAllister ventured to suggest that swells be excluded. Mrs Stevens, sensing, as time went on, the competition between the old exclusiveness and the *nouveaux riches*, sensibly put her money on both horses. The cultural Mecca of the old establishment was the Academy of Music. The new rich had attempted to buy their way into this exclusive circle, offering as much as thirty thousand dollars for a box; but had been turned down. So they set up, in direct competition, the Metropolitan Opera House. In October 1883, the opening night was held. It was reported that: 'the Goulds and the Vanderbilts and people of that ilk perfumed the air with the odor of crisp greenbacks.'[27] Mrs Paran Stevens had thoughtfully taken boxes at both places, and so could spend part of the evening at each.

Mrs Stevens's salon became the place to meet the lions. She gave a series of Sunday evening musical teas; she entertained the foreign aristocrats who were her daughter's friends; she cut an impressive figure as Queen Elizabeth at Mrs Vanderbilt's famous fancy-dress ball. And if her daughter had been the means whereby she achieved these social ends of her own, it was through her son that she managed to get her own back on some of those who had behaved badly towards her.

Harry Leyden Stevens was six years younger than his sister Minnie, being born in 1859. This made him three years older than young Edith Newbold Jones, who was to become famous as Edith Wharton. Edith was a cousin of the Schermerhorns and Rhinelanders, but in spite of these social connections was not at all sociable. She was shy, intellectual, intense, socially rather uneasy; Harry was sporting, handsome, popular, and – on account of these qualities – a leader of the young social set in Newport. They made an unlikely couple but nevertheless, during the spring and summer of 1880, they were seen about a great deal together. Gossips, noticing the friendship, were surprised, but it persisted, and when the Joneses went abroad that November for the sake of Mr Jones's health, Harry did not lose touch. He joined the family in Venice the next September and stayed with them all through Mr Jones's last illness until he died early the next year. He was, wrote Edith's mother to a friend, a comfort to them all. The Joneses returned to America; Harry followed them. By August 1882, Edith and Harry were informally engaged; *Town Topics* reported that the wedding would take place at All Saints' Church, New York, in the middle of October. On 29 October, however, it was reported that: 'The marriage of Mr Henry Stevens, Mrs Paran Stevens's son, to Miss Edith Jones, which was announced for the latter part of this month, has been postponed, it is said indefinitely.'

Speculation was intense. What had caused the break? It was generally supposed that Mrs Stevens, who had never formally acknowledged the engagement, must be behind it. It so happened that the Joneses' intimate circle contained those people who had, in the past, been the rudest of all to the upstart and ambitious Mrs Stevens. Lucretia Jones, Edith's mother, told a friend many years later that: 'Mrs Stevens was intensely resentful of the coldness shown her by members of the Joneses' set and had refused . . . to allow her son to marry into the enemy camp.'[28] Another account, which expands rather than contradicts the first, was given by Edith's fifteen-year-old cousin Helen Rhinelander in a letter to her brother: 'Is it not sad about Pussy's engagement being broken? I have only seen her once and then she did not appear particularly sad. It is evidently Mrs. S.'s fault, or rather she is the cause. We have not heard much about it, only Mrs. S. behaved insultingly to Aunt Lu! Don't repeat this for the world. Aunt Lu told this to Mamma! I doubt Pussy and H. have changed in their feeling for one another, but that Mrs. S. is at the bottom of it all.'

How she must have enjoyed paying back those women who had made her suffer not so many years before! There is another aspect to this broken engagement which may throw light on Minnie's mysterious lack of money so reprovingly noted some years earlier by Lady Waldegrave. Paran Stevens had left a great deal of money, and Mrs Stevens had not necessarily (as Lady Waldegrave speculated) mismanaged the estate and run through it all. But she needed a lot of money herself to keep up the social grandeur and display with which she was making her mark; and, as it happened, the bulk of the estate – over a million and a quarter dollars, not huge by Vanderbilt standards but still very respectable in the early 1870s – had been left to Harry. He would come into his inheritance on his twenty-fifth birthday or on the occasion of his marriage, whichever occurred first. Mrs Stevens was therefore determined that, at the very least, he should not marry before the age of twenty-five. On the date when he and Edith Jones were to have married, he would have been twenty-three; so Mrs Stevens secured the use of the full income for another two years – and who knew what might not happen then? (By a dreadful irony, what did in fact happen was that Harry died of consumption at the age of twenty-six.) It is probable, therefore, that there would have been little to spare for Minnie if her mother had anything to do with it. Minnie had youth and beauty and snap and must make do with those – as Marietta had done before her.

But the business of transatlantic matchmaking was not always pursued in the spirit of grim determination which seems the dominant note in the manoeuvrings of Mrs Vanderbilt and Miss Stevens. The Wilson family, for example, though no less successful – indeed, arguably more so, since their marriages were both elevated and, to all appearances, happy – seem to have approached the whole affair in an altogether lighter-hearted mood.

Richard Wilson – whose first name, it will be remembered, had eluded the compiler of *Titled Americans* – had started life as a travelling salesman in Georgia. He had married the daughter of a well-to-do farmer, and backed by his father-in-law's money had opened a general store in Loudon. This he built up, by successful speculations abroad during the American Civil War, into an immense banking business. The Wilsons had five children, and Mrs Wilson early grasped the principle that the quick way to social advancement was through judicious marriage. Her activities in this field gave rise to a popular joke:

Q: Why did the Diamond Match Co. fail?
A: Because Mrs Richard T. Wilson beat them at making matches.

In fact only one of Mrs Wilson's daughters – Belle – made an aristocratic match, marrying the Hon. Michael Herbert; but her son Orme married Carrie Astor, daughter of the doyenne of New York society – the owner of the ballroom into which the Four Hundred were all that could be fitted – and her eldest daughter, May, married Ogden Goelet, who was soon to inherit about $25,000,000 worth of Manhattan real estate from an uncle; and the combination of these marriages – but especially Belle's – opened the way for Grace Wilson to marry young Cornelius Vanderbilt against the wishes of his awesome mother, Alice of The Breakers, who had other ideas for him. But, given such a background, May Goelet's daughter, also called May, was an obvious candidate for a transatlantic alliance – a fact which she seems to have regarded with the greatest equanimity, viewing the whole affair very much as a game. In the winter of 1902, May wrote to her Aunt Grace from Bad Homburg, the spa then much favoured by the King's set:

I can't begin to tell you what fun I had in London. It simply was glorious. You know how fond I am of dancing, and all my old partners were so kind to me, and I made several new ones.

To go back, though. I must give an account of my proposals. Well, first Lord Shaftsbury [sic] popped almost as soon as he returned to London. He came one afternoon. Mamma happened to leave the room for a few minutes and off he went – like a pistol. I told him it was quite ridiculous as he had only known me three weeks and he couldn't possibly know his own mind – and besides I knew nothing of him nor his past beyond the fact that when he was 21 he had been devoted to Lady N–, which he said was true but that was all over long ago – and he was certain he knew his own mind. I like him very much only I have no intention of marrying him or anyone else at present.

Mamma is terribly afraid I will accept Lord Shaftsbury, though! The Duke of Roxburghe is the man that everyone says I am engaged to. I didn't see him at all at first as he never goes to balls, but at a dinner at Mrs James' he came and talked to me and the following night we met at Lady Curzon's where we were dining. Such a nice dinner. Lord Castlereagh took me in (the Londonderry boy) and we talked together afterwards so I didn't have a chance of saying a word to the Duke.

Mrs Benson is crazy to make a match between Captain Holford and myself! And Lord Grey who married Captain Holford's other sister is very anxious to arrange it too. The Prince said to Lord Grey, 'It's quite time George (Captain H.) was getting married. I know just the right person for him – a charming girl, Miss Goelet. It really must be arranged.'

Now the funny part is that Capt. Holford has never said a word for himself. He wants to find out, you see, if we are willing before he commits himself in the least. Dorchester House, of course, would be delightful and I believe he has two charming places in the country. Unfortunately, the dear man has no title, though a very good position – and I am sure he would make a very good husband.

Well, the next offer was from George Cornwallis-West, Princess Pless' brother. Such a dear, attractive, good-looking boy, and quite the best dancer in London. Anyway he fancies himself very much in love with me. So foolish of him. I am so sorry about it – but what can one do? I like him ever so much as a friend – but why they have always to wish for something more, I can't imagine.'[29]

But, of course, she could imagine, perfectly well. May in fact fulfilled society's predictions. Unable to resist the idea of being a duchess, she married the Duke of Roxburghe and went to live at Floors Castle, his seat in the border country.

But whether forced, anxiously sought or lightheartedly indulged in, there is a quality about all these matches which makes one feel that the cynicism they inspired was amply justified. Were all such matches institutions in which it was considered somehow indecent to engage the deeper feelings?

Perhaps it is not surprising that few love-matches figure in the annals of the dollar princesses. It must, after all, be more a matter of luck than anything else if a marriage contracted for advantage, of one sort or another, should also turn out to be a love-match. But occasionally we do hear of such. In the case of Jennie Jerome and Lord Randolph Churchill, the union was one of passion on both sides – it was incidental that Jennie's father was a rich American, and neither family was particularly enthusiastic about the marriage to begin with; but Jennie and Randolph were not to be deterred by parental attempts to keep them apart long enough for passion to recede.

Then there was the instance of Mary Leiter and Lord Curzon. Here it seems plain that it was the lady who made the running – not because she was fascinated by Curzon's position, but by his person. Mary met George Curzon at a ball during her first London season, and during the weeks she remained in London that year, they met repeatedly. Over the course of the next three years, though he was constantly in her thoughts, his attention was far less undivided. They met from time to time the next season in London; it became evident that he liked her and found her attractive, but that she was deeply in love with him. For the reigning belle of Washington this was a new experience. He visited America, even passed through Washington, but did not call on Mary. Instead he visited another Virginia belle of whom he noted in his diary: 'Upon me Amy shone with the undivided insistence of her starlike eye. Oh God, the nights on the still lawn under the soft sky with my sweetheart!'[30] Piqued, Mary would occasionally remind him that her everlasting devotion was by no means to be taken for granted. 'There has been very much of a princeling who came with equerries and a suite to study American institutions, and I had the misfortune to be the only institution he wished to adopt,' she wrote once; and again, when in Italy she was courted by both the Marchese Rudini and the Count of Turin: 'There is an absolute assurance about an Italian one rarely finds elsewhere. There is no competition and no jealousy. None of them dreams that his importance is to be questioned.'[31] But she succumbed to none of these advances. Eventually, during a hurriedly arranged dinner in Paris, eighteen months since their last meeting and three years since they had first become acquainted, Curzon, somewhat (it seems) to his own surprise, proposed to her and was accepted. He wrote later, when death and retrospect had gilded every moment he spent with Mary:

I had entered the hotel without the slightest anticipation that this would be the issue. She told me her story. How she had waited for nearly three years since the time when we first met, rejecting countless suitors and always waiting for me. I told her that while I felt from the beginning that we were destined for each other, I had not dared to speak, and had even run the risk of losing her because there was certain work in my scheme of Asiatic travel which I had resolved to do, and which I could not ask any married woman to allow her husband to carry out. Some of it, notably the journey to the Pamirs and Afghanistan, still remained undone; and even now when we

became secretly engaged, it was on the understanding that I should be
at liberty to complete my task before we took the final step.[32]

So poor Mary was condemned to another two years of secrecy
before she could make her engagement public, let alone marry.
She swore to him that, if he should die on his journey, she would
marry no other man but would retire to a convent; he promised
her that she could trust him absolutely.

What were Curzon's motives for embarking on this marriage?
Mary's biographer, Nigel Nicolson, on the whole believes that
they were not cynical – as they might, indeed, appear. There was
no doubt that Mary's money could be – and was – of the greatest
help to Curzon in underpinning his high-flying political ambitions; but to set against that advantage would be the jeers of his
friends, all of whom would assume that he was indeed marrying
only for money. Then there was the fact that the in-laws with
whom he would thus be saddled were just the sort of Americans
whom he most disliked – whom he had once described to a friend
as 'the least attractive species of the human genus'. Besides, if
he had been only after the money, he could have married her,
and it, when they first met, and not risked losing the prize by
keeping her waiting five years. But if he was not passionately in
love with her, as she was with him, from the first moment they
met (and as he later, in rosy retrospect, affirmed that he had
been) his devotion increased with acquaintance – and hers never
faltered. Perhaps of all the transatlantic unions that of George
Curzon and Mary Leiter, the shopkeeper's daughter whom he
made a vicereine and grew to love with such unwavering devotion, is the most truly romantic; just as that of Consuelo Vanderbilt and the Duke of Marlborough is the most gothic.

Mary Leiter had taste. George Curzon was worth waiting for;
he was one of the most extraordinary men of his time. But there
can be no doubt that, for many nobly connected scallywags,
American heiresses represented a way to a marriage and an easy
fortune which they would never have had a hope of securing
amongst their own circles.

Take Sir William Gordon-Cumming, villain of the Tranby
Croft scandal in which he was accused of cheating at cards –
the most dreadful offence a gentleman could commit – and in

73

connection with which the Prince of Wales himself, who had been present, was threatened with being subpoenaed as a witness in a court of law (the ultimate horror in that society which believed, above all things, in discretion). Even before this incident Sir William had shown himself to be not a particularly pleasant fellow. For example, in 1875, the year after Jennie Jerome was married to Lord Randolph Churchill, we find her sister Clara writing home to her mamma: 'Jennie wants me so much to be nice to Sir William Gordon-Cumming and wants him to make up to me. I think *entre nous* that it wd take very little to make him devoted to me, although he is a married man who never speaks to a young girl and only flirts with married ladies. He began *très sérieusement à faire la cour* to Jennie but last night he would not leave me in the hall. But I could not think of him at all as he is very poor and awfully conceited and not *sympathique*. I don't think I could really like a man like that.'[33]

Indeed, who could? In 1882, when the youngest of the Jerome sisters, Leonie, on her first visit to London was walking in Hyde Park, Sir William gave further evidence of his appalling lack of taste by coming up to her and saying, 'Over here husband-hunting?'[34] Between Clara's encounter and the Tranby Croft events in 1891 he had shed his wife; and if he accused Leonie of being on the hunt, that may have been because he had the very same thing in mind. On 10 June 1891, the very day that he was cashiered from the Scots Guards on account of Tranby Croft, he married Miss Florence Garner, a young, beautiful and extremely rich American girl. It was reported that Miss Garner married 'against the wishes and protests of her family'. But presumably for her a sir was a sir; and there could be no doubt that Sir William had known all the best people, even if they no longer cared to know him.

So, for their various reasons, they got married – and, say the fairy stories, 'lived happily ever after' – thus subsuming in a merciful formula those events of the greater part of our lives to which the excitement of the wedding is often such a misleading preliminary.

6

Great Expectations – France

The world was radiant, the lights were lit, the music playing; she was still young, and better-looking than ever, with a Countess's coronet, a famous château and a handsome and popular husband who adored her. And then suddenly the lights went out and the music stopped when one day Raymond, putting his arm about her, said in his tenderest tones: 'And now, my dear, the world's had you long enough and it's my turn. What do you say to going down to Saint Desert?'[1]

It is of course a truism that arranged marriages are no more likely to be unhappy – or happy – than those entered into for love. Marriage, it is to be hoped, lasts longer, and comprises more, than the first fine careless rapture. But that presupposes certain things about the arranged marriage: notably that it will ensure that the protagonists share a common background and have received a similar upbringing, so that they may be expected to place importance upon the same things and view the world in a similar way. It is hard to over-estimate the importance of such things in a happy marriage; but they did not enter into those arrangements made between the dollar princesses and their princes.

How did they feel as the moment approached when they must face life alone together? The cautious pessimism expressed by Anna Gould when she refused to become a Catholic, since that would preclude the possibility of divorce, must have been shared by a good many of the girls and not a few of the men. They came from such different worlds that the surprising thing is not that many of these marriages were unhappy, but that any of them were happy. What, once the formalities were over, had a Boni de Castellane to say to an Anna Gould – or vice versa?

Boni de Castellane has left a full and revealing account of his childhood. It was a life centred upon the family, the land and their traditions and upkeep. He begins his *Confessions*, the book in which he tells his side of the story of the marriage with Anna, with an account of the ancient lineage of the Castellanes and a description of their château in the Loire valley, Rochecotte, 'a temple dedicated to ancestor-worship'. Of the château he says: 'Everything there served as a link in the chain of the Past, and silently recalled some definite landmark in the history of a family which attached more importance to the traditions of good breeding than to any accepted ideas of the day.' And again: 'Memory triumphed, the invisible were all-powerful.'[2]

When Boni was a child the house was dominated by his grandmother, a niece of the famous Prince de Talleyrand, who had brought her up and whose devoted disciple she was. At her *petite levée* she handed out the orders of the day and dealt with the problems of her tenants and servants; she passed two hours at her toilette; she passed her evenings in conversation with a few trusted old friends and the local abbé; young women were expected to keep respectfully quiet in deference to their knitting elders. Through this lady the Castellanes were related to half the aristocracy of Europe – the Courlandes, the Hatzfelds, the Radziwills, the Potockis. To Rochecotte came a constant stream of relatives bearing historic and occasionally royal names, there to pursue the tradition of family life.

In this idyllic spot, young Boni's education was divided between the church and schoolroom – intimately connected – the countryside and the hunting-field. Above all reigned religion: 'religion was the foundation on which the Château had been raised.' Money was never an end in itself, but was important only insofar as it contributed to the upkeep – ample and in superb style – of Rochecotte and the other family estates. One did not think about it; it was simply assumed that it would always be there.

How different was the childhood of Anna! If, with the Castellanes, everything was taken for granted, with the Goulds nothing was. How could it be when their father, Jay Gould, had started from nothing to become the most hated and feared man in Wall Street, referred to by the press as 'the modern Mephistopheles' and indeed regarded by not a few as nothing more nor less than the devil reincarnated? It was bad enough, and socially disorientating enough, to be the children of a man reputed to have made his first fortune out of a patent mousetrap; when that same man was also supposed to have driven his first financial partner to suicide, was known as the 'Great Bear', had been the ruthless cause of 'Black Friday' when so many had been ruined in the course of his attempt to corner the gold market – when he was said to have wrecked and ruined every enterprise with which he had been connected, except himself – then social equivocation might be supposed to reach a peak.

Such a man might be expected to be a monster in every respect. However, contemporaries noted with some surprise that this was not the case. If he was a monster in his business life – a judgement which was occasionally disputed but more generally accepted – Gould's preoccupations in his private life were surprisingly gentle. A sickly man, plagued with consumption, his two great pleasures were his orchids, for the propagation of which he built acres of elaborate greenhouses at his country estate at Irvington on the Hudson River, and his children, to the details of whose upbringing he devoted endless care and attention. A contemporary description pictures him 'surrounded by children who climb upon his knees and ask him all sorts of questions about the sights to be seen through the car windows'.[3] Callers were always made aware that Mr Gould was an extremely busy man, and if they had nothing of importance to communicate, they should leave him to his work. His children were aware of his preoccupation – he frequently apologized, in his letters to them, for having failed to write because he was so busy – but no detail of their lives was too small for him to take an interest in. There were a number of children – George, Edwin, Howard, Frank, Helen; Anna was his youngest daughter. Their mother died when Anna was very young, and Helen, her elder sister, to some extent took her place.

Anna's childhood was passed under a strict regime of supervision which must have more than offset any moments of indulgence. She might be rich, but all this meant was that she had more responsibilities and must set a better example. 'Dear Anna, I fear you think I preach to you,' wrote sister Helen one birthday. There followed a birthday reminder about growing into a woman, with a woman's responsibilities. 'You do not know how much I love you,' the letter ended. 'I am anxious that you should be a noble, unselfish woman.' It was the Puritan ethic in its purest form.

Certainly she was not allowed to throw her money around. Any expenditure must be accounted for, any bill paid on the nail. When the family visited Egypt on their yacht *Atalanta* – presumably in search of a mild climate for Gould's illness – Anna kept a record of her daily expenditure in the back of her diary, noting every dime. A 'grab bag' cost her ten cents, two ice creams, seventy-five cents. 'Today saw Pyramids – stayed in Giza Palace Hotel,' she recorded; but the trip was far from being a wild round of pleasure. A note written on the *Atalanta* says succinctly: 'Much milder – ate all my meals today.' Back home she attended Miss Bennett's school at Ogontz, Pennsylvania; and here, too, her father's main concern seems to have been to make sure that she should not think herself any better or different from the other girls just because she was richer than they were. He wanted to know who her friends were, scolded her for infringing the rules ('I think you should ask Miss Bennett's forgiveness'), and would not let her beg special favours. 'I see from a letter from your bank that you have overdrawn your account by $8.60,' he wrote severely. 'I hope by the time I get back you will have done something about it.'⁴ – This from a man of whom it was written that: 'No other man in the world . . . deals with such immense masses of money in the ordinary course of his business. To purchase a railroad outright and give his cheque for the full amount is not an extraordinary transaction for Jay Gould.'⁵

At the same time, Anna was never left in any doubt of her father's affection. The letters were by no means only concerned with money. 'Your affectionate Pappa' tells her that Helen has the gripe, Ed's leg is better, Howard is recovering; when he goes to Florida, again in search of health, he worries about her being in the big house alone when the family is away, and apologizes for having been too busy to write; her brother Frank says: 'Papa is waiting for a letter from Anna and wonders if she is writing to him now.'

And then Jay Gould died, and Anna, just coming up to marriageable age, was left without a guiding hand, uncertain of her place in society, and fair game for the fortune hunters who would certainly pursue her. Her sister Helen was deeply religious, interested only in good works and completely unsuited to chaperone Anna through the shoals and reefs of high society, even had she been interested in doing so. Her brother George and his wife were very social indeed – some of the taint having washed off the Gould millions by the time they reached the second generation – but they had their own position to confirm, their own life to lead, and although they would keep an eye on Anna when they could, they could not do so full time. What, then, was to be done?

The answer was to turn to Mrs Paran Stevens, who was prepared for just such eventualities. Did the papers report that Anna's uncle Abe Gould ('Rough and Ready and Full of Peculiarities, but He Has a Host of Staunch, True, Friends') had recently been noticed wrestling for the right of way down a narrow passage with an Irish hod-carrier – and winning?[6] The Four Hundred might turn up their noses at anyone connected to such a roughneck – but Mrs Stevens knew what it was like to suffer at the hands of the Four Hundred; and, besides, a little more money was always welcome.

For since her daughter Minnie's establishment at the heart of European society as Mrs Arthur Paget, a leading member of the Prince of Wales's set and at home in all the capitals and fashionable watering-places of Europe, the Stevens family – always enterprising – had set up what amounted to a transatlantic marriage bureau, of the very highest class, of course. For a price, and to suitable candidates, introductions and chaperones were provided. It was, for example, Mrs Paget who, in her London home, 35 Belgrave Square, 'a fine house with lofty rooms in which there was an immense amount of nondescript furniture and numerous tables that were littered with signed photographs in silver frames',[7] agreed to introduce Consuelo Vanderbilt to the Duke of Marlborough. Consuelo's main impression was of 'a pair of hard green eyes'. Minnie's comments on the occasion were certainly to the point: 'If I am to bring her out she must be able to compete at least as far as clothes are concerned with far better-looking girls,' she informed Mrs Vanderbilt.[8] (This unflattering view of Consuelo was not generally shared.) At her behest, tulle and *jeune fille* decorum gave place to satin and a deep *décolletage*. Satisfied in these respects, Minnie fulfilled her part of the bargain; it was at a dinner party at her house that Consuelo first met the Duke. He sat on the hostess's right, with Consuelo on his other side – 'a rather unnecessary public avowal of her intentions,' Consuelo thought.

Back in New York Mrs Stevens was doing her bit to help the family business. At her house, eager young men on the make could meet the right sort of girl. *Town Topics* helped her in this enterprise, since if anyone had felt it slightly indelicate to ask the kind of questions which were inevitably at the forefront of their mind, all answers were supplied in full by that obliging publication. For example: 'Lord Garmoyle was given a dinner last Sunday evening by Mrs Paran Stevens. His friend and companion, by the way, Lord Godolphin, holds the title by courtesy only, inheriting it from his father, Lord William Godolphin, also a courtesy title. Lord William Godolphin is the fourth son of the seventh Duke of Leeds. The baronetcy is quite ancient, having been created in 1620....'[9]

As heiresses went, Anna Gould represented both a catch and a challenge for those formidable ladies. For while she was probably as rich as Consuelo Vanderbilt (who was up for disposal at about the same time), she possessed none of Miss Vanderbilt's other advantages, being socially nowhere and plain into the bargain. She was small and thin, and her face was all nose and eyes; her complexion was sallow, her hairstyle unbecoming ('arranged in the form of an aeroplane's wings' was how one observer described it[10]) and – the kind of detail of which any girl is hideously conscious – 'her back was a mass of long black hairs'. Then she had no conversation; she had not received the kind of education which teaches a girl the importance of such things. What she did have was a certain rigidity of character, a strong respect for the letter of the truth, a deep sense of the value of money and consequently of her own value as the possessor of large quantities of that useful commodity, and a conviction that, as an heiress and an American, her position in the world was second to none. The satisfactory disposal of Miss Gould was a problem that required some concentration. To this end, Mrs Stevens supplied a permanent chaperone, Miss Fanny Reed, a member of her own family. Miss Reed had a flat in Paris in the rue de la Trémoille, and here she received the eighteen-year-old Anna with a view to introducing her in Paris society.

Society flocked to her door to view Miss Gould, for Anna's fame had travelled before her. 'Gossip credited Miss Gould with the possession of boundless wealth. She was worth milliards instead of millions, and there was likewise much speculation as to her matrimonial future.'[11] In other words, every hard-up nobleman in Paris saw himself doing Miss Gould a favour by marrying her; and Miss Reed, set *in loco parentis* by the Goulds, felt her responsibilities keenly.

Boni de Castellane was at this time twenty-seven years old, spoiled and immensely vain. In Paris, his style was a byword. He '...had the radiance of the dawn.... His complexion was like a sixteen-year-old Swedish girl and his profile like Louis xv's modelled by Caffieri.'[12] His obsession with appearances – above all, his own – made him an object of jealousy and notoriety. This did not disturb him – on the contrary, it was an effect he relished. 'If Boni had received a louis d'or every time his name was uttered, he would no doubt be as rich as ... Anna Gould, so irresistibly did he appeal to his contemporaries' imaginations,' wrote the Duchesse de Clermont-Tonnerre. From him, Marcel Proust drew many of the qualities of his golden young man, Saint-Loup.

Boni felt quite sure that nobody could make such superlative use of great wealth as he could. He was an accomplished ladies' man, and was convinced that the capture of Anna Gould, and thence the easy attainment of his dreams, would be mere child's play. Miss Reed hated him. The extent of her dislike can be deduced from the extraordinary malice of his descriptions of her. Nevertheless, he was not discouraged. He frequented her salon and finally achieved the introduction he was after. 'My name', he records, 'did not appear to make much impression on Miss Gould' – she was talking to the Prince von Battenberg at the time; but viewing her as she sat there, shy yet quite self-possessed, dressed in the unbecoming grey crêpe de Chine which Miss Reed considered suitable for her, the ineffable Boni considered that she had 'possibilities', and 'thought that it would be most fascinating to complete her education in the best finishing school in the world – marriage, and afterwards to present her to an admiring world.'[13]

We have already seen how Boni achieved this aim – and how little chance the unsophisticated Anna and the outflanked Miss Reed stood against his determined wiles. Miss Reed, after all, could only advise; and the George Goulds, who were Anna's official guardians, were charmed by Boni – whose stock-in-trade was charm. So the wedding was arranged, the date fixed for 4 March 1895. Boni's mother presented Anna with a pearl necklace which had been in the family for many generations. The necklace was five rows of pearls with an emerald clasp. Anna was not impressed, commenting only that the pearls were not large enough to be fashionable; the necklace's history meant nothing to her. It was a foretaste of things to come. Boni was mortified, and infuriated by the hullabaloo inevitably attendant upon such a wedding in New York. 'Women journalists laid siege to Anna's bedroom; jewellers and art-dealers lived at my front-door; my valet waxed rich and I waxed angry.'[14] But there was no drawing back now – even if he had wanted to, which, of course, he did not.

The wedding was of the most elaborate. It took place at the Gould house on Fifth Avenue and was solemnized by Monsignor Corrigan, Catholic Archbishop of New York. The ceremony took place in the morning and was followed by a lunch, served at little tables; the bridal table, pictured in the *New York Tribune*'s multi-page spread, was in the shape of a fleur-de-lis. The menu, too, was French – at least, it was written in that language; but the meal was essentially American, its outstanding feature being artifice rather than gastronomic delight. Apparent potatoes turned out to have cutlets concealed within them; apparent chickens were made entirely of sausage meat. The ladies found gold vanity cases hidden beneath their napkins, the gentlemen, gold cigarette cases. Mrs George Gould was not being outdone by anybody.

Amid this splendour sat Boni's relatives, wondering. 'My

mother, in her red velvet gown, sables and Alençon lace, looked
like an ancestral portrait purchased by a millionaire,' he wrote.
'No words can convey any idea of her distress of mind.' His
father was altogether more inclined to take things as they came,
his greatest distress of mind being caused by those newspapers
which insisted upon calling him 'the Old Marquis'. Jean, Boni's
brother, who was one of his witnesses, loved the luxury of it all;
as for Boni, 'I only lived for the moment when I should embark
for Europe, and there regain my lost Paradise of Tradition and
Beauty.'[15]

One man's paradise, however, is not necessarily his wife's. If
the suave and cosmopolitan Boni had been taken aback by some
aspects of life in America, it seems clear that Anna found it much
harder to adapt to life in France, which was, after all, to be her
home from now on. Until now she had been on her own ground,
with Boni more or less at a disadvantage. Moreover, she had
been the prize; he had needed to marry her more than she had
needed to marry him. There were (in American eyes) in-
exhaustible numbers of Bonis, but few girls with a fortune like
Anna's. But now all that was reversed. He was regarded as the
catch; she, looked upon with cynicism. True, she had reserved
the right to divorce – but despite this apparent cynicism, what
girl of nineteen looks forward to such an eventuality just after
her wedding to a man by whom she is dazzled – as Anna clearly
was dazzled by Boni? And now all eyes would be upon her –
French eyes and not necessarily friendly – to see how she would
acquit herself as Madame de Castellane.

How should this lady acquit herself?

However it was, of one thing Anna could be sure. The life of
a *comtesse* was nothing like that of a society woman in New
York. It was not just a question of rank. The whole concept of
married life was fundamentally different on the different sides
of the Atlantic.

Indeed, their legal status as married women in France must
have come as an unpleasant shock to Anna and her compatriots,
for the disposition of property and rights of the spouses were
not here, as they were in England, a matter of arrangement.
Marriage in France normally assumed community of property –
but the husband had the sole right to administer the joint estate.

If he so wished, he could take possession of his wife's personal property, although this did not apply to real estate, of which he could only take the usufruct. Even where there was separation of property the wife could not alienate her own real estate without her husband's consent. And even where the couple were legally separated, the wife still needed her husband's signature for all her business affairs. About the only right she gained from a legal separation was the right to live where she pleased – otherwise, legally, she had to live where her husband told her to, and he could use force to make her do so. But this was about the only right she did gain. She could not sell her property; he retained full rights over the children, and, should he die, she could only act with the consent of his two nearest relatives. She had, as a widow, custody of the children, but if she decided to re-marry, the family council met to decide whether the new situation was acceptable to them and whether she would be allowed to keep the children. In short, marriage in France was an institution for the promulgation of the family – something larger than either of the participant individuals, and much more important than the mere happiness of either; whereas in America it was already an institution within which the two individuals hoped better to further their own ends, whatever those might be.

It was not surprising that American brides should find the state of affairs in France bewildering and infuriating. They had been brought up to consider themselves the social and financial equals of their male relatives; they had been expected (like Anna) to account for themselves financially and regulate their own affairs; they were aware – none more so – that their financial independence represented the basis of their social independence.

What was surprising was that Frenchwomen, to all appearances no less intelligent or independent-minded than American women, not only put up with these restrictions but appeared perfectly happy in spite of them. How – why – could this be so? Edith Wharton, who had lived for many years in France, attempted to explain such mysteries to her compatriots in a curious little book called *French Ways and their Meaning*. Mrs Wharton knew a number of American girls who had married into the *gratin*, and her observations of their difficulties and comparisons between the French and American approach to marriage are, as one might expect, illuminating. Why, asks Mrs Wharton, is the French woman different from the American? Is it a question of dress, cooking, feminity? No; 'the real reason is quite different, and not nearly as flattering to our national vanity. It is simply that, like the man of her race, the Frenchwoman is *grown up*.' Later she enlarges on this, and we see the other side of the American belle's coin. For if her life was at its zenith when she was a young girl, enjoying that freedom and independence which we have observed and which no European girl could hope to attain, it was downhill all the way from there.

In America there is complete freedom of intercourse between boys and girls, but not between men and women; and there is a general notion that, in essentials, a girl and a woman are the same thing. It is true, in essentials, that a boy and a man are very much the same thing; but a girl and a woman – a married woman – are totally different beings.... A girl is only a sketch; a married woman is the finished picture. And it is only the married woman who counts as a social factor.

Now it is precisely at the moment when her experience is rounded by marriage, motherhood, and the responsibilities, cares and interests of her own household, that the average American woman is, so to speak, 'withdrawn from circulation'.... On her wedding-day she ceases, in any open, frank and recognized manner, to be an influence in the lives of the men in the community to which she belongs. In France, the case is just the contrary.[16]

American girls then, treasured their girlhood and hung onto it as long as they could; but in France, 'young girls' lives were so disagreeable that they all rushed headlong at marriage like a herd of sheep at the door of the pen,' observed the Duchesse de Clermont-Tonnerre.

Seen from the viewpoint of the French husband, it is not surprising that American wives seemed less than satisfactory. Wrote Boni about 'my wife's compatriots': 'The overseas girl does not easily accept guidance. She enjoys almost complete freedom.... Her manner with men is full of assurance.... Once married, she is a less tender mother than the Frenchwoman.... The American wife soon tires of her husband and indulges in passing emotions which do not display any savoir faire....'[17] However, he hoped that in this particular case, an exception might be found to the general rule. He makes much of Anna's 'promise' and 'possibilities' at the time of their marriage; she seemed socially unformed enough that 'I hoped that after I had helped to complete her soul's education' they might get on excellently. But, immersed as he was in the peculiar social values of his own world, he could not imagine how strange these appeared to Anna; and when her manner indicated this, he at once took offence.

It was in attitudes to the family and the conduct of family life that France differed perhaps most of all from America; it is not surprising, therefore, that it was the family which caused the first upsets between the newlyweds. On their return to France it was natural that they should visit the family estates – those of the Juignés, who were Boni's maternal grandparents, and of course Rochecotte. Anna hated these visits, and her dislike was quite incomprehensible to Boni. Naturally all the tenants and the family wanted to see 'what kind of an American I had married'. But Anna could not bear being the object of such unfeigned curiosity to the peasantry, servants, nuns, children, and all the rest of those whose families had for generations been connected with the château. At Rochecotte, Boni's mother had arranged a traditional welcome for the young couple – a procession of schoolchildren headed by the schoolmaster, a municipal address of welcome at the railway station, wreaths, bunting, streamers, a triumphal arch, a choir of children. 'I looked at Anna, hoping for some expression of pleasure. None was forthcoming – she was unmistakably bored!' wrote Boni. Anna's taciturn little face was not designed to convey the finer nuances of expression. It seems unlikely that she was bored – but she was almost certainly bewildered, and perhaps dismayed at this view of the kind of life in which she would now be expected to play her part. After all, the entire Castellane family lived at Rochecotte for part of the year at least: she would undoubtedly be expected to do the same. She may have been horrified, as Consuelo Vanderbilt was, by the feudality; or she may simply have recoiled from the notion of *la vie de famille*, so simple, so established, in which she would play such a subordinate role compared with the older women; which would be so tedious – of which she would never really feel part, and which she would continually be conscious of helping to finance: her sole reason for being there. At any rate, 'from that day,' recorded Boni, 'she disliked Rochecotte with an ever-smouldering hatred'. She refused ever to stay there; she was, Boni realized – his dismay growing as the realization sank in – adamant. 'She would never consent to lead our patriarchal *vie de famille*, when during part of the year we made Rochecotte our communal home.'[18] Certainly not – had she left her gay life in America in order to moulder in the country?

She was the more disinclined to submit herself to such an existence in that she had no sympathy whatever for that aspect of life which was its mainspring: respect for rank. Anna had been brought up in a society where wealth was paramount, however much some people might try to pretend things were otherwise, and titles were nonexistent. Why should she suddenly bow down to a lot of people, ugly and patronizing old women, boring old men, just because they were members of old families? Boni introduced her to one haughty duchess after another, but Anna was not cowed as a young bride should be in such circumstances. This piqued him. He stood in some awe of these people – why should not she? 'Day by day, evidence of my wife's curious self-satisfaction became more and more apparent.... Anna was utterly unimpressed by rank. She disregarded it completely; it mattered nothing to a Gould – she was sufficient unto herself.' She did not seem to realize that this was France – that she was no longer in her own peculiar country. Boni's parents tried, and failed, to make contact. How could they when there was no common ground? He himself suffered snubs on her behalf. He and a friend put up George Gould for membership of the Polo Club; George was not only rich but a great fancier of horses, and Boni imagined that these qualities would be sufficient to admit him – that, and his new connections. Not a bit of it. He was blackballed – out of sheer jealousy, Boni surmised: the club members were determined to show that they, at least, were unimpressed by mere wealth.

But if there were some things which all Anna's money could not buy, there were others which it most definitely could. As Boni put it, 'the voice of inanimate beauty was calling to me across the ages'. He had always been a fancier of antiques and now that money was no object he went on the spending spree he had always dreamed of. The antiquarians welcomed him with wide open arms. 'Why, M. Boni, you've become a veritable Croesus,' they remarked delightedly and looked out their choicest wares to spread before him. Boni bought them all. He began with some Boucher tapestries, went on to some pictures – Reynolds, Gainsboroughs, a Van Dyck, Rembrandt's 'Man in a Fur Cap'. Then there was a blue marble table and a pair of celadon vases to set upon it; a buhl clock; a dinner service of green Sèvres – 'it was impossible for me not to acquire it'. Eighty thousand francs bought a fourteenth-century carpet from Lisbon Cathedral, twenty yards long with wreaths of acanthus on a pink background. He bid against Pierpont Morgan for some Fragonards, but Morgan won, and on his death they were acquired by Henry Clay Frick. Boni hated the thought of such treasures leaving Europe for America. 'It causes me positive physical and mental distress,' he said; American collectors had not the first idea of how to arrange and set out the pieces once they had acquired them.

Not that Boni was yet able to demonstrate how this should be done. No existing house in Paris was (Boni considered) grand enough for them to live in the style which he was determined they should keep up. He therefore bought a site and designed an elaborate palace to go on it in the avenue du Bois de Boulogne; meanwhile the young Castellanes set up house in a rented mansion in the avenue Bosquet, where indeed they spent the first two years of their marriage, and where two of their sons were born. The temporary house did not please Boni: 'its proportions were faulty and its high windows and mediocre staircase were not in keeping with the size of the rooms.' As for Anna, when complimented upon her surroundings in the early days of her marriage, she would invariably reply, '*C'est aimable à dire*' ('Kind of you to say so') in her American French; of the avenue Bosquet mansion she said, 'This is only a warehouse,' and when asked what her future home would be like, she replied, 'It'll be like the staircase at the Opéra, only bigger.'[19] Neither Boni nor his friends could ever get used to her laconic style.

But neither the rented house nor Anna's taciturnity could dampen Boni's determination to shine. Anna's twenty-first birthday was approaching, and Boni decided this would be an occasion for a party to end all parties. This party would go down in the annals of Parisian history. It was to be arranged by Boni and his even more stylish uncle, the Prince de Sagan, and they decided that the only possible setting was the Tir aux Pigeons in the Bois de Boulogne, where a stage could be set up on the banks of the lake and there could be fireworks and an illuminated ballet 'of the most beautiful description'. However, even the *gratin* had to get permission from the municipality to use this site. Accordingly, Boni and the Prince called upon the president of the municipal council and the Prince explained their plans. The president had never heard anything like it. Such a thing had never been; was it possible that such a thing could be? Irritatedly he turned to Boni and snapped, 'Sir – be good enough to explain *precisely* what is the real object of this fête!'

I said never a word, but my uncle, adjusting his famous monocle, gravely considered our interlocutor in much the same way that an explorer scrutinizes a rare specimen of savage – his impertinence was something at which to marvel. Then, smiling an icy and mocking smile, he addressed himself to the President.

'You wish to know what is the object of this fête, sir? This fête is given simply for our amusement,' and he repeated the words 'for our amusement' several times in succession.[20]

Boni was in his element. He ordered eighty thousand Venetian lamps from Murano and hung them in the trees, where they swayed like pale, glassy fruits. Firefly lights illuminated the walks and avenues leading to the Tir aux Pigeons. Sixty footmen in scarlet liveries were to be grouped on the grass to produce a patch of colour in the right place (this was a touch of which Boni was particularly fond, and which he was to use often when arranging a *mise en scène* of this kind). Fifteen kilometres of carpet were to protect the guests from the rigours of damp grass.

And then it rained. It poured with rain all day. Everyone save Boni was in despair, but our hero remained unperturbed, convinced that, for him, the moon could do no less than shine. His optimism was rewarded. At five o'clock he ordered the carpet to be laid regardless of the weather: and at that moment the clouds broke and the sun showed through. Steam rose from the earth; 'the Tir aux Pigeons looked like a vast vapour-bath!' The guests flocked in. Three thousand invitations had been sent out for the main party, which would be preceded by an intimate dinner for two hundred and fifty particular friends, to be served in a marquee decorated with red roses. Ladies in misty ball gowns floated through the vaporous evening in the moonshine; there were fountains of fire, an orchestra of two hundred musicians; twenty-five white swans were set free by M. Groult, a wealthy manufacturer of vermicelli. Boni and the Prince de Sagan were enchanted; and Anna? She enjoyed herself, but Boni was dismayed to realize that it was merely the party she enjoyed – its extraordinary nature was, he thought, quite lost on her.

But in other respects Boni was having his effect on Anna. If he could not educate her to hedonism, he could educate her to elegance. Paquin and Doucet designed gowns especially for her, which were not repeated for anyone else. From being small, swarthy and insignificant-looking she emerged dainty and superbly turned out. Boni 'managed to transform her – by means of depilation, massage, make-up and a hair-dresser,' commented Elisabeth de Clermont-Tonnerre cattily; she considered that Anna would have made an adequate Red Indian chieftainess, but was not quite in the Parisian style.[21] In fact Anna, before the onset of Boni, had no style of her own, Red Indian or otherwise. It was not something one learned at Miss Bennett's; nor had she learned it at home, with a busy father, no mother, and only the austere and religious Helen to discuss such things with. But for Boni, his wife formed an integral part of the decor of his life. When receiving guests at the head of his pink marble staircase, admiring the effect created by the carefully placed groups of footmen, he had to know that his wife, too, enhanced the scene. Fitters came specially from the rue de la Paix to adjust her veil properly. Even her everyday appearance had to blend with the background. An old schoolfriend recalled visiting her in Paris at about this time:

> I saw a delicate-looking vision of pink and white approaching me, and recognized – though the original is greatly changed – a little girl whose face was familiar to me ten or twelve years ago. She was gowned in a loose robe of pale pink chiffon over a pink Louisine slip – a beautiful frock, very daintily made, with many tucks and plaitings, and perfectly in keeping with the apartment.... Mme de Castellane wore a garden hat of leghorn, tricorne in form, and adorned with

roses of varying shades of pink. I noticed also her shrimp pink satin slippers and open work stockings of the same shade.[22]

An ordinary call became something of a theatrical occasion at the avenue du Bois de Boulogne. One rang the bell at the enormous wrought-iron gates and a large, splendid-looking porter – the Castellanes only employed the largest size of footman – wearing livery of blue and gold, with flesh-coloured silk stockings and black pumps with silver buckles, asked if one were expected. He was 'quite the most magnificent personage I had spoken with for many years,' remarked one visitor.[23] On receiving an affirmative answer, six or eight more footmen, all wearing similar uniform, materialized and conducted the visitor through the house to the private apartments. Anna's bedroom was sumptuous – 'too formal in taste, I should say, for the average woman', opined the same visitor; but then Mme de Castellane was not the average woman; her husband's whole efforts were directed to ensuring that she should, precisely, not be that. The bed had once belonged to Marie Antoinette. The canopy was trimmed with white ostrich feathers at each of the four corners, with a large cluster of the same at the centre top. This canopy was lighted from beneath by hidden electric bulbs. The coverlet was embroidered satin, of a shade of grey so pale as almost to be white.

Within this sublimely tasteful setting, did Boni and Anna enjoy the transports of married love? The presence of their three sons, George, Jay and Boni, would seem to indicate that they did; but this was not, it appeared, enough for Boni. When, after eleven years, their marriage came to an end, Anna alleged – and produced evidence to prove – that he had been almost uninterruptedly unfaithful to her. He had, she declared, carried on liaisons during that time with at least twelve other women, members of Parisian high society and well-known *demimondaines* such as the notorious Otéro. The date when she first discovered this distressing habit of his was put variously at a few months, or three years, after they had been married. Whichever it was, the incident evidently came as a nasty surprise for both parties. Anna, leaning affectionately over the shoulder of her husband as he was writing, read (before he could cover it up): 'You alone are lacking to my happiness – Boni.' Anna was horrified, but not more so than Boni, who, realizing that his wife had read this – the concluding line of a letter to his current mistress – sprang up and slapped her face, notwithstanding the fact that there was a servant in the room. Other incidents made it quite clear that this was no isolated occurrence. One morning when she went to her husband's bedroom, knock and call as she might, there was no response. Going in to wake him from this sound sleep, she found that the bed contained, not her husband, but a dummy made to resemble him. As she left the room she met the real thing – coming down the corridor from the bedroom of one of their guests. Not long after this, riffling through an unlocked writing-desk at the Château de Grignan, which they had just bought, Anna came across a letter to her husband from this same lady. Thick with *tutoiements* and endearments, 'I must see you in our nest,' it ran. 'Five days have passed since that happy Wednesday, and no word from you. But I know, I am certain, that this is against your will. Write, my dear friend, to console me. I love you, I love you.'[24] Other letters, from other ladies, also – somehow – fell into Anna's hands: 'I kiss you tenderly on your neck, quite close to your ear. Can you feel my embrace?' ran one – a thought which, quite apart from its context, probably shocked the former Miss Gould to the core.

It was not only in the sexual field that Boni was giving his wife cause for concern. His extravagance was such that, as soon became apparent, even his wife's enormous fortune was scarcely equal to it. When they married, $3,000,000 was settled on Boni; in addition, they had the income from another $15,000,000 belonging to Anna. Talented as he was in the art of spending, it took Boni very little time to run through his own money. In less than a year he had disposed of $1,000,000 on what the American press called 'bric-a-brac', had bought a yacht, the *Valhalla*, for $200,000, had spent nearly half a million dollars getting himself elected to the Chamber of Deputies, and had donated $200,000 for a permanent building for the annual charity bazaar (to be named in memory of Anna's mother: an inscription on the building read 'Founded by the Miller–Gould family'). The Bois de Boulogne-Malakoff site for the new palace cost $740,000, and an adjoining lot, $200,000: the cost of the building (still incomplete when the marriage came to an end) was estimated at $5,000,000. The bills came pouring in: Boni had to turn to his wife's money. Requests soon began to arrive at George Gould's house in New York for more cash: at first, though grumpily, George complied. But soon he felt the time had come to call a halt. Boni and Anna were summoned to New York for a family council in order to discuss the limitation of their expenditures.

As may be imagined, Anna's sympathies were entirely with her brother and against her husband. She might be rich but she was keenly aware of the value of money – her early training had seen to that. As for Boni – what was money for, he wanted to know, if not to buy him the pleasures to which his station in life entitled him and which he was so ideally equipped to enjoy? The very notion of being called to account for his expenditure sent him into a rage. When they received George's letter, in August 1900, Boni flounced out of the house leaving a letter for Anna which read: 'I have 10,000 francs. On this I can live for a year. After that I shall work. I shall resign from the chamber and go to China. P.S. I have in my pocket only 600 francs, of which I leave you, dear, 300 for your lunch.' But he failed to carry out this threat, and in January the Castellanes arrived in New York, where they were frigidly received by the Gould family.

It turned out that one dealer, having failed to obtain payment of several millions of francs owing from Boni, had had the bright idea of attacking the Comte through the Gould Trust in New York, where he was bringing a suit. In vain Boni pleaded with his brother-in-law to let him invest Anna's fortune: with his knowledge, he could swiftly double its value. But this was the one thing the Goulds were not going to permit. If once Boni got his hands on the money it would surely disappear, and then what would be left for Anna and her children? 'Men risk millions on similar speculations, but I have never yet heard of one who recognized the value of brains or who backed them for all he was worth,' grumbled Boni.[25] The only investments recognized as proper by George involved railroads or similar hardware. Boni added magnanimously: 'To do Anna justice, she had every right to expect she would not be worried over money matters, but if she had proved herself more sympathetic towards me at this crisis in my fortunes, I should have become her slave for life.' But Anna was not sympathetic. She allied herself firmly with her brothers in this respect. When Boni showed George Gould a wonderful set of four armchairs and a settee upholstered in yellow tapestry with decorative parrots and garlands of flowers, which he had bought for a mere 60,000 francs, Gould dismissed it contemptuously: 'The whole caboodle isn't worth twopence. Why ever do you buy these things?' Nearly (but not quite) speechless with rage, Boni gave the historic reply of his uncle, the Prince de Sagan: 'For my own pleasure.' George Gould was struck with horror at such blatant hedonism.

Certainly it is easy to see that from the point of view of the Goulds, the whole Castellane adventure seemed to be turning out disastrously. Fanny Reed, who had been against the whole affair from the beginning, smugly pointed out that Anna would have done better to follow her advice. Anna agreed. Boni fumed. And yet – there is more than one way of looking at even such an apparently clear-cut case of cold-blooded fortune hunting.

Let us examine first of all, as being simplest, the pecuniary complaints. Undeniably Boni ran through enormous amounts of money. When, in the course of his *Confessions*, he says, 'But was I actually a spendthrift? *Most assuredly – No!*' the reader's inclination is to ask, if not that, then what? And Boni's own feeble attempts at self-justification do not add to his credibility any more than they added to his credit. 'I did not imagine that it would be impossible to spread the payments ... over a certain time. I certainly never contemplated settling my accounts directly they were presented,' he says. But in fact, the money was for the most part neither wasted nor irrecoverable. Boni's suggestions to George Gould were not stupid. With so many wealthy Americans in the market the price of the highly limited supply of fine *objets d'art* was bound to go up. In making such acquisitions the most important qualities are expertise and taste, with both of which Boni was unarguably endowed. His view of the antiques market was, simply, ahead of its time. It is not now considered eccentric to buy works of art as an investment. The sad thing is when the buyer does not enjoy them, or allow them to be enjoyed, while they are appreciating in his possession – and this was the one sin Boni did not commit. But the notion that an enjoyable luxury might also be viewed as an investment went against the grain of the Goulds, whose view of what did or did not constitute sound finance had been formed in the narrow school of Wall Street, puritan and unimaginative. Of course, Boni's presentation and behaviour did not help him in his quest to be taken seriously. He was the very picture of a wastrel. The Goulds were to the depth of their Scottish souls revolted by his conceit, his extravagance, his Catholicism. How could they trust the judgement of such a man in any way? Why should they bother to do so?

Of course, the Goulds' opinion of Boni's financial acumen was not enhanced by their view of his behaviour in other respects. We know that Anna early on found out about his multifarious love affairs – and found out, too, that she had been the last to find out: always a mortifying discovery. But if Boni's amatory habits were common knowledge in Paris, this was not the case in New York – nor would it be, unless she chose to make it so. It is hard to know whether she did. The urge to complain of her miserable lot must have been great – but then, the humiliation! After all, Boni was her choice and hers alone. And the Goulds, brought up in an austere and religious atmosphere as regards family matters – Anna herself, the product of Miss Bennett's academy in Ogontz, Pa. – were not among those who might regard such lapses as the inevitable concomitant of modern marriage.

Who did? Well, as might be gathered from the quality of some of the ladies named in the divorce suit, Boni's circles most certainly did. Here, for example, is Edith Wharton's view of such behaviour:

Marriage, in France, is regarded as founded for the family and not for the husband and wife. It is designed not to make two people individually happy for a longer or shorter time, but to secure their permanent well-being as associates in the foundation of a home and the procreation of a family.... The notion of marriage as a kind of superior business association, based on community of class, of political and religious opinion, and on a fair exchange of advantages (where one, for instance, brings money and the other position) is so ingrained in the French social organization that the modern girl accepts it intelligently, just as her puppet grandmother bowed to it passively.

From this important act of life the notion of love is tacitly excluded; not because love is thought unimportant, but on account of its very importance, and of the fact that it is not conceivably to be fitted into any stable association between man and woman.... They have decided that love is too grave a matter for boys and girls, and not grave enough to form the basis of marriage; but in the relations between grown people, apart from their permanent ties (and in the deepest consciousness of the French, marriage still remains indissoluble), they allow it, frankly and amply, the part it furtively and shabbily, but no less ubiquitously, plays in Puritan societies.[26]

If this was the view of marriage held by Boni – and it describes his circumstances and attitudes with great accuracy – then it will be seen that as far as he was concerned he did in fact fulfil his side of the contract. For him, marriage was a family matter. He adored his three sons, had pet names for them, spent as much time as he could with them, driving in the park, playing, generally taking pleasure in their company; his greatest terror was that Anna would take them away with her to America. Such behaviour was quite unlike that of most upper-class Englishmen – who would have considered it cissy and unseemly – or that of most moneyed Americans, for Jay Gould had been the exception rather than the rule: most of them were too preoccupied with their moneymaking to spare more than a passing moment for wives and children. His eldest son's great delight was to come into his father's bedroom first thing in the morning and light the fire there – a simple pleasure unexpected in a rose marble setting. Marriage was a family affair. It was also a public affair: and as far as the public was concerned, Boni could feel he played his part. When King Carlos of Portugal complimented him on his house, 'If it please your Majesty, it is the house of Madame de Castellane,' replied Boni gracefully and truthfully. When he and Anna drove out in their superb barouche drawn by satin-coated horses, blue satin footmen in attendance, all Paris was treated to the splendour of the Castellane couple.

As for his infidelities – what had they to do with Anna? The essential thing was that both parties be discreet – in which case they might enjoy the same privileges. Not, one imagines, that Boni seriously expected that Anna would ever be unfaithful to him. Groom her as he might, mother of his children though she was, she was scarcely to be taken seriously as an attractive woman. He had married her because of her fortune; that was fair enough; how otherwise should such a plain little thing have expected to catch a Boni de Castellane? It was a fair deal – more than fair, as far as she was concerned, for there were many heiresses (though, he had to admit, few as spectacularly rich as Anna) and only one Boni.

His friends shared this view, and, perhaps for this reason, had not become her friends. Wrote one some years after the marriage had ended:

> Madame de Castellane had nothing to complain of. She is still living ... in the houses planned, built and furnished by Boni. She had charming children. She has been the queen of the most splendid fêtes in Paris. Did she begrudge her husband a few adventures? Innumerable women ran after him, how could he have escaped them all? Her rivals, if any, glided past and lingered not. Madame de Castellane's great grievance, descending as she did from American magnates, was a dread of her fortune being frittered away. That is what was drilling through her flinty little heart, the heart of an independent American woman.[27]

(It is interesting to note that this was the view of a woman, not a man.) This was the generally shared view of *le tout Paris*.

At first, nevertheless, Anna made a valiant effort to put a brave face on things. 'She would defend me and my misdoings to others, but she would never defend them to herself,' says Boni.[28] Poor Anna! In the end she turned more and more to American friends who could understand and sympathize with her lot. There was a Mrs Black 'whose accent, together with her whole personality, suggested the very Farthest West'; there was the eternal Fanny Reed, 'that *âme damnée* of my married life'. Boni hated these women. He felt they were against him – as indeed they were. They took sides – they took Anna's side. With them her grievances were rehearsed and solidified, bringing ever nearer that day which Boni so dreaded – which he refused to believe would ever arrive – when Anna would finally take that course of action which she had, from the beginning, reserved the right to take.

Was it possible that she would actually divorce him? Neither Boni nor his friends could believe it. In their staunchly Catholic circles, such a thing was unheard of. One's private conduct was a matter for oneself, but one preserved appearances. But that was not Anna's tradition. 'I *hate* him, I *hate* him,' she cried – and that was enough for her. Boni's friends felt that was no explanation; Anna's, that it was all the explanation she needed. The final straw came at the end of January 1906. For some time now, Anna had been threatening to leave on account of Boni's latest affair, with the charming young Duchesse d'Uzès. She had been persuaded not to walk out before the grand reception they had long planned for the King and Queen of Portugal on 12 December 1905. But Boni continued to see Mme d'Uzès, and when, in January, Anna scolded him about it, he responded by spinning her an extraordinary story. He swore that he was slowly dying of cancer of the breast. Would she leave him to die alone like a dog? He made her put her hand under his coat to feel the malignant growth. Anna could feel nothing out of the ordinary. Boni insisted that they call a doctor; any doctor would confirm that he had not long to live. A doctor was called; he declared that Boni was sound as a bell, as healthy as any man of his age could expect to be. On hearing this Anna turned away in disgust. She would never again, she said, believe anything he told her. That evening she packed a small bag and, accompanied by her maid, left for the Hotel Bristol.

Boni was appalled. The debts, the humiliation! He refused to accept the situation. There must be reconciliation. He tried to force his way into the Hotel Bristol, but the concierge had been briefed to keep him out. Then he ostentatiously moved out of the house at the avenue du Bois de Boulogne, placing it at Anna's disposal; she graciously agreed to move back in. She had by now engaged the services of Edmund Kelly, counsel at the American Embassy, to secure a judicial separation for her, and to this end Kelly had engaged Maître Cruppi, a leading Paris lawyer. She had meanwhile been awarded provisional custody of the children.

The Castellane family were horrified. They told the newspapers that 'we are all earnestly hoping that the unpleasantness will not go any further than a temporary separation.' They had always suspected that this adventure would lead to no good, and now they had been proved right. But maybe it was not too late to smooth things over. They said that 'it would be useless to deny that she left her home four or five days ago and took up residence at the Hotel Bristol. Her withdrawal followed an excited interview in which she accused Count Boni of infidelity, but since then we have persuaded her that infidelity was too strong a term and that he has been only indiscreet.' The indiscreet one had taken refuge in the bosom of his family. 'Count Boni is with us,' the family spokesman said, and went on to explain that: 'his attitude is that of unaffected penitence. He is figuratively on his knees to the countess.'[29] It was hoped that this attitude would enable a reconciliation to be effected, but Anna was not interested. She would certainly not have him back in order to soothe the feelings of Boni's mother. Last time she had been in New York she had written that she proposed to stay a little longer among her own people, and added: 'I will not return at all unless you can promise me that the marquise de Castellane will not come to my house more than once a week. She is constantly there, criticizing everything. She said my three boys, in the black suits I bought them, looked like butlers. Let the marquise stay at home with her saints.'[30] When friends of the family remonstrated with her that it really would not do to divorce, all she would say was, 'I don't see why.'[31]

So much for family feeling and the proprieties. Boni therefore made an effort to fan the embers of conjugal affection. He began to bombard his wife with love-letters. 'I cherish the remembrance of the kiss you gave me on Jan. 27 at 3 o'clock,' ran one. 'You have been my life. Your absence will be my death.' But Anna remained unmoved. She replied that she had suffered too much and had lost all affection for him and all confidence in his honour and veracity; she found him disgusting. In March she decided to sue, not for a separation, but for a divorce.

At this, Boni lost his head completely. When Anna had first walked out he had written, in sentimental vein, 'I hope I may die soon, but I shall at least have the recollection of my love for you.' Now he announced that this eventuality was imminent. In the middle of September, despite the fact that she had forbidden him to write any more letters, he sent one informing her that he could not long survive and hoping that she would at least bestow on him one last visit in his extremity. 'I kiss you passionately,' he concluded. Receiving no response, he sent another missive complaining that – if not actually dying – he was suffering miseries worse than death. He was stranded in the midst of second-rate Englishmen, and Anna passed him by 'like the Milky Way passing across the sky'. But Anna was not to be deflected from her purpose. The divorce suit was heard at the beginning of November.

It was his last chance, and he made the most of it. Maître Cruppi was heard first, and recited the never-ending litany of the Comte's misdeeds, referring to, and quoting from letters indited by a positive alphabet of ladies (Mme. A., the Baroness B., the Countess of C., Lucie D., who was no better that she ought to be ...); mentioning various vast sums placed at Boni's disposal and the amazing speed with which he had spent them.

The creditors, who were owed in all some $540,000, had their way. They were anxious that they should not be landed with a sole debtor – Boni – who would be manifestly quite unable, not to say unwilling, to discharge his debts. They asserted that Anna was quite as responsible for them as the Count, as was George Gould, as trustee. Certainly it seemed reasonable that she should foot the $136,000 of dressmakers' bills. It was recounted to a fascinated court that the Countess had spent $120,000 in a single month; the ceiling of her bedroom cost $160,000, with furniture to match. Anna had offered Boni, in order that he might live as befitted the father of her children, $30,000 a year and $200,000 towards his personal debts – but he refused this, demanding $50,000 and all his debts paid off. It was ridiculous, argued his counsel, Maître Bonnet, that he should be forced into bankruptcy in the knowledge that his children would eventually inherit some $20,000,000. But Anna stood on her rights: if he would not accept her first offer, then he should not have anything at all. In vain did Maître Bonnet argue that the debts represented household expenses and could not be regarded as personal; in vain did he recount the distressing tale of how, when some bailiffs had called at the Castellane château the previous year, they had been told they could not touch the furniture – which they had come to seize – because it was pledged to George Gould for a loan of $40,000, but that they could (said the Countess) help themselves to all the Castellane portraits (including the one of

Boni) and ancestral relics, including the baton wielded by the Maréchal de Castellane in the service of Napoleon. Maître Bonnet concluded his case with the surprising news that he brought the Countess a message containing the assurance of the undying love of her unhappy husband. At this, Anna's lawyer told the court about the death scene which had precipitated her departure for the Hotel Bristol.

So, in a torrent of recrimination and melodrama, the marriage of Anna Gould and Boni de Castellane came to an end. Society waited with interest to see what the protagonists would do now.

Boni, for his part, showed surprising resource. Burdened with debts, deprived of income and expectations (he had already anticipated his inheritance), no longer able to live in the grand manner, he put to solid use those brains, taste and expertise with which he had failed to impress George Gould. He undertook interior decorating commissions for his friends and sought out desirable antique pieces for visiting Americans and, living among his wares, was enabled to maintain a certain style and elegance – if not the grandeur with which he had dazzled Paris for a decade. This way of life also enabled him to embark upon potentially profitable friendships. For, far from being cast down by his experiences at the hands of the Goulds, the unquenchable Boni was eager to try his luck once more. In 1909, Elsie de Wolfe, Elisabeth Marbury and Anne Morgan, three wealthy American socialites who had bought the Villa Trianon at Versailles, gave a party there to celebrate a music pavilion they had built. Boni was the *metteur en scène* for this party – who better? And what better prospect, as far as he was concerned, than Anne Morgan, only daughter of the formidable Pierpont Morgan, connoisseur of *objets d'art* and mountainously rich? Boni let it be known that he was interested, and reporters stood on tiptoe awaiting the announcement of the engagement. But Miss Morgan was not interested; as far as men were concerned, she never was interested. Undaunted, Boni continued his quest.

As for Anna, she did not, as might have been expected, return to the America she understood and the bosom of her family. After eleven years running the most dazzling household in Paris, who could return to Newport? Commonplace little Anna might not

have liked her husband, might not have enjoyed the extraordinary theatrical elaboration of life which he organized around
her, might have seemed completely unimpressed by the dukes and
princesses who surrounded her, but it was what she had known
all her adult life, and no doubt she realized that she would like
New York even less. So Anna determined that the only thing to
do was to marry again.

Her choice of second husband was in a way characteristic.
There was a definite touch of malice about the erstwhile Miss
Gould, and while Boni blustered, she had been laying her plans.
In the months between the separation and the divorce hearing
it became clear to everyone what those plans were. Anna was
going to pay Boni out as neatly as might be, and gain a much
better title into the bargain, by marrying his cousin Hélie de
Talleyrand-Périgord, Prince de Sagan, the son of that Prince de
Sagan with whom he had organized that legendary party at the
Tir aux Pigeons. Boni was furious. At the funeral of a cousin
of theirs, Charles de Talleyrand-Périgord, he clubbed Hélie with
his walking-stick as they were leaving the church. But Hélie had
the last laugh: he married Anna and the considerable remains of
her fortune. By then, presumably, Anna had found out what
marriage in those circles comprised. Hélie had found this out
early in life: the Prince of Wales had a habit of calling on his
mother in the afternoons when his father was out, and on one
of these occasions young Hélie crept into the dressing-room
adjoining his mother's bedroom, filched the Prince's clothes and
threw them into the fountain in the garden. When his father
came home and found out what had happened his fury was immense. He told Hélie that no gentleman ever behaved like that,
and packed him and his tutor off to South America, thus ensuring
the safety of the Prince of Wales's dignity for the nonce. This
marriage was reasonably successful, but *le tout Paris* was in no
doubt as to its motivation. The young Marcel Proust observed
to his friend Reynaldo Hahn, that after the walking-stick incident,
'Hélie ought to be spelled Elie, like the Prophet who in similar
circumstances flew up to the heavens, a resource which unfortunately wasn't available to our Hélie. But in my opinion
Gould for him spells principally Gold.'[32]

'Of course,' said Elisabeth de Clermont-Tonnerre pursuing her

Red Indian analogy, 'Boni might have pacified the imperious little chieftainess, but when could he have found time to fathom those Anglo-Saxon reactions which are so disconcerting to Frenchmen steeped in tradition?'[33]

7

Great Expectations – England

Q: Is more expected of English wives than of ours, and are American girls happy under the new restraints?
A: Nothing more is really expected of them socially; but an American girl sees that she must inform herself thoroughly on a variety of subjects unfamiliar to her, in order to compete with her capable English rivals, after the first two or three years, when the brilliancy and audacity so charming in a girl loses its novelty, or she will be looked upon as a butterfly imported with the radiance of her plumage diminishing year by year.
Chauncey M. Depew, introduction to *Titled Americans*,
1890

The contrast in tone between French and English society towards the turn of the century was very great. It is almost inconceivable that an exotic like Boni de Castellane could have flourished, let alone have been taken seriously, in England. 'The last time I saw your enchanting father,' said Lady Cunard once to a mystified young man who, as it happened, was *not* Boni's son, 'he was dressed entirely in scarlet feathers with a purple velvet cloak!' Yet Boni's speeches in the Chamber, especially those on the Moroccan question, were listened to with respect. Boni was an exotic, but he was not a fool. His knowledge and love of art were genuine, but his interests were not confined to the arts and society. One might not agree with his political opinions ('How about an anti-Semitic party?' he once demanded of his chiropodist, extending a toenail for varnishing), but his political concerns were, equally, genuine. Several times during the course of his

Confessions he remarks, with apparent surprise, that Anna, on this occasion or that, appeared 'unmistakably bored'. The surprise was justifiable; for life with Boni, in all its unlikely variety, was not conducive to boredom. Other emotions it may have aroused in many people, but not boredom, for which Anna (to her misfortune and his) seems to have shown a preternatural predisposition. His last plan, never realized, was to have lions and tigers held on a leash by purple-robed Indians parade through the grounds of his formal Louis XVI château, Le Marais.[1] It was (Anna grumbled) just another example of his hopeless extravagance.

But it could be argued – as Boni and his friends argued – that the Gould fortune was a fortune on an extravagant scale, and one that required real imagination if it were to be spent to the best effect. What, after all, was money there for if not to be spent? – and this way it was being spent to undeniably extraordinary effect. Others spent just as freely but less imaginatively; they enjoyed themselves less, but because they were dull, they were not objected to. Take, for example, the Duke of Marlborough. Consuelo Vanderbilt's fortune was just as spectacular as Anna Gould's, and her husband quite as anxious to spend it for her as Anna's. 'I was surprised by the excess of household and personal linens, clothes, furs and hats my husband was ordering,' she wrote; and he insisted on buying jewels for her on the same scale, any family heirlooms having long since been more or less advantageously disposed of. But life amid all this luxury was not fun. Their evenings alone together, of which, at Blenheim, there were many, sound especially awful:

How I learned to dread and hate these dinners, how ominous and wearisome they loomed at the end of a long day. They were served with all the accustomed ceremony, but once a course had been passed the servants retired to the hall; the door was closed and only a ring of the bell placed before Marlborough summoned them. He had a way of piling food on his plate; the next move was to push the plate away, together with knives, forks, spoons and glasses – all this with considered gestures which took a long time; then he backed his chair away from the table, crossed one leg over the other and endlessly twirled the ring on his little finger. While accomplishing these gestures he was absorbed in thought and quite oblivious of any reactions I might have. After a quarter of an hour he would suddenly return to earth or perhaps I should say to food and begin to eat very slowly, usually complaining that the food was cold! And how could it be otherwise? As a rule neither of us spoke a word. I took to knitting in desperation and the butler read detective stories in the hall.[2]

Of such details are marital murders compounded.

From her very first introduction to the society which her mother had ordained her to inhabit, at the Lansdownes' viceregal palace in Calcutta, Consuelo had had her doubts as to how stimulating she might find it. The Viceroy's daughter, it turned out, was an ignoramus – a condition forced upon her not by any particular lack of intelligence but by sheer lack of education. Consuelo, who was something of a bluestocking, was shocked. English girls of her age were still educated, she found, by what Lady Mary Wortley Montagu had described more than a century before as a 'good homespun' governess. This left plenty of resources to expend on sons, while giving daughters as much education as they were likely to need. It followed that English wives could not be expected to join in their husbands' lives to any considerable degree – which was just the way most husbands liked it. Wrote George Curzon to Mary Leiter when they were engaged: 'The terrace of the House of Commons is as crowded with women as the Royal Enclosure at Ascot, and the encroachments of the Sex fill me with an indignation that no blandishments can allay. Give me a girl that knows a woman's place and does not yearn for trousers.' And again, when she had written to tell him that she had been standing next to Woodrow Wilson when he made his great speech on tariffs: 'How shocking to think of you actually on the floor of the House in the middle of the Members! It violates all my notions of the correlation of the sexes. There will be none of that over here, Mary.'[3]

Did Mary experience a slight sinking of the heart, a momentary vision of the life they might imply, as she perused such sentences? Probably, in the excitement of receiving a letter at all – no matter what the contents – she did not: anticipation of bliss, such as Mary's in contemplation of her beloved George, does not look beyond the immediate achievement: in this case, the wedding. Besides, one can form little idea of what one has not experienced. It is true that girls such as Mary Leiter and Consuelo Vanderbilt had seen, had to some extent joined in, the life they were proposing to enter. But they had not experienced what for them must be the dominant reality of life in England, which was that women's lives were subordinate there to those of their husbands. They were subordinate not, as in France, by law; but, which is much harder to overcome, in reality: a reality so utterly woven into the fabric of life, so completely accepted by the participants, that it was barely noticed if it was noticed at all. Certainly it is unlikely to have been noticed during their brief forays into society by those daughters of the New World where, in all spheres but business, women were, in fact if not in law, the dominant partners. This was a state of affairs resented by some American men. 'The English woman knows that tradition, the law, and Society, demand of her that she shall make a home for a man; the American woman has been led astray by force of circumstances into thinking that her first duty is to make a place for herself,' wrote the American Price Collier; and added: 'Wherever in the history of the world woman has assumed, or been accorded, this unfortunate and artificial prominence, it has meant decay.'[4] But whether it was America or England which was in its decadence, their attitudes to women unarguably constituted a difference between them; from the point of view of Consuelo and Mary, *the* difference.

Subordination was not, of course, a word one attached to the condition of being Duchess of Marlborough, one of England's premier duchesses. It was a position Consuelo assumed with immense charm and tact. 'Everybody raves about Consuelo,' wrote Mary Curzon from London to her family in Washington. '... She is very sweet in her great position, and shyly takes her rank directly after royalty. She looks very stately in her marvellous jewels, and she looks pretty and has old lace which makes my mouth water. I never saw pearls the size of nuts.' But shy as she might seem, Consuelo was quite aware of her position and all that it entailed. She had known from the first that all eyes would be upon her, that her slightest slip would be noticed – and that not a few ladies would be only too delighted if she were to make such a slip.

Their opinion of Americans, or at any rate of America, was

made plain from the start. Lady Blandford, Consuelo's mother-in-law (for whom she was later to feel great affection, and who was always to stand by her during the vicissitudes of her marriage, perhaps because her own painful experience had made her only too aware of what an unhappy marriage could be like), opened their acquaintance with 'a number of startling remarks, revealing that she thought we all lived on plantations with Negro slaves and that there were red Indians ready to scalp us just around the corner.'[5] Other visiting Americans experienced similar displays of eye-opening ignorance. A cousin of Consuelo's was asked, to her surprise, about the war between North and South America. 'But we never had a war with South America.' 'Oh yes, you did,' the questioning nobleman assured her. 'It was in 1861.' For him, the southern states of the Union were all one with the separate continent.[6] Mary Leiter had the same treatment from her father-in-law, Lord Scarsdale; she wrote to *her* father:

> I never cease to wonder how G sprang from his parent, I never knew a more trying person to live with.... Last night at dinner he said, 'Do you have sea fish in America', 'I suppose you don't know how to make mince pies in America', 'I suppose you don't know how to serve a good tea in America. We only know how to do it in England.' G said to him the other day, after I had said, 'Why don't you ask if we are civilized or white in America' – 'Papa, what sort of notion have you of America anyway – I never heard such absurd questions in all my life.'[7]

But Lord Scarsdale only had the same notion of America which seemed to be shared by most of the English. 'Your Grace will no doubt be interested to know that Woodstock had a Mayor and Corporation before America was discovered,' said the mayor of Woodstock to the newly married Consuelo during his speech of welcome to the bridal couple. She held her tongue and smiled politely that time, but she knew that if she were ever to establish herself, she could not always hold her tongue. At the end of a dinner party, it was the custom for the ladies to rise at a signal from the hostess, leaving the men to their port, cigars and dirty stories. 'At one of my first dinner parties,' Consuelo writes, 'to my surprise I found the ladies rising at a signal from my husband's aunt, who was sitting next to him. Immediately aware of a concerted plan to establish her dominance, and warned by my neigh-

bour Lord Chesterfield's exclamation, "Never have I seen anything so rude; don't move!" I nevertheless went to the door and
meeting her, inquired in dulcet tones, "Are you ill, S.?" "Ill?"
she shrilled; "no, certainly not, why should I be ill?" "There
surely was no other excuse for your hasty exit," I said calmly.'[8]
From then on, Consuelo had no more trouble of that sort.

This was not to say, however, that her life was ordered as she
might have wished. For, duchess or not, Consuelo was to learn
that every Englishwoman was expected to bow to two authorities:
tradition and her husband.

Tradition dogged her steps from the first. When she first arrived
at Blenheim, her impression was that the society into which she
had been transplanted was more closely connected to the eighteenth than to the fast-approaching twentieth century. The
Duchess's duties were what they always had been. She ministered
to the needy and sick on the estate, by visiting and reading to
them – something she rather enjoyed – and by distributing food
to them. Uneaten food from the Blenheim table was placed on a
sideboard and crammed into tins at the end of the meal for
distribution to the needy. Tradition dictated that all – meat,
vegetables, salads, sweets – went, undifferentiated, into the same
tin: charity food might be nourishing, but why should it be
delicious? This was something that Consuelo managed to change,
to the relief of the recipients. Other traditions were more un-
bending. There were not enough bathrooms in Blenheim for the
numerous guests who regularly spent Saturday to Monday there;
in the tower where the housemaids lived, the 'Housemaids
Heights', there was not even running water. Consuelo possessed
the means, and the desire, to remedy these defects; but she was
not allowed to do this. Housemaids had done without running
water since Blenheim was built; they could continue to do so.
Equally, they could continue to draw and carry the hot water for
up to thirty baths a day. Consuelo hated the round bathtubs
placed in front of the fire in the bedrooms. She disliked their
'ugly intimacy' and felt sorry for the housemaids subjected to this
needless labour. But the Duke liked them and would not have
the bathrooms built; and that was that.

Other aspects of life, too, were adjusted to the Duke's, rather
than the Duchess's, convenience. One such was social life. This

came as a revelation to an American girl – for if there was one domain completely dominated by women in America, it was the social domain. What time or use had their husbands for the elaborate games played by society matrons, for the unremitting efforts of those not yet chosen to achieve the desired degree of admission? They were too busy making money: to be in business in America was an all-consuming affair, and any breaks were intended purely for recuperation. Both men and women cultivated their respective spheres with a single-minded energy which would have been rather frowned upon in Europe, with its dread of the crude and the obvious.

As might be expected, things were by no means so neatly separated in Europe. There, even social pastimes tended to be dominated by the men – the result of many generations of gentlemen cultivating their leisure. The key to the apparently arbitrary ordering of the English social round lay, as the American Price Collier accurately observed, in the pattern of occupations of gentlemen of the upper class. Common sense might dictate that summer be spent in the country, winter in the city: but not so far as the British aristocracy was concerned. 'In summer there is no shooting and no hunting, but there are Parliament, polo and cricket in London. Society meekly adapts itself to man's duties and diversions.... Society is so patently ... for the women in America, that to the American it is with some awe that he sees even social matters dominated by, and adjusted to, the convenience and even the whims of the men here.'[9]

So Consuelo and the Duke spent their first summer in London in a hectic whirl, inundated with far more invitations to balls, dances, dinners and pleasure rides, than they could possibly accept. Things had not changed much since Henry Adams described the London season thirty years before. He had written to his brother in July 1863:

The rush and fuss of society is still going on and will last another week. We have been here and there, knocking about at dinners, balls, breakfasts, from Rotten Row to Regent's Park, and entertaining at home in the intervals. We had a tremendous ball at a neighbour's on Tuesday and the dawn looked in while we were still at it. We watched the gathering light from the conservatories and looked faded and pale. But the ball-room was the most magnificent that I ever saw, and I really had a very tolerable time, for once, though only enough to remind me of the want of that happy absurdity which I feel in American society. Sleep in these times is scarce. One rides in the Park two hours in the morning, dines out in the evening, and goes to a ball; rises to a breakfast next day; goes to a dance in the afternoon and has a larger dinner at home, from which he goes to another ball at half after eleven. Luckily this comes only by fits and starts, for two or three days together, and leaves the intervals tolerably clear....[10]

Weekends during the summer, and whole weeks, or more, during the winter, were spent in large groups, sporting when the season permitted, at various country houses. When she was obliged to act as hostess to one of these parties, which was often since Blenheim was one of the greatest of all the country houses, Consuelo found that their organization, for an American girl not brought up to such things from her earliest years, could be nerve-wracking. The Marlboroughs would return to Blenheim from their rented house in London on Saturday morning, their guests following in the late afternoon. During the intervening hours Consuelo and the housekeeper would make the rounds of the thirty guest rooms: all must be supplied with stocks of writing-paper, coal, bedside reading and other necessaries. Menus must be sorted out, the right guests given the right rooms, and (most important of all) seating arranged in the correct order of precedence for the grand dinners – a detail also extending to the procession into the dining room. Who should be on whose arm, who seated next to whom and how far from the host and hostess? These decisions would be reflected in the servants' hall, where vicarious precedence was solemnly observed. Servants, indeed, were almost more snobbish than their masters. 'The house-keeper, the butler, the head-coachman, the master's valet and the mistress's maid, are the nobility and gentry of the servants' hall, while footmen, grooms, maids and the like are commoners. To the average American these distinctions may be merely laugh-able. Let him come to England and keep house for a year and he will find them adamant.... If he accepts them, well and good; if not, he will have no servants.'[11] There could be no risk of such an eventuality occurring in an establishment such as Blenheim. Consuelo must soothe the rivalry between the butler and the chef and try to overcome its direr consequences; the housekeeper must be pacified, the maids kept happy. It was an incessant preoccupation. 'English servants are *fiends*,' wrote Mary Curzon to her mother. 'They seem to plot among themselves. They are malignant and stupid and make life barely worth living, and I should like to hang a few and burn the rest at the stake.' No doubt they felt they could take advantage of rich Americans unschooled in the ways of English social life.

During the summer, weekends were languid, passed between meals, church, and discreet assignations – invitations to walk in the grounds tête-à-tête, the amassing of which conferred status and the lack of which caused more than one lady to spend the afternoon in her room rather than be viewed in ignominious solitude. During the shooting season things were more vigorous: the ladies joined the guns for a plentiful lunch and stayed to watch the afternoon's sport, crouching shivering behind a convenient hedge. The alternative to this discomfort was sitting in the drawing room in the company of other languid ladies, writing those letters which later biographers have found so invaluable.

Considerably more active were those weekends spent hunting. Hunting was a sport in which both sexes could join, and all who could hunt were expected to do so. For those who enjoyed it, it was like a drug – continuously thrilling, impossible to have too much of it. Moreover, ladies knew they looked their best in their tightly tailored riding habits; and what could be more alluring to an English gentleman than a beautiful woman who also showed courage and dash in the hunting-field? From Melton Mowbray, heart of the Leicestershire hunting country, George Wyndham wrote to his niece Lady Cynthia Asquith, about his son Percy: 'It amuses me that Sibell [his wife, Lady Sibell Grosvenor] has always taken the most melancholy view of his [Percy's] coming to hunt here. To her Melton is the haunt of man-eating Delilahs.'[12]

But Lady Sibell's notion was not so far-fetched as all that. Where but to Melton had come the beautiful and vivacious Nancy Shaw – later to take England by storm as Nancy Astor – fleeing from a disastrous marriage in Virginia and accompanied by her sister Phyllis Langhorne – and to what end? It might well have been supposed that the spoiled and petulant Robert Shaw, whom Nancy had married at the age of seventeen, only to come running back to the family house at the first opportunity, had

put her off the idea of marriage for good. This however was not
the impression received by her English friends. Wrote H.H.
Asquith:

> You must not reproach me, my dear Mrs. Shaw;
> It's not like a Redskin selecting a squaw;
> For there's no tougher problem, in logic or law,
> Than to find a fit mate for a lady called Shaw.

> ... More than once I have felt sure that I was on the eve of the Great
> Discovery, and just as I am arranging that the gentleman should be
> photographed, I awoke and found that it was only a dream. I have not
> abandoned the quest, but I am less hopeful than I was. So many
> qualities are needed ... Am I too fastidious? Or even a little jealous?
> Impossible![13]

Meanwhile, whatever her other motives for crossing the Atlantic,
Mrs Shaw hunted like a lion – an unexpected quality in a
Virginia belle, perhaps, but then there was plenty of hunting back
home near Richmond. Hunting was Nancy's passion, and the
best hunting was at Melton. She and Phyllis took a house there
and became the rage. Sir Humphrey de Trafford, doyen of the
hunting field, was but one of the many who were enthralled by
Mrs Shaw's multifarious charms. He wrote, from his house at
Market Harborough, letters filled with news of dogs and useful
hints about horses and grooms: 'I will mount you, bring your
saddle. There are two puppies for you, Snow and Flo.' 'You
understand you have to give your groom a suit of clothes besides
27/- a week. This is apart from the livery which you could use or
not as you like.'[14]

But for most of the American contingent, nurtured not in the
wilds of Virginia but in the more exacting and less athletic
atmosphere of what was considered correct for an aspiring
American young lady, hunting was something more to be endured
as a social necessity than enjoyed for itself. It was enjoyable but
by no means irresistible, as Consuelo Marlborough found:

> I shall always remember the first meet with the Quorn hounds
> when, perfectly fitted in a Busvine habit, a tall hat and veil, I mounted
> 'Greyling', inwardly trembling with excitement and fear. Marl-
> borough ... was a fine horseman and it was up to me to follow him.

Ladies then rode side-saddle, and the Leicestershire people were hard riders. Mrs Willie Lawson – 'Legs', as she was known for the length of them – Miss Doods Naylor, Lady Angela Forbes and a host of others were eyeing me critically [how easy it is to picture those formidable females!], and so far, thanks to my tailor and a good seat, had found nothing amiss. But the great test was still to come. Hounds were moving to covert. There was a gate through which a crowd was pressing: there was also a fence with arching branches with a drop the other side. Marlborough chose the fence. With my heart in my mouth I followed. Greyling jumped in perfect form and I ducked in time to avoid the branches. When I looked back and heard Angela Forbes say, 'I am not going over that horrid place,' I felt my day had begun auspiciously. . . . I remember Lord Lonsdale who, with a passing word of praise for my dashing debut, thought it necessary to explain he had been held up by a riderless horse and an unhorsed lady. But it was our stud groom who gave me most pleasure by his praise and the pride he took in Greyling's performance. 'You fairly let him go,' he said, 'and he's a beautiful jumper.'[15]

But Consuelo never contracted the hunting fever, and on the whole found winters in Leicestershire cold and boring. She began by studying German philosophy, with a teacher from London, to pass the time, but this was regarded with suspicion as being exceedingly intellectual. This was a winter when she could not hunt at all, because of being pregnant. 'Only this interest . . . got me through the first depressing winter, when my solitary days were spent walking along the high road and my evenings listening to the hunting exploits of others.' There was no escape from this purgatory. Marlborough occasionally made short trips to London or Paris when icy weather prevented hunting, but it was considered inadvisable for Consuelo to travel with him; she sat disconsolately in her room, which had a view over a pond in which a former butler of the house had drowned himself. 'As one gloomy day succeeded another I began to feel a deep sympathy with him.' Other winters, even when the children were born, were little improvement. She did not hunt much, and although she would have enjoyed passing the time by playing with her babies, strict British nannies frowned on such indulgences. So, in defiance of public opinion, she passed the time reading. One year, horrified by the reports of unemployment and its attendant miseries at Blenheim, while she was living upon the fat of the land, albeit not particularly happily, in Leicester-shire, she sent funds to get some relief work going in the shape of roadbuilding on the estate. But when the Duke found out what she had done, far from being pleased he was furious. Wives, even duchesses, did not take that sort of initiative. They left such things to their husbands, and provided any support necessary.

Such a reaction did not make Consuelo feel ashamed or mortified – it simply made her furious. It was not the sort of thing an American girl expected to put up with; it offended her deeply. Some American girls, of course, did put up with it; this she could not understand; it was against all her principles – and theirs too, if they but stuck to them. Of Mary Curzon, she wrote: 'I thought that she had shed her American characteristics more completely than I was to find myself able to do. Wholly absorbed in her husband's career she had subordinated her personality to his to a degree I would have considered beyond an American woman's powers of self-abnegation.'[16]

Mary was quite conscious of what she was doing. 'I hear on all sides that Margot has hurt Asquith's career by making him so late in attending the House, and I don't want anyone to say that marriage has hurt George,' she wrote to her sister Nancy;[17] and fulfilled this criterion so absolutely that when, in 1898, Curzon's name was recommended to Queen Victoria as the next Viceroy of India, Lord Salisbury, the Prime Minister, was able safely to reassure Her Majesty when she queried, 'Would Mrs Curzon, who is an American, do to represent a Vice Queen?' Yes; she would do admirably. But despite the efforts Mary made in the direction of subordinating her natural independence of spirit, and despite the fact that it was what George had seemed to want ('There will be none of that over here, Mary.') Mary, too, was not happy during the first years of her marriage in England.

After the glittering procession of her years in Washington, cul-minating in the grand climax of her wedding, the loneliness and isolation of Mary's first years in England made a sad contrast. 'It is not all a bed of roses to live in a strange country and I am as strange to the people and their ways as they are to me. G's devotion and thoughtfulness for me are touching, but ... I have many lonely hours when my joy is to write to my dear ones,' ran one of her numerous letters to her family. Part of the trouble was that, being plain Mrs Curzon (Curzon was not created a peer until 1898), as compared with, say, the Duchess of Marlborough, inclusion in social life was not completely automatic; and Mary had no particular friends of her own in England. There was George; and for a long time, there was only George. George, of course, had his friends; he was a member of that group of witty, intellectual and self-absorbed men and women known as 'the Souls' – discussion of the existence or not of the soul being one of the dominant features of their conversation. Mary, as Miss Leiter, the glamorous visitor from America, had once been welcomed into their midst; but as Mrs Curzon they seemed less ready to accept her on her own account. There may have been a touch of jealousy in this, several of the ladies having taken more than a passing interest in George – and if there was indignation in America at penniless aristocrats making off with all the most desirable heiresses, there was equal annoyance at yet another promising prospect being lost to the English girls who had for so long been weighing up their chances in this regard. But this initial drawback could doubtless have been overcome with wit, charm and determination. Mary, however, caught up in a vicious circle of loneliness and isolation, seemed to have lost her gift for social life – a gift which, after all, stems so largely from self-confidence.

In all this, George was not much of a help. At this time he was working more obsessively hard than ever in an effort to put himself in a position to achieve his great ambition to become Viceroy of India. The position would fall vacant at the end of Lord Elgin's tenure of office in 1898. Curzon would then be thirty-nine – very young to hold so exalted a post – but he was determined to have it, and would spare no effort to achieve it. To this end he worked sixteen hours a day; and when work was over his inclinations, understandably, were towards a quiet domestic life rather than active sociability – of which, anyway, he had never been particularly fond. His work took priority over even the most outstanding fixed points of the social year: 'I am not going to Ascot,' wrote Mary in June 1896; 'G's work defeats every form of amusement.' She put on a brave face, but it was apparent that – naturally enough – she was longing to enjoy a bit more of the fun which she saw going on all around her. 'Consuelo is the rage of the season and everyone makes a great fuss of her,' she wrote; it was a sad contrast with her own situation: 'We only dine out on average once a week. I don't suppose that any-one else in London goes out so little. I feel as though I should like to go sometimes but now people begin to stop asking us for we go out so little and when people don't see you they quickly forget you. I don't mind really not going out, for it's impossible with George's work, and I feel shy of going alone.' Poor Mary! She had not even the satisfaction of running her own household, for George's work obsession extended to the pettiest of house-hold details. He fussed about with a duster making sure that not a speck remained to sully his precious oriental treasures; he chose the furnishings; he kept the household books.

We have been making up our autumn accounts and G has been making up all his wonderful books – and he says to me, 'Would you like to know how much we have spent on coal?' I say, 'Yes.' 'So much,' says George. 'On hay?' 'Yes.' He tells me. On household living? On luxuries? On servants? On visitors? On wine? On every detail of everyday life, out comes the exact amount to a farthing. It is really astonishing and a very good thing, for we know to a sixpence where we are, and we don't owe a penny, for G pays every bill at once and takes off 10% discount, which makes no mean item in the long run.[18]

When their children were born, George even took upon him-self to engage the nurses. How Mr and Mrs Leiter must have wondered, and worried, as they received the almost daily letters from their daughter recounting this strange way of life, so different from the way things were ordered in America – so different from what they had visualized as a destiny for their brilliant daughter.

Such forays as Mary did make outside her home at this time did not seem to be particularly enjoyable or successful, either. In July 1895, there was a general election, and George had to go up to defend his seat at Southport in Lancashire. Mary went with him: it was her job to charm the electors. This she did, smiling at them until her cheeks ached, but she hated it and them. 'I loathe this place more than any other I have *ever* been to, but this I can only say to you,' she wrote home. 'The people are an idle ignorant impossible lot of ruffians. I smile at them and look sweet because it would be the end of us if they knew all that I thought.'[19] That was the unglamorous end of politics. The glamorous part happened in London where the great hostesses, Lady Londonderry, the Duchess of Devonshire, Lady Lansdowne, the Marchioness of Salisbury, the Duchess of Buccleuch, Lady Spencer, Lady Tweedmouth, held sway and encouraged the politicians to meet and talk, to work out the reality which would be given concrete form at Westminster, in their drawing rooms. But these ladies had no interest in making things easy for Mary, who had impinged upon their prerogative by usurping the ear of George Curzon, the most promising young politician of his day. 'My path is strewn with roses, and the only thorns are unforgiving women,' she wrote; and again: 'London life is a continuous striving, striving, striving to keep going, the little people praying to be noticed by the great, and the great seldom lowering their eyelids to look at the small.' The ladies managed to ruin her first grand dinner party, given for the son of George's friend, the Amir of Afghanistan: three of the most influential, Lady Londonderry, the Duchess of Sutherland and Lady Dudley, accepted and then, at the last minute, failed to come. 'George and baby are the only people who exist for me in England,' she wrote to her mother the next year, in March 1896, when her first daughter, Irene, was three months old. 'I am so much more sensitive and reserved than English women and I never feel any sympathy with them, and I don't feel that they do with me, so that my life centers on my own house.' She suffered from continuous headaches; she grew thin and sad. George did little to encourage her to be more outward-looking. 'He cares only for work and me. Other things don't count for much and he gets to care less and less about people and going out.' So much so that, a month later, she wrote: 'We dine out very little, so little that I only got one evening dress this year.'

Not surprisingly, she was violently homesick. Her life of gaiety and luxury in Washington, the easy affection of her loving family, seemed like a dream. 'I never knew how much I loved you all until I had to be separated from you; after all, one's own blood is the dearest thing in the whole world, and I shall feel my separation more and more as years go on,' she wrote in October 1895. '... England can *never never* take the place of home to me.' Of course the passing years had just the opposite effect from this;

Mrs Arthur Paget, *née* Minnie Stevens, dressed for a fancy-dress ball in 1897. She was reputed to run, with Consuelo Manchester, the London end of the Stevens introduction service organized in New York by Minnie's mother, Mrs Paran Stevens.

The Prince of Wales's set dance a Highland fling. On the Prince's left, Minnie Stevens; on his right, Emily Yznaga, sister of the Duchess of Manchester.

The ninth Duke of Manchester with his bride, *née* Helena Zimmerman, whom he had recently married in secret. Having failed in his quest for an Astor or a Vanderbilt he had to make do with Miss Zimmerman, but she turned out richer than people had thought.

The eighth Duchess of Manchester, *née* Consuelo Yznaga. An early 'dollar princess', her parents-in-law had been horrified at the prospect of their son marrying 'a little American savage'. Consuelo was no less horrified when her son 'Kim', who had succeeded to the dukedom eight years previously, married Helena Zimmerman, described as 'the daughter of a well-known American millionaire'.

The Duchess of Roxburghe, *née* May Goelet, in court dress (1912). Miss Goelet was one of the granddaughters of Mrs Richard T. Wilson, who was known as the most successful matchmaker of her day. May inherited a share of $25,000,000 from her father, Ogden Goelet, and a foothold in English society from her aunt Lady Belle Herbert (*née* Wilson).

Gladys Deacon, the toast of intellectual Europe and second wife of the ninth Duke of Marlborough.

Below 'Sunny', the ninth Duke of Marlborough.

Below left Consuelo Marlborough, *née* Vanderbilt, Sunny's first wife, with her two sons Lord Blandford and Lord Ivor Spencer-Churchill (1907).

Miss Winnaretta Singer, heiress to the
sewing-machine millions.

The Princesse de Polignac, *née*
Winnie Singer, with her husband,
Prince Edmond de Polignac, and their
friend (soon to become their enemy)
Comte Robert de Montesquiou. The
Princesse's salon was one of the
centres of Parisian musical and
intellectual life.

Anna and Boni de Castellane *en famille*.

After the divorce — Boni maintains his dignity in the face of the odds (cartoon by Sem).

Miss Natalie Barney outside the Temple de l'Amitié in the garden of her house at rue Jacob, Paris, where for sixty years she held a literary and lesbian salon.

U.S. AMBASSADOR CONSOLES DEBS.

As some slight mitigation of the disappointment of
American rejects for presentation at court it is suggested that Mr. Kennedy might present them instead
to Lady Astor, who is getting to be pretty
important around here, too.

Lady Astor reigns supreme.

Lady Cunard embowered in
a paradise of artifice.

but even three years later, when things had changed, she could write to her sister Nancy who seemed to be about to get engaged: 'Take time to make up your mind; for one quickly realizes the realities of life when married, and those quiet peaceful days in your lovely rooms at Dupont will be gone for ever.' Through it all, what kept her going was her passion for George, which remained undiminished. In the same letter to Nancy, she wrote: 'I always think that the sweet test of affection is if you feel that when he comes into a room the band is playing the Star Spangled Banner and that the room is glowing with pink lights and rills are running up and down your back with pure joy. Then it is all right, but don't ever give your heart away until you feel *all* this, which I feel when George appears.' Nevertheless, it seemed sad that the belle of the balls, the intimate friend of the White House, the dazzling beauty of American society, should have been destined for sullen domesticity amid hostile servants in the English fogs.

And yet – one might ask – why should they have expected anything different? Why should they have expected to be happier – to be as happy, even – amid other people's ways and strange faces than staying at home among their own friends, near their own family? Mary lived for the (relatively frequent) visits of her parents; even that mother with whom Consuelo had such a strained and ambivalent relationship was welcomed with relish and relief when she came over to be with her daughter during her first confinement. In America there would have been no such loneliness.

Indeed, it was noticeable that many of those American girls who made the greatest personal success in purely social terms after their European debuts were not, in some ways, American at all. Their parents were American, and their attitudes were of course influenced by that; but they had been largely brought up in Europe. This was true, for example, of the Jerome sisters, who spent much of their youth with their mother in Paris while their father remained in New York earning the wherewithal to keep them there. There the three vivacious girls were popular members of the circle surrounding that sad monarch who was to be overthrown in 1870 – an upbringing which effectively ensured that they would not, at any rate, be dazzled by mere titles unsupported by talent or attraction. And it was true of Gladys Deacon.

If ever anyone had a golden social youth it was Gladys Deacon – although it cannot be said that she had a very promising start in life. She was the daughter of Edward Deacon, a millionaire banker from Boston; her mother was a daughter of Admiral Baldwin of the US Navy. But the family life of the Deacons was not of the variety that such a background might promise. In 1892, when Gladys was eleven years old, her family was the centre of an awful scandal. Her mother had a French lover, a M. Abeille; and one night at Cannes, when the lovers were in bed, Gladys's father broke into his wife's bedroom and fired three shots at Abeille, who was trying, unsuccessfully, to effect an exit through the communicating door into the next room. Deacon swore in court that he had intended only to wound – but the fact remained that Abeille died. In America or England Edward Deacon would have been tried for murder, or at the very least for manslaughter. But in France such an attitude to his wife's adultery was condoned by the law – indeed, it still remained open to him, under French law, to prosecute his wife for adultery. This he declined to do, but returned to America the next month with two of his four daughters. Gladys stayed in France with her mother.

Gladys grew up into an exceedingly beautiful girl. Boni de Castellane, who praised her beauty one night at dinner, was advised by the lady next to him 'to take jumping lessons'. For Elisabeth de Clermont-Tonnerre she was 'as beautiful as a Greek warrior, with eyes perhaps too large and too blue'. Mme de Clermont-Tonnerre first met Miss Deacon when she was asked by the Comtesse Greffulhe, one of the leaders of Parisian society, to bring her to the Polo Club. She was expecting the usual little speech – 'How kind of you, Madame, to call for me' – and was pleasantly astounded when a blazing-eyed beauty emerged from the hotel and launched without more ado into a critique of Thomas Hardy. 'Hardy's type of insight must seem monotonous to you, but it penetrates regions that have never been explored before,' the astonished Duchess was informed.[20]

Such an opening would have been met with blank amazement in London, where a hostess might invite a famous writer to dinner but could certainly not be expected to have read his books, let alone to embark upon literary criticism. In London, politics reigned supreme. The leading hostesses – Lady Londonderry, the Duchess of Devonshire, Lady Lansdowne – were political; they did not – perish the thought! – actually take part in politics themselves, but politics took place at their houses; statesmen met other statesmen and arrived at decisions later to be ratified. Then there was the social set, who received only those who were 'in' and liked gambling, shooting, eating and drinking, vying with one another to provide the very best of all these amenities. The unaccustomed quality of indulgence in the intellectual life may be judged by the very existence of a group such as the Souls – the acknowledged centre of all that was intellectually inclined in society. It was a small group, select and self-conscious.

> Their intellectual tastes, their aesthetic manner and their exclusive aura tended to render them ridiculous to those whose feet were firmly planted in the prosaic walks of life [wrote Consuelo Vanderbilt].

> It was at a big dinner given by their friends in honor of Lord and Lady Curzon of Kedleston on his appointment as Viceroy of India in 1898 that I first floated on to their Olympian heights.... Looking at the assembled company, I think there is some justification for the name of Souls, since many have since become immortal. There are present two future Prime Ministers – Asquith and Balfour – John Morley, the future Lord Haldane, Minister for War, and countless other cabinet ministers.... There was usually a sprinkling of rising young men or lovely women so to speak on trial. Sometimes they became initiates – more often they disappeared.[21]

This curious and exclusive attitude to the pleasures of the intellect was quite different from what might be found in Paris, where it was assumed that intellect might be expected to hold its own socially even without benefit of birth; where leading hostesses were identified, indeed, by the particular group of writers, painters, musicians, who met regularly at their salons. This is not to say that people were unconcerned with such things as precedence in France. On the contrary, wrote Edith Wharton, 'in France there is no democratic dinner-table over which it does not permanently hang its pall.' But even the rules of precedence reflected French attitudes to the intellectual life, for who shared the top rung with dukes and ambassadors? Why, members of the French Academy – those immortals whose election, though it might be the subject of intrigue, had to do with intellectual achievement and not with birth. And as one moved down the dinner table, away from the host and hostess who sat in the middle surrounded by the great, the high-born and the established, one arrived at the *bouts de table* – those at either end whose contribution was to entertain rather than to glorify. The *bouts de table*, declared Mrs Wharton, 'are at once the shame and the glory of the French dinner-table; the shame of those who think they deserve a better place, or are annoyed with themselves and the world because they have not yet earned it; the glory of hostesses ambitious to receive the quickest wits in Paris....'[22] To the intellectual lion, everything was forgiven. When Mrs Wharton gave a dinner party, she showed the guest list to a friend whose uncle, a duke, was the received authority on matters of precedence. The niece reported that her uncle had to confess himself defeated. 'My dear child, Mrs Wharton ought *never* to have invited them together,' he sighed despairingly. He *thought* on the whole she had better place the guests in a certain way, but, such were the complex shades of precedence, even he could not be sure.[23] But, Mrs Wharton found, even had she committed some glaring *faux pas*, all would have been forgiven – because she was a successful writer, and a translation of her most recent novel, with a flattering introduction by Paul Bourget, had recently been published. In New York, in London even, such an achievement would have intimidated rather than attracted the fashionable world. But not in Paris.

In such a society American girls, however rich, were at a double disadvantage; they had neither lineage nor culture, so what could be expected of them? An Anna Gould merely confirmed such prejudices. On the other hand, so little was expected of American girls that the display of a reasonable intellect, a working knowledge of the French language, could produce quite a disproportionate effect. When, as with Gladys Deacon, these attributes were allied to great beauty, wealth, and an acquaintance with the best people, the effect was irresistible.

Miss Deacon's success, as a girl and a young woman, was phenomenal. Her looks, coupled with the force of her personality, dazzled an extraordinary selection of the most sought-after men of her day. The Crown Prince of Germany – 'Little Willie' – fell hopelessly in love with her, to the horror of his relatives. In 1904 she was briefly engaged to the German philosopher Hermann Keyserling: the shock of the end of the affair prompted him to embark upon his first major work, *Das Gefüge der Welt* (*Flight from the World*). Hugo von Hofmannsthal, poet, dramatist and librettist to Richard Strauss, wrote of her: 'Gladys D. She is about 25. Is and always will be in a certain sense the most splendid person that I have ever seen. Her eyes like blue fire. Her daring, occasionally amounting to insolence in her talk, has possibly even increased....' She had an affair with Bernard Berenson.[24]

However, the person who remained most lastingly taken with Miss Deacon was Sunny, Duke of Marlborough – who was unfortunately (for all parties) married to Consuelo Vanderbilt. At the time of their first meeting Gladys was only sixteen. The Duke invited her to Blenheim when Consuelo was recovering from the birth of their first child. 'I was soon subjugated by the charm of her companionship and we began a friendship which only ended years later,' wrote Consuelo[25] – a sentiment shared wholeheartedly by her husband. By the time she was thirty Gladys, then described by Edith Wharton as 'an attractive eccentric woman', was reputedly the Duke's mistress; and in 1921, when she was forty and Consuelo had finally agreed to divorce, the pair were finally married.

Although she was now Duchess of Marlborough, Gladys Deacon's success was never an English success. Her style was not that of London; even her wedding – which was after all, also the wedding of an English duke – took place in Paris, among those society intellectuals so lovingly described by Marcel Proust. Proust himself was a guest at the dinner given for the newlyweds by Madame Hennessy: the Duke took a great fancy to him, and invited him to Blenheim. 'I'll put you in a sleeper at the Gare du Nord, I'll tuck you up in a cabin on the boat, and you can stay in bed at Blenheim,' he coaxed, and urged the sickly writer to try the Coué system – 'Just repeat to yourself "I feel marvellous" because if you believe you're well you'll be well.'[26] But Proust did not come to Blenheim and (despite Coué) died the next year.

And now – at her moment of triumph – came the truly appalling part of Gladys Deacon's story.

Tragedy is not uncommon. But that classic form of tragedy in which punishment is not only irreparable but self-inflicted and entirely appropriate, is rare in real life. Gladys's tragedy, in the end, was her great beauty. Even after her marriage, people were still falling in love with her; but, like many women whose beauty has been exceptional, its loss or diminution through age was a prospect she found unbearable. Her particular type had always been acknowledged to be the classical Greek; and, some time after her marriage, she decided that the time had come to correct such small imperfections as existed. She spent some time measuring the proportions of the faces of statues in a Roman museum. Eventually, she was persuaded that, but for one small detail, she had the face of a perfect fifth-century Greek beauty. The defect was that the noses on the statues continued in an un-broken line from the forehead: Gladys, however, had (like most of the world) a small indentation on the bridge of her nose. Deter-mined to correct this blemish she embarked upon plastic surgery, then in its embryonic stage. Paraffin was injected under her skin. It slipped.

Now, instead of the slight indentation of previous years, or the desired smooth line, there was a lump at the bridge of her nose. Princess Bibesco, seeing her at the salon of Rosa de Fitz-James in Paris – one of her old haunts – said she 'looked like a Gorgon' with a rudimentary horn above the bridge of her nose. And not only that: the wax ran down under the skin to her neck, which swelled up horribly, so that she had to go around swathed in clouds of tulle to the chin in an effort to disguise her de-formity. But the disguise was not enough, said Princess Bibesco, 'to prevent the curious from noticing the ravages caused by an excess of admiration for the ancient world by a daughter of the New World.' Said another guest: 'I thought she was a marvel. She is only a curiosity.'

But the exterior does not – or should not – affect the interior; the frightful ravages of an excess of vanity need have no effect on the functioning of the intellect. And indeed Gladys held forth, on this evening, as she had done on so many previous evenings, on the comparisons to be drawn between French and English poetry. However, the crowd which had been spellbound by the beauty displaying that she had, also, a mind, were no longer interested. Now, wrote Princess Bibesco, 'it was not new but just very boring.' Had it been new before? That critical observer Gertrude Stein had not thought so; Miss Deacon may have sent pleasant shivers of outrage down some well-bred spines, 'but after a winter of Montmartre Gertrude Stein [who met her with the Berensons in Florence] had found her too easily shocked to be interesting.'[27] To beauty, however, everything is forgiven intellectually – just as to the intellectual Mrs Wharton, everything had been forgiven socially. Gladys retired from the world and took to dogs, who could not remember her as she had been. Our last glimpse of her (although she died as late as 1977) is in the pages of Chips Channon's diary – those curiously riveting pages which, in their obsession with social glory, are so very American. In 1943, Channon recorded 'a Proustian incident':

In a Bond Street jewellers, I saw an extraordinary marionette of a woman – or was it a man? It wore grey flannel trousers, a wide leather belt, masculine overcoat, and a man's brown felt hat, and had a really frightening appearance; but the hair was golden dyed and long; what is wrongly known as platinum; the mouth was a scarlet scar. Bundi began to growl, and as I secretly examined this terrifying apparition, I recognised Gladys Marlborough, once the world's most beautiful woman ... the toast of Paris, the love of Proust, the belle amie of Anatole France ... I went up to her, and smiled, and put out my hand which she took shrinkingly and then, breaking into French (as she always did) said, 'Est-ce que je vous connais, Monsieur?' 'Yes,' I said, 'I am Chips'. She looked at me, stared vacantly with those famous turquoise eyes that once drove men insane with desire, and muttering, 'Je n'ai jamais entendu ce nom-là', she flung down a ruby clip she was examining and bolted from the shop ... and I remembered how we had been allies for twenty years or more; how she used to telephone me every morning; how I used to give her sugar in the last war when she was still dazzlingly beautiful; and how we used to lunch with Proust; and of the story that D'Annunzio fainted when he saw her, such was her beauty; then of the Blenheim days.... Le temps qui coule.... What an adventure.[28]

The possible morals are many. One might be that energetic American girls need something more than the vacuities of social life, however exalted, to occupy their minds.

8

Setting the pace: society

'Does anyone know a Lady Cunard? She is a most dangerous woman.'[1]

The histories considered so far seem to lead ineluctably to the conclusion that only by a certain distortion of the spirit could an American girl successfully fulfil her new-found role as a member of the European aristocracy. How could it be otherwise? She came from a society where competition ruled, where energy was the quality most at a premium, and where both men and women were expected to make their own way under these conditions. She arrived to take her place in a society where traditions ruled, where things were what they always had been, and where the guiding inclination of her husband, his friends and family was to ensure that this should continue to be so. They probably regarded her father as a vulgar upstart, albeit a useful one; he probably regarded them as useless products of an outmoded and decadent social system, although he liked the fact that they were able to give his daughter a handle to her name.

But although many of them might bow gracefully to the inevitable, the fact remained that American girls, whoever they might be married to, could not suddenly do away with that energy with which they had been born, to which they had been brought up, and which their in-laws so often found worrying and slightly distasteful. It might be vulgar, but it was only through the exercise of that kind of vulgarity that their fathers had put together the fortunes which constituted the entire reason for their presence, after a family gap of several generations and a social gap better left unexplored, back on the eastern side of the Atlantic. Given no outlet it might – as the story of Gladys Deacon so dreadfully showed – lead to misery. And what satisfaction could the endless and in the end trivial social round afford to a truly energetic nature?

It was true that in the United States the social round did absorb these energies. But there, social life was not static. Its whole history showed that, given wealth, time and determination, there was no reason why Mrs John Doe should not reach the topmost eminence where Mrs Astor, Mrs Vanderbilt and Mrs Stuyvesant Fish ruled – for the moment – supreme. Energy and perseverance would win out in the end – marriage to a princeling playing its part, as often as not, in the ultimate victory.

But could sheer force of character compete against the weight of tradition in Europe? One must disallow oneself the solid consciousness of achievement vouchsafed to that Mrs Vanderbilt who could tell a European visitor: 'This whole house was copied for us by Stanford White from the Temple of Jove. I'll show you Fred's bedroom, early Italian Renaissance, so rare we could only have one room done that way. Also the guest bedrooms, we had one man here last week-end who said the chairs were so valuable he just had to sit on the floor.'[2] That was just the kind of thing that all the ladies of London were waiting to pounce upon with scorn. Should one, then, conform to the tenets of sub-dued tastefulness? Mary Curzon's experience seemed to show that conforming, however slavishly, did one little good among the established cliques whose main concern seemed to be with asserting their social imperviousness.

Despite these discouragements it is remarkable how many of the leading lights of European society were, by the turn of the century, Americans. By that date Mary Curzon was Vicereine of India; Jennie Churchill was one of London's leading social and political hostesses; and Chauncey M. Depew could write, in an article intended to encourage other American girls to tread the same path, that: 'there are few more successful and brilliant women in London than Lady Mandeville (Miss Consuelo Yznaga), Mrs Col. Paget, formerly Miss Minnie Stevens, called one of the handsomest women in society, and the Duchess of Marlborough, who in less than one month won her way to the front ranks, all of whom are New York girls.'³ Jennie Churchill, Consuelo Marlborough and Mary Curzon are, in this instance, of less interest to us. Each in her different way rode to her position upon the success or birth of her husband – although each, through her own particular personal qualities, made the most of what was available to her. Consuelo charmed, Jennie dazzled, and Mary, by her unwavering, loving and astute support of her husband, both personal and political, earned herself his undying adoration and the belated, but nonetheless welcome, admiration and recognition of his friends.

Consuelo Mandeville and Minnie Paget did not possess such advantages. No one was going to ride anywhere to speak of on the back of Lord Mandeville or Colonel Paget – the one a black-guard, the other a nobody: a charming nobody, no doubt, but a nobody nonetheless. The best that could be said of them was that – as Minnie Stevens had so clearly grasped when she decided to settle for Mr Paget – being married to them was better than not being married at all. Once that was done you had the entrée, and the rest was up to you. As George Moore wrote to his beloved Maud Burke, marriage was 'a necessary springboard for a woman'.

Moore was not, in this instance, proposing himself for the role of springboard. Once, when an *ingénue* of seventeen had asked him whether he were married, he had replied, 'No, I have always preferred adultery.'⁴ As for Maud, she had told him, 'If we were married we should be very happy – for six months.' For Maud, like Minnie, like Consuelo, like Moore himself, did not equate marriage with happiness. It was merely, in this society, the neces-sary prelude to self-fulfilment – if one saw self-fulfilment in social terms, as Minnie, Consuelo and Maud undoubtedly did.

George Moore's passion for Maud was to last for the whole of his life, from the year of their meeting – 1894 – until he died in 1933. He fell in love with her the first day he saw her, and she, a young girl just over from California, was enchanted at this tribute from such a literary lion. She reciprocated his passion, and they passed some idyllic months together, travelling round Europe and, later, in a 'wilful little house' in Park Lane which he per-suaded her to take. But although she would not agree to marry him, the question of marriage was not dropped.

The question was whom she should marry – who of all the people we know could supply her with the springboard she required. I mentioned a name and her eyes brightened. 'Do you really think so?' Then I knew my hour had sounded. Things of this kind move speedily when they begin to move, and it was in one of those wilful little houses that she said to me, one midnight, 'Swear to me that whatever happens, we shall always be friends'. I swore it and begged her to tell me what was on her mind. The air seemed ominous, and there was sadness in her and a shroud of evil on the night.[5]

Certainly it might be thought that the night was not an especially auspicious one for the person whose name had been mentioned – presumably, Sir Bache Cunard. No less suitable mate could have been found for him than Maud Burke, who was to achieve fame on her own account as Lady Cunard.

Only Americans, one feels, could have been so wholly business-like about the question of establishing and maintaining their position in society as Lady Mandeville, Mrs Paget and (later) Lady Cunard. No European would have been capable of such an attitude; besides, no European who had thus needed to make her way would have found herself in a position to do so. She would have been dismissed as an adventuress and assigned, in all probability, to the *demi-monde* – rich and influential, maybe, but not received.

Were Minnie Stevens, Consuelo Yznaga, Maud Burke, not, then, adventuresses? If the word has any meaning that, of course, is exactly what they were. Though not literally penniless they were, in terms of social coin, very nearly so – undeterred by which they made their way by grim determination to the top of the social tree. The likeness was recognized by George Moore who in one of his letters to Maud mentions Mrs Paget: 'Minnie Paget I saw once again, she sent for me; I am obliged to you for the introduction, for I think I shall always see her with pleasure; she is of our kin and one must keep to one's kin.'[6] It was a reaction quite different from that of Consuelo Vanderbilt, who had noticed only Mrs Paget's 'hard green eyes'.

Maud Burke was not a woman to be deterred by hard green eyes. Indeed, hardness is a quality often attributed to her by Moore, her most devoted admirer (but would he, he asked himself, have loved her if she had been different?), and it is a quality he specifically connects with her eyes, to which he applies the unusual epithet 'marmoreal', as well as her heart. She, like Minnie, like Consuelo, knew about the realities of life – a life requiring the ostentatious expenditure of enormous sums of money. Money was not always forthcoming, in which case something must be done – of course, as discreetly as possible. By the time Lady Cunard died in 1948, many of her paintings had been openly sold, some of the rest were copies, and all her jewels were paste.

It was well known that the one factor which, more than any other, had helped Minnie and Consuelo to their social eminence was their membership of the Prince of Wales's set. What American parent, sending her daughter on the hopeful odyssey to London in the 1870s, could have hoped for such a remarkable piece of good fortune as the existence of the Prince of Wales's set? Just as the aristocracy instinctively distrusted everything that the American girls represented, so the Prince instinctively welcomed what they had to give. He was not xenophobic – he was, after all, pretty much of a foreigner himself. His mother's court, after the death of Albert, was austere and restrained in tone; but the Prince was in reaction against his mother's court and all it stood for. He was a hedonist who enjoyed good things and the trappings of extreme wealth. The comfortable but faintly shabby lifestyle of many of the great country houses of the day, always nigglingly conscious of the need for 'retrenchment' in the background, held no attractions for him. He preferred the untrammelled luxury which could be offered by the rising class of industrial magnates. If the style was right he was not worried about the ancestry – indeed, he seemed actively to prefer this kind of company. 'If he had been born into a humbler station, he might have become a successful businessman,' remarked *The Times*; while Asquith commented: 'In this great business community there was no better man of business.'[7] He also, as was well known, had a particularly appreciative eye for a pretty woman. What could be more to his taste than a rich American girl, full of snap, style and dollars? Consuelo, Minnie, Jennie Churchill, soon became indispensable members of his set – and hence automatically, leading figures in society. This, as far as the old aristocracy was concerned, was the most galling part of it all. One might not – one undoubtedly did not – wish to know the kind of people the Prince surrounded himself with; but one did without question wish to know the Prince. One cannot cut one's future king, no matter how much one may disapprove of his choice of friends. And one cannot expect to remain on good terms with a man and snub his closest acquaintances. After Edward vii's death, the depths of this resentment could be glimpsed. Such erstwhile confidants of the old King as Sir Ernest Cassel and Sir Edgar Speyer were given to realize how little they had really been accepted. But while Edward was alive, first as prince and then as king, however ambivalent feelings about his coterie might be, however much its members might be notorious for their loose morals, their extravagant habits, their taste for gambling, it was quite inevitable that they should take their places amid the social leaders of the day.

This had various effects on the lives of Consuelo Mandeville and Minnie Paget. One was that, inevitably, a lot of their time was spent worrying about money. Keeping up with the Prince's tastes was no cheap affair – and there could be no question of not keeping up and remaining in the coterie. Then, also inevitably, they acquired – if they did not already possess – a certain patina of knowing worldly wisdom. This did not sit too uneasily upon their shoulders, brought up as they had been amid the hard realities of Wall Street and the assessing and unwelcoming glances of New York society matrons. If all this led in the end to a certain cynicism, who could be surprised?

The Prince of Wales's set, however, was not for Maud Burke. Partly it was a question of age: she was of a different generation, twenty years or more younger than that first group of American girls who had taken London by such unexpected storm in the 1870s. A middle-aged prince with his less than girlish mistresses, the set pattern of high living, the gambling, the gluttonous over-eating, were not designed to appeal to impetuous youth. They were especially unlikely to appeal to Maud.

Maud Burke was a much more extraordinary person, an altogether more exotic specimen, than forceful Minnie Paget or luscious Consuelo Mandeville had ever been. Her background, to begin with, was altogether more questionable than theirs. To a European, no doubt, one American family was much like another. One did not ask what went on in the grey American dawn. If one had asked, however, there would have been no difficulty in ascertaining the origins of Consuelo or Minnie. Maud was a different kettle of fish. She came from the far West – from San Francisco, city of the gold-rush. Who was her father? Maud would never say. He died when she was in her early teens, and all she ever told her daughter Nancy about her childhood was a reference to the 'exquisite and adorable' Chinese servants who looked after her.[8]

Manners and morals were altogether freer in the West than on the stuffy East Coast. Moreover, there was a distinct shortage of personable women, while prudence dictated that a woman should not remain alone out there longer than was strictly necessary. Not surprisingly, the charming and sensible Mrs Burke soon found new protectors. One of these was William O'Brien, the silver king, one of the owners of the legendary Comstock Lode. He had been a friend of hers for some time – presumably an acquaintance, as a fellow-Irishman, of Mr Burke's – and it was rumoured in some quarters that Maud might be his natural daughter. Then there was a financier, Mr Coffin, who looked after her investments; and a real-estate millionaire, Horace Carpentier, who had a particular penchant for young girls and was especially fond of Maud. Amid this bevy of 'uncles', Maud passed her teenage years. She in no way resented her mother's manoeuvrings – on the contrary, she was exceedingly fond of her mother and they remained on the closest of terms until the latter's death. There was plenty of money. Mrs Burke and Maud travelled widely, to the East Coast and to Europe, which she grew to love. At the age of twelve she went to her first opera – *The Ring* at the Metropolitan Opera House in New York: she was enraptured by this. At the same time Carpentier was looking after other aspects of her education. He introduced her to the novels of Balzac, which (like opera) became a lifelong passion of hers. She would read and re-read the *Comédie Humaine*: 'When I come to the end, I just begin again,' she said. With Carpentier she read the Greek and Latin poets, Shakespeare, Richardson's *Pamela*; she played the piano for him and sang *Lieder* for him. When she was eighteen her mother remarried, a stockbroker called Charles Tichenor. At this point Maud was allowed to make a second home with Carpentier, to whom she always referred thereafter as 'my guardian'. The young woman who at the age of twenty-two burst upon the consciousness of the middle-aged George Moore was thus quite unlike most of the carefully nurtured young ladies who crossed the Atlantic from the aspiring salons of the East Coast. Far from having been sheltered, Maud had seen life, and seems to have been quite confident of her ability to deal with it on her own terms. The way in which she first encountered Moore gives an example of her abilities in this respect. She and her mother were invited to a luncheon party at the Savoy. It was a large party, and Maud learned that George Moore, the famous novelist, was to be a fellow guest. Determined to meet him, she slipped into the dining room before the lunch began and changed the place-cards so that she would be seated beside him. George Moore recounted the episode as he remembered it to Maud's daughter, Nancy Cunard: 'She was with her mother, Mrs Tichenor. Oh! She was a *lovely* girl and I was immediately attracted to her. She wore a grey shot-silk gown; shall I ever forget it? She was looking at the cards on the table and it seems she did not like the neighbours she was to sit between, or else she wanted to talk to me. So she bent over the table and changed the cards, saying "*I* am going to sit next to Mr George Moore!" '[9] One account says that Moore held forth on the future of the English novel, and his desire to win freedom for it as Zola had for the novel in France; Moore himself says, 'Her conversation was brilliant!' The one actual snippet of this conversation that comes down to us is the moment when Maud leant over to Moore, put her hand upon his sleeve, and cried: 'George Moore, you have a soul of fire!'[10] It is the gesture of a modern Californian – but then, Maud was always ahead of her time. Moore was entranced by her. He was at the miserable tail-end of an affair with the writer Pearl Craigie (whose pen-name was John Oliver Hobbes) – and instantly switched his affections. For the rest of his life, he would be in love with Maud.

Quite how extraordinary Maud and her mother were, by the standards of the day, can be seen in what happened next. Quite simply, Moore and Maud spent the next few months together, undisturbed by any interference from Mrs Tichenor. It was during this period that Maud made the remark about being 'happy for six months' if they were married.

It was an extraordinary thing to do at that epoch – to let her unmarried daughter risk her reputation like that – but then, probably there was no 'let' about it. Could anyone have stopped Maud when once she had determined on a course of action? Moore has left an account of her character at this time:

Her courage, independence, her intellectual audacity, no doubt captured my admiration.... I admired her cold sensuality, cold because it was divorced from tenderness and passion.... I loved but an immortal goddess descended once more among men. Her sensuality was so serene and so sure of its divine character that it never seemed to become trivial or foolish. While walking in the woods with one, she would say: 'Let us sit here,' and after looking steadily at one for a few seconds, her pale marmoreal eyes glowing, she would say, 'You can make love to me now, if you like.'[11]

It was not that Maud was uninterested in marriage. As yet unsure exactly what she wanted to do, she agreed with Moore that to do anything, marriage was 'a necessary springboard'. She had been hoping to marry the Polish Prince André Poniatowski. They had met while he was on a visit to the States, and had corresponded when he returned to Europe; when he announced that he would be coming over to the West Coast, Maud was convinced that it could only be that he wanted to marry her. So convinced was she that she announced their engagement – much to Poniatowski's fury, for not only did he not wish to marry Maud, but he was interested in quite another girl in San Francisco. He went so far as to make her announce that the news of the engagement had been mistaken – a mortifying experience for anyone, but especially for one as proud as Maud. She gave it to be understood that Carpentier had stopped the match; nevertheless, when Poniatowski's real engagement was announced, it was a relief to leave for New York.

An inconclusive affair in London, a non-engagement of the most humiliating kind in San Francisco – it was time for Maud to be married. But whom should she marry? What sprite of contrariety could have suggested the name of Sir Bache Cunard? Was it – as he hints – Moore? If so, he could hardly have imagined that he would be taken seriously. Sir Bache, grandson of the founder of the Cunard Line, had, it is true, an American mother; but that is the beginning and end of what he may have had in common with Maud Burke. However, he was rich; he had a large country house; he could offer her security and (it seems) as ample a springboard as she might require. His sister, knowing her brother, begged Maud to break off the engagement. What could they have to offer each other, he the quiet country squire, she the restless sophisticate? But Maud refused. 'I like Sir Bache better than any man I know,' she said defiantly.[12] As for him, he was dazzled. He had never met anyone like Maud. They were married in New York on 16 April 1895, the wedding being pulled forward without explanation from June, the original date. Perhaps Maud was afraid of contracting cold feet. Then they set out for Sir Bache's house, Nevill Holt in Leicestershire, in the heart of that foxhunting country which Consuelo Marlborough was so heartily to abominate.

Certainly she abominated it no more than Maud, who was now condemned to inhabit it permanently. In later life Lady Cunard loathed the country, never setting foot there except under duress, and certainly never modifying her style of dress for the occasion: teetering on high heels she doubtfully inspected cows, wrapped in leopard-skin she sat gingerly upon the grass. Presumably this aversion arose from her fifteen years at Nevill Holt, which in 1911 she quit never to return. Had she known of it in advance it is doubtful whether even the rebound from the indignity of the Poniatowski affair could have persuaded her to spend so much of her life in such loathsome surroundings.

The loathing, of course, was purely in the eye of the beholder. Seen by those less prejudiced – Maud's daughter Nancy, for example – Nevill Holt sounds charming.

In grey and yellow stone and old stucco, the long stretch of the house is attached at one end to a church; the whole of its length merges into this. Fine, ancient stables stand apart at an angle. A later-day loggia, known as the Cloisters, and a Georgian wing are at the back where a large Victorian dining-room had also been added. Handsome indeed is the main entrance, that front porch with its crenellations and Thomas Palmer's richly-carved oriel window of 1453 to the left of it. All the front – a long, narrow, harmonious tapestry unrolled to the full – is visible and of a piece.... A great lawn between two avenues of very tall beech-trees, a terrace looking towards sunset, walled gardens, secular oaks and elms as one reached the house through the chestnut avenue with its iron gate standing ever open between the stone piers that bear the arms of the Nevills, a bull's head arising out of a crown – such is the walk in memory around Holt....[13]

Within this edifice Maud (so she felt) mouldered. Sir Bache was a genial, foxhunting squire; his friends shared his sporting interests. What had Maud to say to such people? The thought that she might join in their pursuits was inconceivable: she did not even enjoy venturing outside if it could be avoided. Her Californian upbringing ensured that she could ride well enough, but she did not like hunting. Sir Bache, up in his tower workshop, did all he could to please his exquisite young wife. He fashioned a decorative gate for her, all done in fancy woodwork with the words 'Come into the garden Maud' picked out in horseshoes. But Maud remained obstinately indoors.

Her trouble was that she was both very gregarious and a genuine intellectual. For such a person the life of the countryside can hold few attractions. Marriage might be a springboard, but this marriage seemed destined to propel her only into the centre of the county set – an opportunity she deplored. She spent much of her time changing and rearranging the furniture and reading French and English novels – sad enough pursuits when there is no one to share the excitement of them.

It was, however, unthinkable that Maud should remain solitary for long. It is impossible to hold down a great talent, and Maud had one – a social talent. 'You have come into this life to shine in society, to be a light, to form a salon and to gather clever men around you,' wrote Moore.[14] As the years went on she began to gather around her, at Holt, house parties of writers, painters, musicians. These mixed rather uneasily with Sir Bache's sporting friends, and it was noticeable that the more intellectual men tended to appear when the shooting season took the sportsmen north. 'My picture of Holt,' says Nancy, 'is one of constant arrivals and departures during half the year, of elaborate long teas on the lawn with tennis and croquet going on, of great winter logs blazing all day in the Hall and Morning Room, with people playing bridge there for hours on end. Beautiful and exciting ladies move about in smart tailor-mades; they arrived in sables or long fox stoles, a bunch of Parma violets pinned into the fur on the shoulder. Summer-long, in shot silk and striped taffeta they stroll laughing and chatting across the lawns. ...' Winter and summer the house was filled with flowers; its ancient bones were hung with Italian damasks, strewn with cushions, brocades and oriental rugs. Amid all this luxury the life-size silver fox presented to Sir Bache when he retired as master of the hunt stood awkwardly – just as he stood awkwardly amid so many of his wife's guests. One of the few with whom he felt immediately at ease was, curiously, George Moore. Did he not know about Moore's passion for Maud? Or was he, with an urbanity with which few seem prepared to credit him, simply making the best of an unalterable situation?

It says much for Moore's charm that he won the heart of the conservative Sir Bache, who was so upset when Maud addressed one of the footmen direct (instead of through the butler) or when she waved merrily at him from the street, catching his eye as he stood in the window of his London club. If that was bad form, what could be said of Moore's form? Nancy Cunard recalls Moore's answer to the question as to how he liked young American widows. Various such appeared at Holt, seductively clad in floating teagowns, smoking cigarettes through long tortoiseshell holders, as averse to sporting pursuits as their hostess – preferring even to bridge the delightful occupation of flirting on sofas. 'I fancy,' said Moore, 'they are not averse to a *stepaside* now and then, and what is the ha-arm in that? And by the way, there is a beautiful story going round now about ... Oh, what is that woman's name? ... She was losing her husband's affections, you see. So she went to Paris and took lessons from some of the ladies in the Chabanel. A French cocotte has a good deal to teach, you may be sure. When she returned she began to put these lessons into practice in bed with her husband. Oh, it must have been a dreadful moment when she heard him say: "Dora, *ladies never move*".'[15] And Moore went off into one of his chuckles: 'Khk, khk, khk.'

Certainly the conversation at Maud's parties was *risqué* enough. Occasionally one of her husband's friends would be shocked, and would endeavour to make Moore aware of his bad taste. Invariably Moore would turn the affair into a joke on his accuser, at which everybody – everybody else – laughed. One person who was never shocked was the hostess, whose own racy tongue became legendary. Her aim was to disconcert – she was rarely disconcerted. Her introductions became legendary: 'This is Michael Arlen—the only Armenian who hasn't been massacred.' 'This is Lord Alington, dear. He drives in a taxi at dawn from Paris to Rome, wearing evening dress and a gardenia, without any *luggage*.'[16]

As the years went on, Maud found her style. It was not a style likely to reconcile her to her present life, nor one which enhanced the existence of her husband and daughter. Maud had no time for children. She said once, 'No great woman has ever had children. Elizabeth had none, and how about George Eliot, George Sand? Motherhood is a low thing: the lowest.'[17] As to George Sand she was of course wrong, but the meaning remains clear. Nancy on her side did not like her mother. There was no warmth in the relationship. Nancy referred to Maud as 'Her Ladyship' and the two grew ever more distant. Nancy's own reaction to motherhood was demonstrated by her early decision to have her womb removed in order to avoid any possibility of such an eventuality – and any danger of inflicting the same sort of relationship upon her own child as the marble-eyed Maud had inflicted upon her.

It is indeed hard to connect Lady Cunard with such a basic function as motherhood. It smacked too much of the uncontrollably natural, the grossly physical. Perhaps that is what she meant when she called it a 'low thing'. Maud was sensual, but she was never gross, nor (so far as she could ensure) natural. The enduring impression left by the many references to her and descriptions of her which appear in the letters, memoirs and diaries of her day is one of studied artificiality, the creation of a persona as a work of art. The name Emerald, which she took in 1926 ('WHO IS EMERALD. ARE YOU MARRIED.' telegraphed Moore in alarm on receiving a letter signed 'Maud Emerald') – emeralds were her favourite jewels – suited her perfectly in all respects. She was small and delicate, and was often compared to a bird, capped with a crest of fair hair. 'Like a jewelled bird uncaged,' was Lady Diana Cooper's view;[18] and the same comparison was made by Lady Cynthia Asquith in her diaries.

Meeting Lady Cunard on a visit to Glynde in Sussex, she wrote:

> Maud was looking more like an inebriated canary than ever. I love her slight concessions in the way of country clothes! She was in amazing, startling, soprano-soliloquy form and has come on amazingly since I first saw her – she's a priceless woman – like most of the great laughter-raisers, she often doesn't know when she is being most amusing and sometimes blinks with astonishment when one laughs at her sweeping absurdities. She fell upon a volume of Donne's poems – new to her – and read 'The Flea' aloud and thought him some poet: 'Do you know Donne? – he's a most lecherous poet!'[19]

Her conversational style was inimitable. She mocked, she exaggerated, she drew sparks. Thus, for instance, she went on one typical teatime: 'Maud eclipsed herself. She protested how she hated a *tête-à-tête* with either man or woman – naturally what she likes is so-called general conversation – which means her soliloquizing to a large audience. Not only did she detest being *alone* with a man, but she emphatically maintained that she *had* never been. This startling statement was repeated at every meal.... She talked of Nancy with comic detachment, saying she liked her because she was a "good mover".'[20] Margot Asquith recalled hearing her startle a gathering by announcing, as if to herself, that 'to be kissed on the *mouth* is a woman's most intimate experience.'

Such a person could not be condemned for ever to the back-woods of Nevill Holt. That Maud endured it for as long as she did – for fifteen years – is in itself something of a surprise. After all, neither Consuelo Vanderbilt nor Anna Gould, both marrying in the same year as Maud (1895), managed to bear their husbands' company beyond 1906. Perhaps the answer lies in Sir Bache's complaisance. Maud entertained whom she wanted as she wanted. She and George Moore were almost certainly lovers after her marriage, and Moore was not the only man to entertain a passion for the extraordinary young Lady Cunard. A story is told of a Russian prince who was well known to be in love with her. One evening at Nevill Holt, when the men were sitting over their port, they began to play a variation of the 'truth' game. Each person had to say whom he was presently in love with. When it came to the prince's turn the rest of the company sat with bated breath, since Sir Bache was present and everybody knew who was the current object of his guest's desires. But with supreme urbanity he met the challenge. 'I?' he said. 'Oh, *I* am in love with the page-boy at the St James's Club.'²¹ The crisis dissolved in laughter.

Sir Thomas Beecham, however, was not so easily dismissed. Maud made his acquaintance in 1911, when he was famous both for his growing musical reputation and for a scandalous divorce case in which he had been cited as the co-respondent. It was a combination calculated to prove irresistible to Lady Cunard, and she fell, at the age of thirty-nine, hopelessly and irretrievably in love with him. This could not be a hole-in-the-corner affair conducted behind Sir Bache's back; and she was the more disinclined to go on in this way since she was finding the compromise of living, albeit in her own way, at Nevill Holt increasingly unsatisfactory. She might entertain there, but she could not adequately fulfil her social ambitions – that is to say, herself. Should she leave Sir Bache and get a judicial separation? Before she could make up her mind on this issue, Sir Thomas left with his orchestra for a tour of America. Maud was appalled. What should she do without him? On the day he was sailing, she made up her mind. She ordered her carriage and started post-haste for Liverpool docks. The roads were icy and the coachmen afraid that the horses would slip and break their legs. Maud was unmoved by such pleas. 'Faster! Faster!' she urged. The slipping, sliding conveyance drew up panting at the dockside just as the boat was due to sail. Maud rushed aboard and never set foot in Nevill Holt again.

Lady Cunard had not found it especially easy to gain acceptance by fashionable society. If Mary Curzon had found it an uphill task, how much more difficult was it for Maud Cunard, who had none of Mary's background, was not married to a well-known name, and seemed to go out of her way to invite censure from those haughty hostesses who ruled supreme. It was not until 1907, twelve years after her marriage, that the genial Maurice Baring announced that he felt he could resign from the Society for the Prevention of Cruelty to Lady Cunard. Perhaps that is why she stayed at Nevill Holt so long: one needs a secure social base if one is to strike out on one's own, and once that was achieved it was only a matter of time before the lure of London became irresistible. Presumably there came a time when Maud's house parties had become enough of an institution among the intelligent men, and she had been long enough respectably married to Sir Bache, for the ladies (or most of them) to feel they might relax their barriers – with a few notable exceptions. It is reasonable to suppose, too, that the more general disapprobation was reinforced by a fear of competition. There were enough grand hostesses in London already without Maud installing herself on the scene.

But she was not really setting up in competition, in that what she offered was quite different from the social wares peddled by the political or high society hostesses. Not for nothing had her earliest European acquaintance, her first favourite among European cities, been Paris. Lady Cunard's approach to social life, with its emphasis on intellectual distinction and good conversation, was essentially a French approach; and what she now opened was a salon in the best Parisian style. Her relationship with Beecham being what it was, the emphasis was musical; but intellectual distinction, real or fancied, of any kind, was enough to gain admittance. Indeed, the grumble of some of her *habitués* was that Maud, with her discerning eye for a foible, saw distinction where others could see none, and although she was so anxious to avoid boredom at any cost, thus tended to interlard her salon with bores: 'she will like and praise a politician because he recites Corneille, a great General for some such reason as that "he knows all about butterflies!" or a poet "because he seems to understand fish"....'[22] If she found somebody dull, however, she mercilessly goaded the conversation until she struck sparks of fury. It was a habit which persisted until the end of her life. Chips Channon records an exchange which took place in her seventieth year. At lunch Emerald (as she by then had been known for many years) 'with mischief in her old, over-made-up eyes' declared that no man was ever faithful to his wife for more than three years. 'That', she added, 'is a biological fact.' 'You can never have known my Freeman,' Lady Willingdon, the other lunch guest, retorted. 'Perhaps better than you think,' was Emerald's reply.[23]

Naturally, not everybody liked her. Max Beerbohm had come

to stay with her at Nevill Holt, but had not 'really enjoyed' it, and in later years meeting Lord Berners who had just been lunching with Lady Cunard, Beerbohm enquired politely after her health. 'Wonderful, absolutely wonderful, she never changes,' said Berners, to which Max replied: 'I am sorry to hear that.'[24] But for Harold Acton she was 'like a spiritual dancer in a desert'; the young Osbert Sitwell adored her company and contrasted her favourably with the majority of London hostesses who 'love dullness for its own sake and without hope of reward'.[25] That at least was a bondage from which the flight from Nevill Holt had finally freed her. There she, like the rest of English society, had to some extent been bound by the men's sporting calendar: when Sir Bache invited his friends for a shoot (as opposed to going shooting at a friend's) the intellectual standard of her gatherings had dropped deplorably. Now, however, first in a fine house in Cavendish Square rented from the Asquiths during their sojourn at Downing Street, and later in her own house in Grosvenor Square, she need suffer no such deprivations. She invited whom she pleased. 'The fashionable near-art world', writers, painters, musicians, politicians – all were to be found in her drawing room, where she spared no effort to ensure that they were to be seen at their best. 'I was constantly struck by Lady Cunard's faculty of producing, in a theatrical sense, the people who entered her orbit,' said Harold Acton. 'It was like the action of sunshine on a garden. Not that she could make Lytton Strachey garrulous, but whatever he said was intensely characteristic. George Moore was rejuvenated ... Sir Thomas Beecham pursued his own melodic line....'[26] They were subject to one constraint – the starting time of the evening's opera or ballet. Lady Cunard undertook, with great success, to ensure that the house would be respectably filled for Sir Thomas's seasons of opera. 'There appeared to be no limit to the number of boxes she could fill,' wrote Osbert Sitwell. 'Her will-power was sufficient, her passion for music fervent enough, to make opera almost compulsory for those who wished to be fashionable. She had also grasped the fact that in the London of that time, in order to ensure the success of such an art-luxury as Grand Opera, it was absolutely necessary to be able to rely upon a regular attendance by numskulls, nitwits and morons addicted to the mode, even if they did not care in the least for music.'[27] Sitwell, for his part, found this entailed rather a conflict of interests: he found Lady Cunard's drawing room so full of wit, gaiety and life – 'unlike any other' – that, much as he loved music, he was always sorry when the time came to leave for the performance. Moore, too, found this enthusiasm something of a burden in that it led even more to Maud surrounding herself with people when he would so much have preferred to have her company to himself. He would question Nancy about her mother's activities: 'Had any new magnates been discovered by her mother? Were they coming to heel properly in support of Beecham's opera seasons?'[28] But she persisted: the opera came before everything, even entertaining. It was the one and only thing for which she was never late.

The other leading American hostess in London at this time, Laura Corrigan, approached the problem of gaining acceptance quite differently from Lady Cunard. Laura Corrigan was no creature of artifice. Born Laura Mae Whitrock, the daughter of a carpenter in Waupaca, Wisconsin, she did not linger in her native state. She took a job as a waitress in a large hotel in Chicago, where she caught the eye of the hotel doctor and married him. It was a social advance – but not, she discovered, enough of an advance. In the West, however, with its modern attitudes to divorce and abundance of rich men, this need not be much of a check. Laura Mae soon attracted the attention of a steel magnate, James Corrigan, divorced her doctor, married Mr Corrigan and went to live with him in Cleveland, Ohio.

Riches, however, were nothing special in Cleveland, and by this time (the early 1920s) Cleveland, too, had acquired its bevy of matrons who were determined to show that mere wealth was no entrée to the privilege of their society. At this point Mr Corrigan died. Laura was left with an income of $800,000 a year, and she decided that, even if this was not enough for Cleveland, it was probably enough for London. Accordingly she set sail and in 1928 Mrs Corrigan hit London. She took Mrs Keppel's house in Grosvenor Square – Mrs Keppel who had been the King's mistress and had known everybody – and requested that Mrs Keppel's guest list be included in the lease. Mrs Keppel is said to have acquiesced but raised the rent. Having now acquired her 'little *ventre à terre*' Mrs Corrigan set out to take London by storm.

London, as Lady Cunard had found out, was not so easily taken. Why, the best people asked themselves, should they bother to attend the parties given by this Mrs Corrigan? Laura Mae gave them solid reasons for doing so – coroneted gold sock suspenders, initialled braces with gold tabs, pink monogrammed sheets for brides, rattles with gold bells for their offspring; 'I myself was delighted to receive a comb of gold and tortoiseshell in a pink leather Cartier case,'[29] says Daphne Fielding – and in this enjoyment she was not alone. The haughtiest dukes, the most exclusive marchionesses, could not resist Mrs Corrigan's hand-outs. They might not have been much by the standards of Newport, R.I., but to London they were a revelation. Soon everyone was seen at Mrs Corrigan's. She even won over Lady Cunard by taking an expensive box at Covent Garden and donating largely to Sir Thomas Beecham's Imperial League of Opera – but she offered an irresistible target for Emerald's needle-sharp wit. Was Lady Cunard, Mrs Corrigan enquired, proposing to wear a tiara for a forthcoming opera night? 'No, dear,' came the reply, 'just a small emerald bandeau and my own hair.' This was a reference to the well-known, though publicly unacknowledged, fact that Mrs Corrigan was as bald as a coot and kept a whole wardrobe of wigs designed to suit different aspects of life: perfectly coiffed for evenings, rumpled for breakfast in bed, wind-blown for country weekends, in need of a hairdo before notional visits to the hairdresser. Once, while swimming in the wig supplied for this purpose with a swimming cap, the whole lot came off. Mrs Corrigan solved the problem, says Daphne Fielding who witnessed the event, by holding her breath and remaining under water until her headgear was replaced.[30]

But if it was her gifts of gold garters which first brought the best people into Mrs Corrigan's orbit, it was her good-heartedness which kept them there. 'Good, kind Laura will long live in my memory,' wrote her old friend Chips Channon at her death. 'Her kind old heart just gave out ... I was stunned: all next day people kept ringing up: London was grief-stricken. Laura was an amazing woman – sexless, devoid of any outward physical attractions and never consciously amusing yet she made an international position for herself in the very highest society, which she wooed and cajoled.'[31]

During the 1920s and 1930s the Americans formed a distinct and exalted group in London society. They largely constituted what could be seen as the new Prince of Wales's set. If the future Edward VII had lifted Lady Mandeville and Mrs Paget to the social heights, the future Edward VIII performed the same service for Lady Cunard and Mrs Corrigan.

In a way, the royal cycle was repeating itself. George V and Queen Mary did not share the tastes of the old King: their court was altogether more serious-minded and austere. Into these circles Lady Cunard never penetrated. (Said Mrs Ronnie Greville: 'You mustn't think that I dislike little Lady Cunard. I'm always telling Queen Mary that she isn't half as bad as she is painted.'[32]) But soon the new Prince of Wales, the future Edward VIII, was establishing himself as a social presence – and his inclinations echoed his grandfather rather than his father.

In particular the Prince seemed to have a penchant for American girlfriends. His liaison with Thelma, Lady Furness, one of a famous and glamorous pair of twins, the other half of which was Gloria Vanderbilt, was well known. It was observed that he talked with a slight American accent (not, noted Chips Channon, that that was such a bad thing considering that all the rest of the royal family with the exception of the Duke of Kent spoke with German accents). Then one day Thelma Furness made a fatal mistake. Called away from London unavoidably and forced to leave the Prince for some time, she asked her friend and fellow American Mrs Ernest Simpson if she would keep him entertained. When Lady Furness returned it was quite clear what had happened. Mrs Simpson had usurped Lady Furness's place in the Prince's affections. Thelma Furness was furious, and Wallis Simpson obdurate. It was war to the knife. Mrs Simpson saw to it that Lady Furness was henceforth banned from receptions at York House. London began to form up into factions. On Mrs Simpson's side – and avid for the Prince's smiles – was the American contingent: Lady Cunard, Mrs Corrigan, and that strange phenomenon, the Chicago boy who had come to Europe, become an intimate of Proust and Cocteau, gone to Oxford, and who was now a naturalized Englishman and Member of

Parliament (he once remarked: 'I have put my whole life's work into my anglicization, in ignoring my early life'[33]) – Henry Channon, MP, known to his friends as 'Chips'.

It was not at first supposed that Mrs Simpson's liaison with the Prince of Wales would be any more permanent than his various other such affairs. She was not in her first youth; had been married twice; did not seem especially distinguished or glamorous. She was, according to her friend and devoted partisan Chips, 'a jolly, unprepossessing American', a good cook, witty, wise, and an excellent influence upon the Prince who, he considered, had been Americanized, modernized and rather cheapened by the frivolous Thelma Furness. Nevertheless, he recorded in 1935: 'She is madly anxious to storm society, while she is still his favourite, so that when he leaves her (as he leaves everyone in time) she will be secure.'[34]

When George V died in 1936, excitement over the affair rose to fever pitch. It was evident that the new King was obsessively in love: were Chips and Emerald about to become leading members of the court of a new American queen? The obsession of these anglicized Americans with royalty was something unique and extraordinary. Of Laura Corrigan, Chips recorded that: 'She even talks of royalties when standing on her head, which she does regularly for health reasons.'[35] But it would have been hard to beat his own similar preoccupation. His gorgeous house at 5 Belgrave Square, in which he and his wife, the former Lady Honor Guinness, entertained so sumptuously, was next door to that inhabited by the Duke and Duchess of Kent (*née* Princess Marina of Greece). Chips revelled in this intimacy, as he did in the close friendship he preserved with Prince Paul of Yugoslavia, an old Oxford friend; but he was positively over the moon when the King himself came to dine. 'I was sad when it was over, it was the very peak, the summit, I suppose. The King of England dining with me!' he recorded after the first such occasion; and before the next royal dinner party noted that his parents-in-law, Lord and Lady Iveagh, were both amused and impressed by his 'royal activities'. 'Their gangster son-in-law from Chicago has put their daughter into the most exclusive set in Europe!' It may be questioned whether it was also the most interesting set – but Emerald Cunard asked nothing better than to be bored by the resolutely low-brow King. Emerald was thrilled at the prospect that Mrs Simpson might one day be queen – a possibility regarding which she and many others were at one time quite sanguine. In that case what might not her own prospects be – she who had always been kept out of the palace, and who had so enthusiastically, and from the very first, taken Mrs Simpson's part? Chips Channon let her know that she expected to become Mistress of the Robes – an august position at present held by the aloof and respectable Lady Airlie. And it was not only she herself who might benefit. What might she not be able to do, in her new role as an influential courtier, for all her favourite causes – for opera, ballet, music, and the arts in general? The British court had hitherto been unabatedly philistine in this respect – but all that could change. She began closely to examine the royal tastes: nothing must be done to offend them. Laura Corrigan served cold salmon for supper at one of her dances: Lady Cunard remarked disapprovingly, 'Our King says that cold salmon is vulgar.'[36] Not that poor Mrs Corrigan could be blamed for her ignorance of such points of detail, since she was, to her mortification, less intimate with royal circles than her compatriots. It took her a long time to forgive Chips for inviting her, on the occasion of his first royal dinner party, not for but after the meal. She refused to come at all, and was icy to him for weeks. Chips was saddened but philosophical: 'When royalty comes in, friendship flies out of the window,' he mused; but concluded, 'really one invites the King's friends to meet him not one's own.'[37]

Was there to be no social peak safe from the Americans? – As it turned out, there was; and poor Emerald Cunard, having so publicly and decisively backed the wrong horse, was more than ever unacceptable at court after the abdication. How could the new King and Queen meet the woman who had so eagerly befriended Mrs Simpson, the cause of all the trouble? The Duke and Duchess of Sutherland gave a ball to celebrate the coronation, and this dilemma at once presented itself. Lady Cunard was an old friend – but how could she be invited? The new King himself suggested the solution – that Emerald should indeed be invited, but should not come until after supper, by which time the King and Queen would have left. So she sat in her house at

Grosvenor Square, waiting for the telephone call that would tell her royalty had left and she might appear. It was a sad contrast to all that she had hoped for.

In 1940, Emerald Cunard gave up the house in Grosvenor Square, which had been bombed, and moved, with as much of her furniture and effects as she could fit in, to an apartment in the Dorchester Hotel. Here she was to stay for the remaining eight years of her life. With her move, yet another of the institutions which had distinguished the brilliant life of London between the wars, disappeared; for although she could – and did – entertain in her new apartment, the scale was naturally much reduced. The move prompted her old friend and ally, Chips, to muse on her career:

> It was in her house at Grosvenor Square that the great met the gay, that statesmen consorted with society, and writers with the rich – and where, for over a year the drama of Edward VIII was enacted. It had a rococo atmosphere – the conversation in the candlelight, the elegance of the bibelots and books: more, it was a rallying point for most of London society: only those that were too stupid to amuse the hostess, and so were not invited, were disdainful. The Court always frowned on so brilliant a salon; indeed Emerald's only failures were the two Queens [Mary and Elizabeth] and Lady Astor and Lady Derby. Everyone else flocked, if they had the chance. To some it was the most consummate bliss even to cross her threshold. She is as kind as she is witty, and her curious mind, and the lilt of wonder in her voice when she says something calculatedly absurd, are quite unique.[38]

Lady Cunard and Mrs Corrigan died within a few months of each other in 1948. With them died the social era they had personified. The Americans had not quite made the throne: but they had come near to it.

9

Setting the pace: politics

'I'm a Virginian; I shoot to kill.'
Nancy Astor[1]

If Wallis Simpson's most devoted supporters were drawn from the ranks of the London Americans, that was not to say that all the London Americans supported Mrs Simpson. Nowhere, for example, could she have found a more determined adversary than Nancy Astor. Lady Astor spent much time and energy trying to persuade Edward VIII not to marry Mrs Simpson, going so far as to speak 'hotly and loudly' to him, and went off to America for a visit in the belief that she had succeeded in this mission. The abdication, taking place while she was still away, showed her that she had not. On her return she was asked to broadcast about these sad happenings to her native land. With great emotion, she did so. She was at great pains to stress that the reason the King had had to abdicate was not because, as had been suggested in some papers, his intended was an American, but because she was a divorcee.

For who if not Nancy Astor was the living proof that Americans had become part of the very core and fabric of British life? If Emerald Cunard, that dedicated hedonist, saw as her aim in life the shaping of London's cultural and social life, the reforms Nancy Astor had in mind were of sterner stuff. The two ladies and their camp followers had little time for each other. Chips Channon, one of Lady Cunard's most devoted partisans, referred to Lady Astor as 'that old witch' and noted with astonishment her husband's evident and continuing love for her. In this assessment Winston Churchill, an old acquaintance and himself the son of a forceful American political hostess, concurred. When, by misfortune, they met once at Blenheim (hostesses generally laboured to keep them apart), Nancy, 'with a fervor whose sincerity could not be doubted, shouted: "If I were your wife I would put poison in your coffee!" to which Winston replied: "And if I were your husband I would drink it!" '² When the German ambassador, Ribbentrop, visited Nancy in 1936, she took occasion to chaff him at breakfast on the 'bad company' he had been keeping in England – Lady Londonderry and Lady Cunard. He meekly explained that the two ladies had been 'extremely kind' to him and his friends.³ Feel what one may today about the desirability of this particular guest, it was as inevitable that he should be entertained by the one as by the other. If Lady Cunard ran London's leading salon, its leading political hostess was Nancy Astor, MP.

Early acquaintance with the beautiful Nancy can have given little indication of what the future held in store for her. As we have already seen, her first visits to England were centred upon Melton Mowbray rather than Westminster, and although many of the people she met there were politicians, it was not to talk politics that she made their acquaintance. In her own draft for the *National Cyclopedia of American Biography* she wrote: 'She first visited England for the purpose of hunting, and hunted regularly with the best-known packs in the country. Her vivid personality regularly won her many friends in English Society. ...' As to what else she may have had in mind, Lady Cunard (Emerald's sister-in-law) must have voiced the suspicions of many when she said to the lovely Mrs Shaw, 'I suppose you've come over to England to take one of our husbands away from us.' Nancy replied: 'If you knew what difficulty I had getting rid of the first one, you wouldn't say that.'⁴

Whatever the truth of the matter, the fact remains that Nancy did not, in the end, marry an Englishman in the strictest sense of the word. She entranced various lovers of impeccable aristocratic tinge, notably Angus McDonnell, the future Lord Antrim, who adored her but whose passion she never reciprocated, and Lord Revelstoke, with whom she seems to have been fairly seriously involved. In her relationship with both of these there appears that element of rather gratuitous cruelty which was always to be one of her hallmarks – specifically, her reluctance to let anyone free of her thrall when she no longer really desired them, and especially if someone else *did*. But she married neither of these, choosing rather someone who might most accurately be described as a first-generation Englishman: Waldorf Astor, son of William Waldorf Astor, main heir to the Astor millions, who had left America years before to make his home in England.

W.W. Astor was an extraordinary figure. Evidently uneasy in social relations, his great wealth had allowed him to indulge his quirks to the full: he had never had to temper them with the necessity which besets most of the rest of us. With his great wealth, his energy, his intelligence, his constant disappointment was that he was yet never able to control events and people to his satisfaction. He was not successful in making a career in American politics, and after spending some years as his country's representative in Rome, decided that he preferred the Old World to the new. However, unlike some of his compatriots (such as the sculptors William Wetmore Story and Luther Terry) he did not settle in Rome but chose to come to England, where his sons Waldorf and John Jacob were educated at Eton and New College, Oxford. Meanwhile, after the death of his wife in 1891, when Waldorf was twelve, he became more and more of a recluse. He was obsessed with the notion that thieves would steal his fortune. His house in London on the Victoria Embankment was effectively constructed as a strongroom. He always slept with two revolvers by his bed. He insisted on being in complete control of those within his social orbit. His word was law in the family and, as far as he could ensure, among his guests. He had rebuilt the ruined Hever Castle in Kent, with a mock-Tudor village around it to house his guests. These were not allowed to spend their day in any haphazard way, but had to choose their occupations from a menu of possibilities prepared by their host – a practice to which they did not take particularly kindly.

As may be imagined, such crude efforts to impose his will upon others met with limited success. Even where he had most influence – within his family – he was unsuccessful. Mr Astor was a reactionary of reactionaries; his son Waldorf was not, and told his father so in no uncertain terms. Such was his love for his son that William Waldorf was able to accept this from him, even if he did not like it. Employees were less fortunate. When he bought the *Pall Mall Gazette*, he appointed Harry Cust as editor. Cust turned out to be quite brilliant at his job, and soon turned the *Gazette* into the country's leading evening paper. But when he did not share his employer's opinions he refused to kotow to them – even rejecting some of his articles as not up to standard. Accordingly, in 1896 Astor demanded his resignation, and when this was refused, dismissed him. The *Pall Mall Gazette* sank like a stone. W.W. Astor battled on.

Of his grandfather, Michael Astor wrote: 'What he had strived to do all his life was to live in style, evocative of a classically moulded tradition. Where he had no roots he had attempted, assiduously, to create some. In bringing his family across the Atlantic he had, in a sense, been pioneering. It had been a difficult row to furrow, and his children, not he, would reap the benefit.'[5] Waldorf certainly did so. At Oxford he excelled at sports of all kinds, was a member of the exclusive Bullingdon Club, and won his Blue at polo and fencing. Then it became known he had a weak heart. The sports had to be given up. But Waldorf was a determined and intelligent fellow. He must find other interests, and set off to America in search of them. On the return voyage he found what he had been looking for: Nancy Shaw, on her way back to Melton for another season's hunting. Wrote Nancy many years later:

I am not a good sailor, and I remember putting Amos Laurence off when he came one day and said young Waldorf Astor was on board and wanted to meet me. I said later on perhaps. So Waldorf wooed Father. He knew what he wanted. It seems he had made up his mind he was going to marry me. A clever man can always find more ways than one of getting what he wants. Waldorf knew all the ways. He was very good-looking and he had, and still has, immense courtesy and very great personal charm. He soon had Father eating out of his hand.[6]

All that winter of 1905–6 Nancy played the unfortunate Lord Revelstoke along, but it became clearer and clearer that she would eventually marry Waldorf Astor. On 3 May 1906, she did so. As a wedding present, W.W. Astor gave them the great house and estate of Cliveden in Buckinghamshire.

'From the time when she married Waldorf Astor, Nancy's legendary life began,' writes her biographer, Christopher Sykes. But a glance at the correspondence for the first thirteen years of her marriage shows the life to have been very far from what 'legendary' implies. True, it should have been legendary. She was an acknowledged beauty on both sides of the Atlantic, outshone (so far as *that* legend was concerned) only by her sister Irene, who was now Mrs Charles Dana Gibson, the original Gibson Girl, and the leader of all that was gayest in New York. Nancy knew almost everyone worth knowing. Her husband was young, handsome and immensely rich; anyone that she did not know, he did. What was more, he was intelligent and ambitious. Within three years of their marriage, in 1909, he had become an MP, being elected for the Sutton division of Plymouth. The first of her children by Waldorf, and her second son, was born in 1907; she was to have four more; there were the means and the space to cope with them all with the greatest ease. And yet, Nancy's life during these years was not particularly, let alone rapturously, happy. Fabulous house parties would be arranged at Cliveden; but, as often as not, the hostess would not see her guests, being compelled to keep to her bed on doctor's orders. Her guests would write her little notes describing the day's activities, detailing the outfits worn this year at Ascot (for which a house party was held every year at Cliveden) on the days when Nancy was unable to attend; rejoicing in the fact that she was on the mend — well enough, at least, to receive the notes they scribbled to her on her own writing-paper.

What was wrong with her? Early in 1914, a physical symptom at last manifested itself. She was found to be suffering from an internal abscess, and this necessitated two operations. Convalescing from this illness, Nancy found herself at the lowest possible ebb. What happened next is best told in her own words.

When I was well enough to be moved, I went down to my sea-side cottage at Sandwich to recuperate. I had a nurse to look after me, and I lay in the sunshine on the balcony that looks out over the sea. The world was so lovely and so peaceful, and I began to argue with myself as I lay there. This, I thought, is not what God wants. It is not what he meant to happen. It couldn't be that God made sickness. It turned people into useless self-centred people who became a burden to themselves and everyone else. I lay for hours there, puzzling it out with myself. I felt there was an answer to this riddle but I had no idea what the answer was.

Then a wonderful thing happened. Whenever a soul is ready for enlightenment, and awaits it humbly, I believe that the answer is somewhere to hand; the teacher comes.[7]

As this fragment indicates, Nancy was already deeply religious; she had never forsaken the Virginian fundamentalism in which she had been brought up. It is not surprising, then, that the answer for which she was seeking should have been a religious one; nor, given her circumstances, that when it came, it should have taken the form it did. Nancy found her answer in *Science and Health with a Key to the Scriptures*, the book upon which Mrs Mary Baker Eddy based her teaching of Christian Science.

It is not surprising that Nancy saw in Christian Science the answer for which she was seeking, since Christian Science was peculiarly adapted to answer her particular needs at the time. According to Mrs Eddy's new religion, any unsatisfactory situation, from bronchitis to bankruptcy, may be seen as a product of wrong thinking, and may be remedied by the application of right thinking, with the help, in case of illness, of a Christian Science practitioner who specializes in dealing with such situations. In achieving the desired equilibrium, the Christian Scientist must accord his body certain physical aids; notably, he must abstain from artificial stimulants, such as tea, coffee, or alcohol. So far, there is nothing especially unfamiliar about the ingredients of the religion. It is not alone in stressing the importance of psychology in dealing with physical illness – yoga, for example, does so also. It is not alone in urging abstention: so do many religions. What makes it particularly attractive to the well-off, however, is that it sees no virtue in poverty – that, indeed, being seen as a state brought on by incorrect thought. Thus it does not urge the faithful to discount the good things of this world in hopes of rewards to come, but, on the contrary, teaches that the right thinker will attain both. Now all this suited Nancy's situation perfectly. It may reasonably be deduced that much of her malaise was attribut-

able to 'wrong thought' – the malaise of a hyper-energetic person
without enough substantial activity to keep herself healthily
occupied. Abstention was a principle she eagerly grasped: she
hated alcohol anyway, since her first husband had been an
alcoholic, and it was to this that she attributed the breakdown
of her first marriage. There could be no doubt that she was richly
endowed with the good things of this life: what a relief, then,
not to have to feel guilty on that account! Nancy grasped at
Christian Science as a drowning man at a lifebelt, and a lifebelt
it proved. After 1914 she was never seriously ill again. Whether
this can be attributed to 'C.S.' or to the fact that after that date
her life was a ceaseless round of activity which allowed her no
time to think about her minor aches and pains, it is hard to say.
If the evidence of the end of her life is anything to go by, the latter
would seem to be the case.

Nancy Astor may reasonably be said to have set the pace in
political terms since she became, and will go down in history as,
the first woman member to take her seat in the British Parliament.
But she was not the first of the dollar princesses to occupy herself
with politics. Several – Jennie Churchill, for example, and Mary
Curzon – had been married to outstanding politicians, and there
is reason to think that they may have had more effect on actual
policies than Nancy, none of the achievements of whose political
career equalled in importance the fact of her having attained it in
the first place. This is particularly true of Mary Curzon.

Mary's life was completely transformed by her husband's
appointment as Viceroy of India. It was not just that they were
removed to another, exotic world – as of course they were; it was
also that once there the relationship between them became something quite different from what it had been during the unsatisfactory days at London and Reigate. Then, while he had constituted
virtually the entirety of her life, she had been merely a part,
albeit an important part, of his. In India this relationship was
realigned on a more equal footing. The viceroy literally stood
alone. No one could join him on his eminence, not the Indian
princes, not the civil servants, not the military. The government
he represented – specifically, the India Council – was on the other
side of the world. The only person able to join him upon his

lonely summit was his wife, the vicereine. To this challenge Mary responded eagerly and amply. The excitement of her position, the fact of being needed – more and more needed – by George, restored to her that confidence which had been such an outstanding feature of her American self and so totally undermined by her early years in England. She blossomed. She became Curzon's greatest friend and closest confidante, while for her erstwhile acquaintances in London she was transformed from the rather dull appendage of their beloved George into a figure of glamour and importance, glimpsed in magnificence on occasions such as the Delhi Durbar, which she and Curzon between them so stupendously carried off.

She found, when she returned to England for six months' holiday in 1901 – a holiday on which the Viceroy, who must remain at his post for the full five years, was not able to join her – that, for the inhabitants of that world which had hitherto been so unwelcoming to her, she had become someone to be courted, admired, invited everywhere. Human nature being what it is, she found that, if she had increased in stature for them, they had decreased in stature for her. 'Everyone is doing the same old thing – just flirting and dining and dawdling,' she wrote to George.[8] They, meanwhile, found her irresistible. Arthur Balfour, who was soon to become Prime Minister, called her 'intoxicating, delicious and clever'. For a while he and Mary seem to have fallen mildly in love with one another, a fact which Curzon noted without alarm, divining the situation even though Mary described Balfour to him as 'wizened, worried and exhausted'.

One factor which did not escape those in London who were responsible for policy in India was that through Mary they might gain the ear of Curzon. He was a recalcitrant viceroy, preferring his own bold policies to their less radical proposals, insisting that he, as the man on the spot, was acquainted with the situation as they could never be. But suggestions which he might summarily dismiss, coming direct from them, might be given some consideration if they emanated from Mary. To this end such people as Lord George Hamilton, Secretary of State for India (whom she had described to Curzon when she was in London as 'a hopeless dotard' and a 'small-minded ferret-faced roving-eyed mediocrity'[9]), kept up a regular correspondence with her when she returned. By 1903 she would truthfully write to her father, 'I have become a sort of necessary companion to statesmen, I talk to George literally by the hour about every one of his political plans; and the other Sunday Kitchener [then Commander-in-Chief for India] sat in the garden and talked business with me for 3½ hours.'[10]

The leopard, however, does not so easily change his spots. Mary was not, and never considered herself to be, the intellectual equal of her husband; nor would he have liked it if she had been. 'It is only after vast study and reading that women can become good companions,' she wrote – not the remark of a woman to whom such things would ever come easily. Was it, then, ever likely that she would seriously try and impress upon George points of view which were not his own – and which she, moreover, had not thought of? 'Women can at times mould and change the whole aspect of things. I know of nobody more capable of performing such a feminine duty than yourself,' wrote Hamilton hopefully; but if anyone was to be moulded in the marriage of George and Mary Curzon, it was likely to be George who did the moulding. Hamilton and the India Council might have been hoping to find in Mary a power behind the throne; what they actually found was that throne's staunchest and most unquestioning support. Her concern was essentially with his happiness and health – the preserving of which was essential if he was ever to return and take up, as she felt he must, the leadership of the Conservative Party. Mary might receive letters outlining points of policy which it was hoped she would put to George. She might discuss them with him – but was it likely that, having heard his persuasive advocacy of his own point of view, she would not be converted to it? The thought is almost inconceivable. On the one occasion when she really did oppose him, his will, as always, still prevailed. This was when, at the end of his five-year term as viceroy in 1903, he wished to stay on, unprecedentedly, for another term, to carry through and personally to supervise the reforms which he had begun in his first term. Mary was fiercely opposed to this course of action, on her own account more than his. She found India exhausting; she felt it was undermining her health. She was right – and more right, politically, than she knew. Curzon's first term of office as viceroy was a triumph; his second was to end in political defeat and humiliation, and, a little later, in Mary's death. But, even in this, once he had made his decision she supported him unquestioningly, as he knew she always would. It was the secret of their mutual trust and of their great love. Mary might have been a considerable political influence; instead, she was a perfect wife. Curzon mourned her till the end of his days. He never did attain the political office she had so confidently forecast for him. If he had listened to her in 1903 he might have done so; and she might have lived longer.

It was perhaps unrealistic to expect the daughter of Mrs Levi Leiter to be a dominating and ambitious wife. Mrs Leiter, whatever her other qualities, does not seem to have possessed any form of distinction whatsoever; and where but from her mother is a girl to take her model for her role as wife? Mary Leiter was more beautiful, more distinguished, cleverer than her mother, but she accepted as unquestioningly as Mrs Leiter her role as supporter, not competitor, to her dominating and talented husband.

Such was not the case with Nancy Astor, who wrote of her parents: 'I cannot remember the time when I did not realize that my mother was stronger and more important from the family point of view than my father. . . . Perhaps it was this sense of my mother that made me feel the qualities of women should be freed to give better service to the race.'[11] From the daughter of such a union, a husband might realistically expect a less comfortable ride.

In the dominating mother stakes, however, there can be little doubt as to who, in the world of the dollar princesses, takes the palm. It can only be Mrs Alva Vanderbilt. Of her and her friend Christabel Pankhurst, suffragette daughter of a suffragette mother, Consuelo Vanderbilt Balsan wrote: 'With my mother she [Christabel] shared a common hatred for the genus man, although they both delighted in men's company.'[12] After her second husband, O.H.P. Belmont, died in 1908, his widow consoled herself by devoting her time, energy and wealth to the women's suffrage movement, of which she became a leader, even going so far as to lead public parades up Fifth Avenue (of which she later confessed to her daughter, 'To a woman brought up as I was, it was a terrible ordeal!').

In these activities Consuelo fully supported her mother, and in her loneliness after the separation from her first husband, public life seemed an obvious field for her energies. Of course, philanthropic activities were not particularly unusual among women of her class: they were merely an extension of that concern for the welfare of the estate unfortunates which constituted a part of every great lady's duties. It was natural for the Duchess of Marlborough to do her bit in organizing and helping to raise funds for such worthy causes as the investigation of sweated industries, a home for prisoners' wives, and, later, the American Women's War Relief Fund, the Women's Emergency Corps, and other such excellent works. She spoke, she wrote articles; in 1916 she was asked to deliver the Priestby Lecture on 'Infant Mortality, its Causes and Preventions' – the first woman to be so honoured. She acquitted herself, in this ordeal, with the greatest credit.

Philanthropy, however, had its limits, and Consuelo recognized that reforms of any scale must be instituted by government, whether local or national. Feeling that only women would press strongly enough for those reforms which were her particular concern – especially those to do with the welfare of women and children, and perinatal care and mortality – she formed a Women's Municipal Party whose purpose was to get women elected to local councils. It was evident that the women would have to make an effort if they were to achieve satisfactory representation, since the two main parties, Liberal and Conservative, would always prefer to put up men for the safer seats. The W.M.P. put up independent candidates at elections, to disrupt the party in power by drawing off women's votes; and, of course, was always ready to offer a candidate should one of the main parties be interested. When a vacancy occurred in the North Southwark ward of the London County Council in 1917 it was pointed out that the W.M.P.'s most likely candidate was its president: the Duchess of Marlborough. Slightly appalled, for she had had no thought of going into politics herself – being quite taken up with her various philanthropic works – Consuelo had no option but to agree. It was necessary that she be adopted by the Liberal/Progressive committee, since for the duration of the war elections were suspended and vacancies filled, by agreement, by the party which had previously held the seat. With the help of Mr Strauss, Liberal M.P. for North Southwark, the Duchess of Marlborough was duly adopted, and found herself a member of the L.C.C. The selection procedure had caused her some anxious moments. She addressed the sixty-strong committee for an hour, giving her views on a variety of topics, and was then asked to wait outside while the committee voted.

It seemed to me that it took them as long to decide my fate as it had taken me to state my views, and I was becoming despondent for although I had no desire to stand, there was now a question of pride involved in the issue. At last the door opened and Mr Strauss came in smiling and, grasping my hand, said, 'You are unanimously selected as our member for North Southwark.'

Relieved but still doubting, I asked, 'But why did you take so long?'

'Because,' said Mr Strauss, 'so many had to get up to explain that they could not see how a Duchess could be a Progressive nor how she could understand a workingman's point of view, but since hearing your speech they were convinced of your sincerity and your ability to represent them.'[13]

This American ability to disregard class and communicate easily with all was also to stand Nancy Astor in good stead, and was to be the uncomprehending envy of her English friends.

Into the business of administration and committee work, public health, housing and education Consuelo threw herself with a will; and in March 1919, four months after the Armistice, had to stand, for the first time, for election. On her walks around the constituency, groups of children caused a cheerful diversion by spirited renderings of 'Vote, Vote, Vote for Mrs Marlborough' to the tune of 'Tramp, Tramp, Tramp, the Boys are Marching'. She was standing as a Progressive, with the mayor of Southwark, against two Labour opponents. At one moment during the count it looked as if the constituency would be split, returning the Duchess and a Socialist; but by the end the papers were able to report that 'Southwark is again solidly Progressive, the Duchess of Marlborough being at the top of the poll'. It was noted that Her Grace had a particularly large number of women supporters. This support was gained despite the fact that, during her election campaign, while she was holding her meetings, her chauffeur was holding rival meetings in which he informed eager hearers that although she purported to be so exercised about bad housing conditions in Southwark, she herself in fact owned some of the worst slums in London. This was quite untrue: her only London property was the house in Curzon Street which Mr Vanderbilt had built for her and her husband, to be used as a political base for the Duke, and which since their separation had been her London home. (Indeed, the Vanderbilt fortune was not even built on dubious New York property, like that of the Astors, but, perhaps equally dubiously, upon railroads.) Nevertheless the chauffeur had to be sacked, and in future the Duchess went to her election meetings by tramcar – 'which was no doubt a good electioneering move'. For the next two years she laboured to build a 'land fit for heroes to live in', until exhaustion, divorce and remarriage took her away from England.

To be a power behind the throne or a force on the L.C.C. might be satisfying; it might be constructive; but it was not what people meant when they talked about women 'going into politics'. *That* meant to be accepted on a national level in one's own right. That was what the supporters of women's suffrage on both sides of the Atlantic were fighting for. The law making it possible for women to become members of the British House of Commons was passed in December 1918. Countess Markievicz, the Irish Nationalist, was elected in the poll which immediately followed, but did not take her place. Various women candidates, including Christabel Pankhurst, stood but were defeated. It was, however, evident that women would soon enter Parliament – generally, it was expected, in the shape of Mrs or Miss Pankhurst or some other ardent suffragist such as Millicent Fawcett.

It had not at this point crossed Nancy Astor's mind that she might take up politics. This was not through any modesty – never one of the virtues attributed to her – but simply because the situation did not arise. She was a political hostess; as the wife of a successful MP she was acquainted with most of the leading political figures of the day – the Asquiths, Lloyd George, A.J. Balfour and the rest. Entertaining was something she took very seriously – it had, says her maid, Rose Harrison, become 'a fetish' with her. She also had a lively social conscience. The hospital for

Canadian soldiers which she had established in the grounds of Cliveden during the war had proved a great success, and she had spared no effort to ensure this. But further than that she had not considered taking her political and social interests. There seemed little need for two MPs in the family.

All this, however, was soon to change as a result of the vagaries of Waldorf's father. William Waldorf Astor had, in 1916, to his son's horror and disgust, accepted a peerage. Quite apart from any scruples they may have felt about an American doing such a thing – and both Waldorf and Nancy felt strongly about this – it sounded the death-knell to any serious political ambition so far as Waldorf was concerned. For the first time father and son quarrelled bitterly, but what was done could not be undone: in the not too far distant future Waldorf would inherit the title and would no longer be eligible for the House of Commons. 'A peerage was not in his scheme of things at all,' said Nancy. In the event the blow fell sooner than might have been expected. 'This morning at Plymouth Waldorf telephoned me to come at once – his father was dying,' wrote Nancy on 18 October 1919 to her sister Irene Gibson in New York. 'It's a sad blow in more ways than one. I am not really sorry for him – I never saw anyone with so pitiful a life.... Waldorf ... was curiously fond of his father – and he ... has not seen him ever since he took his Peerage.... Poor old Waldorf has to take it on.... I have just given up ever making plans. I see now that "Take no Thought for the Morrow" is really the only way.'[14] William Waldorf Astor died that day, aged seventy-one. The *Evening Standard* immediately reported that, according to rumour, the Conservative candidate in the by-election which was now necessary would probably be the new viscountess.

Would she or wouldn't she? Speculation mounted. 'Dearest Nancy, I am thinking much of you and Waldorf – I know the first thought must be bitter regret that your connection with Plymouth ceases (unless the *Daily Mail*'s suggestion that you should represent the constituency in Waldorf's place carries on your interest in the seat!),' wrote Lady Antrim, a frequent visitor. Lord Salisbury was equivocal about the notion. 'Of course it is a new idea to me and you know I am a hopeless mass of prejudice. I am torn by conflicting emotions – on the one side friendship

and on the other purblind fossilized Toryism!'[15] On Friday
24 October the Plymouth Conservative Association formally invited Nancy to stand. Two days later she accepted the invitation.

It seems clear from what she said at the time, and from what
she wrote later in her draft autobiography, that she and Waldorf
at first regarded her candidacy as a temporary measure: she was
to keep the seat warm for him while he went through the
necessary measures to renounce his peerage. For eleven years
Waldorf had been a successful and popular MP; he was unwilling
to let the connection drop and eleven years of hard work go by
the board. 'I come before you as a substitute for one all of you
know,' said Nancy in one of her election speeches. 'I am not
here as a warming-pan [laughter] although I hope that by the
next general election your late MP will be here. He thinks I can
do it, and as he said, he thinks he knows me better than anybody
else, and I hope to goodness he does, and when he comes back
at the next election I give you my word of honour that I won't
stand against him.'

Nancy Astor did not feel that there was anything about her
which particularly fitted her to be the first woman MP. On the
contrary, she felt strongly that this honour should have been
reserved for Mrs Pankhurst or Mrs Fawcett. 'I was an ardent
feminist, but they were the ones who most deserved this honour.'[16]
But, ironically, someone in circumstances such as Nancy's stood,
as it turned out, a much better chance of being elected than these
celebrated women could have done. If votes for women had not
been easily won, their right to membership of Parliament had
been secured with even more difficulty and in face of even greater
reluctance. Nancy noted this in her speeches. 'I have heard it said,
"Well, we like women" – and so forth – the same old thing. "But
we ain't so sure they ought to be in the House of Commons."
You all had a perfect right to say that five years ago, but you
have no right now.'[17] But, right or no right, people inevitably
did say and feel such things – and a vote for Mrs Pankhurst or
Mrs Fawcett flew in the face of these feelings of uncertainty. All
the political opinions of Mrs Pankhurst or Mrs Fawcett were
subordinate, at least so far as the public was concerned, to their
feminism. Few people, even if they supported the idea of votes
for women, relished the idea of their MP being the MP for

feminism. But Nancy, although she was, of course, a feminist – no woman who was not could have considered standing for Parliament – stood, besides, for a great many other easily definable principles. She stood, in fact, for what Waldorf had been doing, and had been standing for, over the past eleven years. People knew where they were with her: they were where they had been, only under a slightly different and undeniably more colourful banner. It was no coincidence that the next woman MP, Mrs Wintringham, was also elected by this route – in her case, taking over her husband's seat when he died. It was the thin end of the wedge.

It was not likely, however, that a character like Nancy would hide her light behind Waldorf's bushel, whatever the circumstances. Nor did she. 'If you want an MP who will be a repetition of the other 600 MPs, don't elect me,' she adjured the voters. 'If you want a lawyer or if you want a pacifist, don't elect me. If you can't get a fighting man, take a fighting woman.' Some fields she declared to be her particular concern – notably questions affecting women and children, and, she might mention, she had been one of the first members of the Anti-Sweating League. So much was unexceptionable. Other questions were trickier. In 1919, prohibition had become the law in the United States, and it was well known that Nancy would have liked to see such a law established in Britain. She recognized, however, that to make this stand would undoubtedly be to lose the election, and refrained from doing so. She conducted a vigorous campaign, and particularly enjoyed dealing with the many hecklers who interrupted her speeches. 'Come along! Who'll take me on? I'm ready for you,' she would challenge them, and nearly always came out on top in the ensuing exchanges – as she had known she would. She travelled round Plymouth with Waldorf in an open landau driven by their large coachman, Churchward. On one occasion the crowd seemed so threatening that Churchward, concerned, descended from the landau and made as if to intervene. 'Shut up, Churchward,' yelled Nancy, 'I'm making this speech, not you.' Her methods showed more of the barnstorming spirit of old Virginia than the slight hysteria of feminist England. Her repartee relied more on vigour and gaiety than wit, but it was always spirited. 'Now you Bolshevists at the back be quiet!' she would scold. 'Go back to Lancashire!' she yelled at one heckler. 'I'm an Irishman,' he retorted. 'I knew it, an imported interrupter!' yelled Nancy. 'If I'd imported you I'd drown myself in the sea!' he screamed back. 'More likely in drink!' scored Nancy, only to be countered with, 'I'm a teetotaller!' 'Well, go and have a drink today! It might sweeten you!' she triumphantly ended the exchange.[18] She had always made a point of being elegantly turned out while canvassing. On polling day, while she was holding a woman voter's baby, it began to play with her pearls. 'Always give babies your pearls to play with,' she brazenly remarked to some nearby reporters. Her campaigning style was unsullied by any tinge of the ladylike. She had the considerable advantage of having been born a Virginian, not a lady.

Counting was delayed from the fifteenth until 28 November in order that all servicemen's votes might be included. In the meantime a motion brought before the House of Commons at Waldorf's instigation, to allow the surrender of peerages, was defeated. If Nancy won the seat, it now seemed likely that it would be for herself, not for Waldorf, that she held it.

She did win, of course. Everybody, including herself, had expected that she would. 'I knew I'd win. I knew it before it began,' she said when she was told that the count so far showed victory to be inevitable. Later she said, of her husband: 'I never knew a man so respected as he is by *all* parties, and it's really a vote of confidence in him.' Did she really believe this? She was an extraordinary candidate, and she knew it. Her opponents, William Gay for the Labour Party and Isaac Foot for the Liberals, were very able, but they could not compete with Nancy on her home ground. For that was the point; Plymouth *was* her home ground. Her background might be exotic, she might be an international millionairess, but she belonged to the Plymouth Co-operative Society ('a novel step for a millionairess,' commented the *Daily Mail* suspiciously), she had given a number of creches to the city, had established a clinic for the instruction of young mothers and their babies, and had lived in Plymouth, as well as Cliveden and London, for the past eleven years. This, together with her un-English dash and gaiety, made an unbeatable combination.

Nancy's first letter as an MP was written to her elder sister

Irene Gibson. 'I hear it's the talk of All England! Fancy *me* being the talk of England and America! It's comical. I don't take it seriously so never fear. I take the *job* seriously but not the *personality*.' To her brother-in-law Dana Gibson she wrote, 'This honor has been thrust upon me – I didn't want to do it – but Waldorf wanted me to or our eleven years work would have gone *fut* and a badish Labour man might have won.... The American papers surprise me. I had no notion that they were taking notice too!'[19] But indeed they were, their main obsession being with the question: What will Lady Astor wear in the House of Commons? 'PLAIN BLACK COSTUME DECIDED ON BY FIRST WOMAN IN PARLIAMENT,' the *Boston Globe* was able to inform its readers, while the *Buffalo Times* reflected that 'DAWN OF WOMAN'S DAY IN CONGRESS SOME YEARS AWAY'. Commented Nancy: 'I ought to feel sorry for Mr Foot and Mr Day, but I don't. The only person I feel sorry for is the poor old Viscount here.'[20]

Nancy was introduced into the House of Commons by two old friends, Lloyd George, the then Prime Minister, and A. J. Balfour, who had previously held that office. She was, of course, then and for some time to follow, the cynosure of attention. Her own boudoir was set aside for her. Many of the Hon. Members regarded her presence in the House with distaste; she was un-cowed – indeed, thoroughly combative. She immediately set about conducting a duel with Sir William Joynson Hicks over her choice of seat, which happened to be that traditionally used by him.

It is hard not to feel that, in historical terms, Nancy's most important contribution occurred at the moment of her introduc-tion – not the hallmark of an outstanding political career. She once described an encounter with another member, 'a regular old Noah's Ark man and a typical Squire type. After two years and a half of never agreeing on any point with him, he remarked to someone that I was a very stupid woman, but, he must add, a very attractive one, and, he feared, a thoroughly honest social reformer.' In many ways, this description is not inapposite. Of course Nancy was not stupid, but she does seem to have lacked any trace of social subtlety – a quality not unallied with political subtlety; and political achievement is rarely attained by the direct method – the circumstances of her own election being a case in point. Thus, when told of the death of an old enemy she replied, quite simply, 'I'm glad'; and when she disagreed with a point or a policy she did not labour for her ends behind the scenes or make an irresistible speech, but preferred to make her points by interrupting the speeches of others. Such behaviour and attitudes made her the bane of that other MP of American origin, Henry Channon, who took such infinite pleasure in all those shades, subtleties and usages with which Nancy could not be bothered.

Of course, this is not to say that she did nothing while in the House. Away from the headlines she did a great deal of patient and painstaking work to forward the causes she had particularly at heart – the welfare of women and children, women police, and other such. Many of these causes were, inevitably, of the sort that concern women more than men, since she was for so long the obvious and only spokesman for them. From the first she had declared her intention never to be a 'sex-member', but this excellent resolve had not proved workable. Her reaction to this state of affairs shows how little, even after ten years in the House, she had grasped the essential workings of British politics. In that year, 1929, a general election returned fourteen women, and these were all invited to a luncheon given, kindly and appositely, by Lady Astor, the first woman member. She first of all charmed her guests, saying that she knew how galling it might have been for British women that the first woman MP had been an American, but that she felt there had been certain advantages in her being the 'ice-breaker' – she had met most of the leading members socially and so was not cowed by them, she had a particularly irrepressible personality 'like a popping gas-jet', and so on. Then she moved on to what was evidently the real purpose of the luncheon. 'We were there to be told what to do,' recalled Mary Agnes Hamilton, who had just been elected as a Labour member. 'And what we had to do was to forget that we had been elected as representatives of the Labour Party, and its ideals and plans, and act, henceforth, as part of a Feminist phalanx. The nine Labour women among the 14 women MPs were to drop their Labour allegiance, and form the backbone of a Women's Party.'[21] Quite apart from the fact that two of the new Labour members were ministers in their party's government, this curious suggestion – which fell on deaf ears, and indeed led to a heated argument – shows a complete lack of feeling for British politics and their working, odd in one who had already been engaged in them for so long. Certainly she never felt any particularly strong allegiance to her own party, the Conservatives, as such, preferring to ally herself to particular policies of which she approved.

The political allegiance for which she will go down in history is, of course, that to the alleged 'Cliveden set', that group of Germanophils and appeasers including Lord Halifax and Lord Lothian and the editor of *The Times*, Geoffrey Dawson, who were supposed, in the years before the outbreak of World War II, to be running from the Astors' country house a sort of supplementary Foreign Office to promote their own policies and avoid at any cost the war which many saw as being inevitable. Did the 'Cliveden set' exist? The phrase was coined, and many of the most dastardly plots of its supposed members exposed, in Claud Cockburn's sheet of political revelations *The Week*. Christopher Sykes, Nancy's biographer, goes to great lengths to show that many of the participants in those meetings described by Cockburn could not possibly have been there at the time; that the details of the plots he 'exposed' were wrong; and in short that the 'set' was a figment of his active imagination.

Why then, if it was baseless, did the legend persist? Certainly the Astors made an easy target for suspicion and distrust. They were not, after all, British; they were rich to excess; and although Lady Astor might not be a particularly eminent politician, she certainly entertained those who were. The 'set's' reputed members were all people whom she entertained particularly frequently – and the opinions attributed to them were not far-fetched. In Nancy's case, and in that of her great friend Philip Lothian, they coincided with many personal prejudices – of which she held a great many, and with that extreme vehemence which so characterized her. She could not bear Catholics, she could not bear Latins, she held the gravest suspicions of the French – why, then, should she support such people against nice Herr Hitler, who was so ignorantly maligned and who was, when one met him, always so polite and agreeable (as for instance on the two occasions when he met Lord Lothian)? Yet another of her antipathies, that for Winston Churchill, can only have fortified these opinions. Nancy was not alone in her passionate support for Neville Chamberlain, but her dislike for Churchill was, as we have seen, old-established and extreme. This led her to interrupt his speech in a particularly ignorant way when he was attacking Chamberlain over the latter's spineless lack of resistance to Hitler's invasion of Czechoslovakia. Churchill was at his most stirring; Lady Astor at her pettiest. A little later, her virulent anti-Communism led her to suggest that Sudeten German refugees from Hitler be sent to Russia rather than be given asylum in the West, since they were probably Communists themselves. It was a horrendous error of taste, if nothing more. If Nancy had wished to set herself up as a target for the anti-Hitlerites, she could have done little more than she did to help them. If the tale of the Cliveden set was eagerly seized upon and kept alive, even when the detail of the accusations made out against it could be shown to be false, then Nancy herself must be said to have sent up quite a lot of the smoke which led people to believe that, inevitably, there was a fire somewhere.

She had no political judgement whatever; she could be selfish and petty in an extreme degree; and yet she had – she must have had, she undeniably did have – enormous charm. Part of this had to do with her beauty. Walter Elliot, a parliamentary colleague and a close friend, described her as: 'a figure of physical beauty to take the breath from your throat; recalling so sharply her New World ancestry, and marked off so decidedly from the willowy lovelies who flower in the gentler, more temperate landscapes of the Home Counties. She carried, in every fibre, the crisp chic of the highly-bred American woman. She also had their unusual blend of femininity and sexlessness.'[22] And she was full of vitality – a small, tough figure bursting with life. It seems clear that Parliament provided for her, more than anything else, a means by which life could be filled to bursting – as it had to be filled if she was to be happy. The management of her household and children, the running of her social life and the conscientious attention she paid to her political life, took every ounce of what she had. She thrived on it. A letter to 'Dearest Irene' written from 4 St James's Square, her London house, in 1924, provides a stunning contrast to the sad torpor of her life a decade previously:

I will see the boy when he comes, but you simply cannot think what it is. Every human being seems to come over here with a letter to me from somebody, and there isn't one of them I really want to see except your special friends. Your nice friends at the Ritz, I have tried and tried in vain to find a moment for. I'm having a terribly busy time; we've got the Ascot party on at Cliveden and I have rushed down here to try to do a morning's work and go to the House for the rest of the day, and to add to it all, Nannie Gibbons has been away on holiday, and the new Nursery Governess sprained her ankle yesterday, and has been taken off to a Nursing Home, and we've been forced to bring Nannie back....[23]

The extent to which her life relied on this degree of busyness and external importance was shown in 1946. She was persuaded not to stand for re-election in that year since she was so obviously, and sadly, not what she had been at her best. She herself could not see this, and nor could her great friend Bernard Shaw, then in his nineties; but everyone else, including Waldorf and her sons, was convinced that for her own sake she must stand down. With the greatest reluctance she took their advice, and at once relapsed into misery. Christian Science was of little use to her in this new vacuum. She turned against Waldorf with hatred. She did not know what to do with herself nor where to put herself. She had found her life, and it had been taken away from her. She found – as she had known she would find – that there is no substitute for membership of the best club in the world. The rest of her life was a sad anticlimax. The energy which had kept her going through the crowded years became once more her enemy.

Wrote Consuelo Vanderbilt Balsan: 'Looking back on the little circle I knew of the American women married to Englishmen, there are, I realise, very few who remained definitely American. Nancy Astor was one of these. Her high spirits, her sense of humour, her self-assurance, her courage, her independence, are all of the American variety.'[24] It has been remarked that she seemed to belong to no particular time or place, being always a unique phenomenon except possibly in that nineteenth-century Virginia into which she was born and which had more or less completely disappeared by the time she reached adulthood. The fact that this phenomenon happened to be in the right place at the right time to be elected to Parliament was a piece of extraordinary good fortune for her. It ensured, what might otherwise not have been the case, that the first woman MP was possessed of the appropriate dash and snap for the role; a source of dramatic satisfaction which was probably not without its political importance.

For those who did not know her, Nancy Astor is difficult to write about. The enduring characteristics that emerge solidly from memoirs, letters and diaries are on the whole unattractive: a blind self-centredness and pathological possessiveness, a predilection for prejudice, an inability to see large issues through obsession with smaller ones. What does not survive is what was evidently there but harder to capture: vivacity and gaiety, fits of generosity; a capacity for great loyalty. She tended to be cold and bullying, but she could be kind though rarely (it seems) warmhearted. When her son Michael invited her to address a political meeting on his behalf, and sat down after finishing his own speech, 'Where did you learn to do this?' she demanded. 'I feel like Balaam when the ass spoke.' It was not the remark of one blessed with generosity of spirit.

10

Setting the pace: culture

America created the twentieth century.
Gertrude Stein
Ils sont pas des hommes, ils sont pas de femmes, ils sont des Américains.
Pablo Picasso

The dollar princesses had shown that determination, money and style could achieve social leadership and political influence – a certain political position, even. But the world of the arts was – or should have been – a different proposition. A notable and perhaps rather surprising feature of Lady Astor's career was the fact that she pursued it with at least a modicum of success even though she seems to have been quite without sensitivity or intellectual distinction. She was energetic, she was courageous, she was gay and amusing, but that such a person should achieve even partial success in a profession – as opposed to social success, for which she was by nature and fortune endowed – might be thought to say something about that profession. 'I cannot remember the talk of the eminent statesmen and political persons I met; they made scant impression on me. Like Somerset Maugham, I was puzzled by the apparent mediocrity of their minds,' recalled Harold Acton of Lady Cunard's salon.[1] That, of course, was one place where he would not have met Lady Astor, but there seems no reason to think that he would have modified his opinion had he done so.

But influence, let alone distinction, in the world of the arts was not to be bought. One might, of course, be a Maecenas, but an undiscriminating Maecenas quickly becomes a figure of fun. In this world quality of mind or achievement was all, and the notion of achieving distinction without it, a contradiction in terms. It is then perhaps with a certain surprise that we note that here, too, the American ladies made their mark and, in certain cases, led the way. They did so, moreover, not in London – where at least they spoke the language – but, more surprisingly still, in Paris, which was 'intellectually . . . the capital of the world, and the judgment of Paris was final.'[2] It was a judgment much influenced during the period in question by such Americans as Gertrude Stein, Natalie Barney, and the Princesse de Polignac, *née* Winnaretta Singer.

The first decades of the twentieth century were of course legendary ones for Americans in Paris. They flocked there on the intellectual circuit which included Sylvia Beach's bookshop Shakespear and Company, and the two American salons – Miss Stein's and Miss Barney's. Of visits to these salons, 'It was considered quite an honor and part of one's education, but was really quite a bore,' wrote one such young man years later when he was no longer young; he went to Miss Barney's once and Miss Stein's twice, 'which was once too much'.[3] And probably once too much for Miss Stein too. But although the young men regarded Paris as so essential an ingredient of their artistic formation it is hard to discern what they assimilated there apart from picturesque background material upon which to display their American-ness. Such of the young men as Ernest Hemingway and Sherwood Anderson of course drank at the fount of literary style – Gertrude Stein's style, which as they readily acknowledged so deeply influenced their own, and in the development of which she had been so much affected by her isolation as an English-speaker in a French world. 'One of the things that I have liked all these years is to be surrounded by people who know no english,' she wrote. 'It has left me more intensely alone with my eyes and my english. I do not know if it would have been possible to have english be so all in all to me otherwise.'[4] But Anderson, Hemingway, John Dos Passos, felt no need for such cultural isolation. Miss Stein had liberated them from the nineteenth-century novel, and for them the epitome of the twentieth century in which they revelled was America – of which they became, whatever their subject matter, the literary quintessence. The achievements of their lady mentors were quite different. The cultural world *they* affected was wholly European.

The contrast between the best-known American Londoners and those of Paris is very great. What would such aggressively normal, such essentially conventional women as Nancy Astor or Jennie Churchill have made of the hothouse world of Winnie de Polignac, Natalie Barney, Gertrude Stein? For one of the uniting features of these ladies – quite apart from the fact that all were American and all deeply intellectual – was that, like so many of the leading female figures of the Parisian intellectual world at that time, they were exclusively, though not necessarily aggressively, lesbian.

What, then, (it may be asked) have they to do in a book about dollar princesses – a position from which their proclivities necessarily debarred them? Well, of course, this was not quite the case: at least one of them, Winnie Singer, was a dollar princess in the most classic mould – twice, in fact, since she married two different princes. And for Natalie Barney one may perhaps stretch a point: one of the great loves of her life, and her abiding friend, was the Duchesse de Clermont-Tonnerre. Indeed, in her background of Midwestern wealth – one grandfather made a fortune in railroad cars in Dayton, Ohio, the other in whiskey in Cincinnati – and her Washington upbringing, in order that she might meet the right people, Natalie resembles no one so much as Mary Leiter, who was, in fact, one of her earliest exemplars of the power of female beauty. Young Natalie was out riding in the Washington woods with a friend when they came upon Miss Leiter, then at the height of her career as the belle of Washington, driving a four-in-hand with young Cecil Spring-Rice from the British Embassy (who was at the time madly in love with her). The girls' horses startled Miss Leiter's team, so that she had the greatest difficulty bringing them back under control, which she eventually did, Natalie and her friend meantime staring spellbound at the picture of such loveliness. In the event it was the friend, not Natalie, who fell in love with Miss Leiter (a feeling not reciprocated, it is hardly necessary to say: such strayings were not for the upright Mary). But it might well have been Miss Barney; in which case this would merely have been among the earliest in a long line of lady loves – with most of whom, it seems, the strong-willed Natalie eventually had her way. Had her inclinations been otherwise, there seems no reason why Miss Barney, with her wealth, her attractive person and arresting personality, to say nothing of her intelligence and wit, should not also have had her Lord Curzon. As it was, one of the young men proposed for her, and rejected by her, was Lord Alfred Douglas, which in the circumstances was curiously appropriate.

It is perhaps worth asking whether it is more than a coincidence that so many of the more original female minds of this period were lesbians. The answer may of course be the simple one of limited energy – that women who do not expend themselves in procreation have more time left for creation. This is a possibility, although it must be remembered that in those days of plentiful servants and nurses, motherhood was not necessarily an all-consuming exercise. Nancy Astor, after all, had six children and still managed a job and the most active of social lives.

But there is also a more positive side to the question. The nineteenth century had been a man's century, and nowhere more so than in America. The brute strength of the pioneer and the hardly more subtle brutality of the big businessman had been its hallmarks. The woman's role *vis-à-vis* these heroes was a subordinate one: she kept the log cabin cosy, brought up the children, kept his clothes clean, kept the stockpot bubbling, was his discreet confidante, stood by him when times were hard, and so on. When eventually he made it she took her place in her own world – the social world of whatever city it was she lived in; and we have seen what energies, what devouring passions, were brought to bear upon society wherever it might be found.

No woman of talent, energy and independence could be blamed for rejecting such a prospect; but to do so meant, effectively, rejecting marriage – unless one were to find the most remarkable of men. In such circumstances, it was not surprising that advanced women should turn to those of their own sex. Who else would understand so clearly the frustrations, of all sorts, which fenced them round? And what better than an alliance of like-minded women to overcome them? Gertrude Stein was introduced to lesbianism when she was a student at Johns Hopkins Medical School in Baltimore; and the young women she met at the university there were just the kind of young women one might have expected to find it attractive.

In Europe something of the same logic applied, but, in England at any rate, the difficulties were greater. America might be crude and brutal but it was large in every sense, and the toleration for individual eccentricity was very great. But in England the trial of Oscar Wilde had greatly lessened the margin of toleration. What had been acceptable when unspoken, when people could avert their eyes from what they did not want to see, became intolerable when paraded before the public in all the crudity of the law. Of course women conducted lesbian amours in Britain – very much the same kind of women who conducted them in France and in America; the publication of various recent memoirs makes that abundantly clear. But that bitter cry of desperation, Radclyffe Hall's *The Well of Loneliness*, shows what it was like for many such women living in a country where Queen Victoria had not believed that such things existed and where a large section of the population was determined to persist in this attitude. In Paris, however, things were different – and in fact Radclyffe Hall borrows Natalie Barney's house at 20 rue Jacob, as the paradisal retreat where her heroine Stephen Gordon so nearly finds happiness (only to have it snatched from her by a man). For in France alone of European countries, ruled neither by canon nor by case law but by the Code Napoléon, homosexuality was not illegal. So Paris became the city where lesbians could come out of the closet, and where Natalie Barney could run a salon which was not merely overtly lesbian in tone, but positively proselytizing. (When reproached for seducing a happily married woman and then dropping her, tearing her from a life of peace and leaving her bewildered in a situation where she was liable to be led 'astray' on all sides, Natalie remarked: 'But she was astray before!')

Natalie Barney, although so utterly American in origin, was sent to school for some years in France at a fashionable establishment called Les Ruches, where the kind of *affaires* that went on seem to have had the same steamy and intense quality as those described by Colette in her novel *Claudine à l'Ecole*; and from then on she never looked back, becoming a veritable Doña Juanita and remaining so for the rest of her long life. Her father's dearest wish was that she should return with him to Washington and marry a nice young man (such as Lord Alfred Douglas) but this was a prospect which, as far as Natalie was concerned, compared most unfavourably with the gay and independent life she was leading in Paris. Since 1899 she had been established in a charming villa at Neuilly with a garden in which she could organize the theatricals and *tableaux* in which she delighted. Here Colette, whom she had met in 1900 out walking her various animals in the Bois de Boulogne, might appear as a naked faun while Natalie spoke the verse of the poetess Renée Vivien who was her great love for ten years but who finally faded away in November 1909 ('*Mademoiselle vient de mourir*,' announced the butler as a distraught Natalie rushed up the stairs); here Mata Hari might ride mounted on a white horse as Lady Godiva (Colette noticed that her flesh, which appeared a luscious brown in artificial light, turned out a mottled purple in the harsh light of day). In 1909 Natalie moved from Neuilly to a two-storied *pavillon* with a garden containing a little Doric temple at 20 rue Jacob. Here she resolved to establish her salon.

Natalie was well known in principle to a great many Parisians and others since she was the original of Flossie, the American seductress in Liane de Pougy's autobiographical novel *Idylle Saphique* which appeared in 1901. Liane de Pougy was one of the *grandes horizontales*; when Natalie saw her driving in the *bois* she immediately determined to get to know her and seduce her, and when it was explained to her exactly who this object of her desires was, her determination was all the greater. She would woo Liane away from the courtesan's life. In this she did not succeed, but, as the book graphically describes, in all other respects she did. *Idylle Saphique* was a great success when it was published in 1901. Natalie's father, Albert Clifford Barney, was mortified by it and more than ever desperate to get his daughter back to America and respectability. But he failed to do so, and died the next year; after which Natalie was free to live as she wished.

Natalie's literary success in the third person was greater than that which she achieved in her own right. She was completely bilingual, and she preferred to write (mostly verse and epigrams, some dramatic dialogues) in French; but as a writer she was obviously second-rate. Bilingual though she may have been, it is the rarest of writers who succeeds in anything but his mother tongue. In this sense, Joseph Conrad was an extraordinary freak. When Edith Wharton, after living many years in France, wrote a story in French, she was advised, although it was published, to stick to English in future. The assiduous efforts of her friend Pierre Louÿs finally got Natalie's works published; but it was as an intellectual impresario, rather than as a writer, that she was talented. She functioned best at second hand.

Her greatest coup in this respect was undoubtedly the conquest of the aging and reclusive sage Rémy de Gourmont. Gourmont was a well-known essayist and critic. He wrote about anything and everything, including science, and is perhaps most closely paralleled in English by his great friend and avid disciple Havelock Ellis. When he was young he had been handsome and sociable, but at the age of thirty had been struck down by lupus, a skin disease which had left him horribly scarred. He retreated into his rooms, surrounded himself with books, and came out as little as possible. Natalie was introduced to him in 1910 by her friend Pierre Louÿs. Was it the challenge of the situation that appealed to her? Or its grotesquer aspects? At any rate, the meeting was an enormous success. Natalie was charmed by Gourmont and he fell hopelessly in love with her. For the remaining five years of his life she held him in thrall. He would hold her hands while they talked – of course there could be no question of anything more. He called her '*l' Amazone*' – referring both to her preference for women and to her passion for riding: to be dressed '*en amazone*' is to wear a riding habit. She inspired his *Lettres à l'Amazone*; their genuine private correspondence was later published as *Lettres intimes à l'Amazone*. It is as Gourmont's amazone that Natalie Barney will be remembered; for that, and for her salon.

The running of a successful salon in Paris was then almost a *métier* in its own right. Each salon had its lions, its specialities. Natalie's specialities were women writers, which one might have expected, and distinguished scholars, which one might not; she was introduced to many of these – such as Salomon Reinach, Charles Seignobos – by Dr J.C. Mardrus, the husband of the poet and novelist Lucie Delarue-Mardrus, her great friend and, for a time, her lover. Mardrus was the learned translator of the

Arabian Nights. He was well aware of the conflicting demands of motherhood and literary creation, and at one time went so far as to suggest that Natalie might bear his child, thus both giving the satisfaction of a child in the household and leaving Lucie free for her writing. But Natalie was not tempted by this proposal.

The salon was held on Fridays between five and eight. Sometimes there was just a gathering of people, but sometimes a programme might be arranged. In 1927, for example, we have the programmes for January and June:

January 7: in honor of Madame Aurel.
January 14: in honor of Madame Colette, who will play a scene from *La Vagabonde* with Monsieur Paul Poiret [the dress-designer].
January 28: Lucie Delarue-Mardrus, poet and novelist.
February 4: Gertrude Stein presented by herself.

May 6: in honor of the Duchesse de Clermont-Tonnerre and the English poetess Nina Loy.
May 13: a novelist, a poetess, an unknown, etc.
June 3: Rachilde, then Ford Madox Ford will discuss American women of letters, including Djuna Barnes.
June 10: retrospective of the works of Renée Vivien and Marie Leneru.[5]

Many of these were or had been Natalie's lovers, for she lived in a constant whirl of intrigue and new amours. Her long-standing attachments – Romaine Brooks the painter, Dolly Wilde, the Duchesse de Clermont-Tonnerre – had to accept that, at the same time as swearing undying love, Natalie would be embarking upon continuous small *affaires*.

Perhaps it was this gay and overt cynicism, verging sometimes upon sadism, which endeared Natalie to that extraordinary figure of the Paris artistic, aristocratic and homosexual world Comte Robert de Montesquiou. Despite her magnetism and her brazenness, Natalie had not found it easy at first to gain acceptance by all those she would have liked to know. Anna de Noailles, for example, had returned a book of Renée Vivien's poems with a note stating that 'she was not interested in the writings of such people'.[6] But Montesquiou, the precious and self-conscious model for the sensualist Des Esseintes in Huysmans' novel *A Rebours*, liked Natalie (who almost alone among his

friends remained his friend until he died) and was able to introduce her to a number of useful and interesting people including
that bearer of one of France's oldest names, the Princesse de
Polignac. This meeting must have taken place some time in 1893,
since the Polignacs were only married in that year, and soon
afterwards, they and Montesquiou fell out – the customary end
to his friendships.

Natalie Barney and Winnie de Polignac met officially for the
first time at a reception of Montesquiou's – but, Natalie's biographer assumes, this was not the first time they had met. Their
tastes in young women were similar – but, unlike Natalie, the
Princesse de Polignac was exceedingly discreet. Nothing could
have been more alien to her than Miss Barney's generally shame-
less way of conducting her *affaires*. They may have met; but if
they had it is unlikely that the poker-faced Winnie would have
given the slightest indication that it was the case. But whether
they had encountered each other previously or not, the fact that
these two women should meet officially for the first time at the
house of Robert de Montesquiou gives an indication of the bizarre
mobility of the world in which they lived.

For the Princesse de Polignac, too, was an American. She was
born in Yonkers, New York, in January 1865, the twentieth child
of the wealthy manufacturer of sewing-machines Isaac Merritt
Singer, and christened Winnaretta Eugenie. Winnaretta was the
second child of his second marriage, to Isabella Boyer Summer-
ville. Between these two marriages Singer had conducted three
acknowledged (and countless unacknowledged) liaisons and
fathered sixteen illegitimate children, all of whom he recognized.
At the time of Winnaretta's birth by no means all of this story
was public knowledge – the full ghastly tale not being revealed
until after Singer died, when one of his common-law wives
decided to contest his will. But enough had leaked out to ensure
that Mr and Mrs Singer would never be received by respectable
society in New York. They endured two years of ostracism, and
then set sail for Europe, where, since Mrs Singer was half-
French – the daughter of Louis Boyer, a tavern-keeper, and his
English wife – they decided to settle in Paris. Here they set up
house on boulevard Malesherbes, where they produced two more
sons and a daughter before the events of 1870 forced them to

move on. Their next stop, and Singer's final home, was at Paignton in Devon, where he built himself a fabulous house which he called The Wigwam. Here the old man was able to indulge his taste for the theatre, which he had always preferred to the business world – he had turned to inventing sewing-machines only as a desperate last resort when it became clear that, as an actor, he would never be anything more than a spectacular failure. Now he had his own private arena, in which he could hire circuses to perform, where he could stage-manage stupendous parties for his children, and where he could generally play the part of sugar-daddy to the whole populace of Paignton. The Wigwam was still incomplete when he died there in 1875, at the age of sixty-four.

Singer had enjoyed his years at Paignton, and his children were happy there. His widow, however, was not satisfied with the social prospects presented by such a location for either her children or herself. She was in her thirties, still very personable; the children were rich, and both her daughters good-looking. Who knew whom they might not marry, given the correct environment? Paignton was not such an environment. The family's only social contact there was with tradesmen, or at most with such members of the professional class as the architect who had worked on The Wigwam. The county had snubbed every effort to strike up acquaintance. Accordingly, Isabella decided that she and the children would decamp and go to live once more in Paris, where she set up house at 7 avenue Kléber. Here she soon re-married. Her new husband was Victor Reubsaet, a Belgian musician; it was rumoured that they had been well acquainted before her marriage to Singer. Any doubts as to the social desirability of this alliance were quickly disposed of, as far as Isabella was concerned, by Reubsaet's convenient inheritance, in swift succession, of two faintly dubious titles: that of Vicomte d'Estemburgh (or Des Tambourgs), which was Belgian, or so it was said; and that of Duc de Camposelice, which emanated from the Vatican. Thus prepared, the new Duchess made her bid to establish avenue Kléber as a centre for the social and musical world of Paris.

Winnaretta shared her stepfather's passion for music, for it turned out that she was herself musically extremely gifted. Her tastes were sophisticated – for a fourteenth birthday treat she had requested a performance of Beethoven's Fourteenth Quartet, opus 131; she adored Wagner; she had been an enthusiastic friend of Gabriel Fauré ever since, at the age of sixteen, she had met him in Normandy one summer. But in other respects she, and her sister and brothers, found their mother's new household distasteful. 'I warned Madam and begged her not to marry that man,' mourned George Woodruff, the head of the Singer operation in England and an old family friend. In a letter to Singer's American executor, David Hawley, he wrote that Winnaretta's younger brother Paris (later to become known as the lover of Isadora Duncan) 'says they go for weeks without speaking to each other and he has heard the Duke tell his Mother that he got all the property in his own name and if she did not mind what she done [sic] he would turn her out.'[7]

That was unfortunate, but it was Isabella's affair. But it seemed the Duke was not satisfied with his wife's money – he wanted to get his hands on her children's as well. A plan was devised whereby the boys might thwart these designs. Each of them, as he reached the age of sixteen, ran away from home and was made a ward of court. But for the girls, Winnie and her younger sister Isabelle, the situation was not so easy. They could not run away from home – not if they wanted to retain any social credibility. The only escape was into marriage.

For Winnaretta, the question of marriage was not an easy one. She had already discovered that she was not attracted to men, so that any marriage would be contracted, so far as she was concerned, for purely social reasons. She had plenty to offer a future husband: a huge fortune, an attractive presence, an interesting mind. The least she might expect in return was a title, an established social position, and the right to lead her own life. Her route to this desirable situation was, she decided, to be Prince Louis de Scey-Montbéliard.

Nobody was under much illusion as to the reasons for this marriage. George Woodruff, in a fatherly note, advised her most strongly not to get married before she had ensured that all her property was settled safely in trust for her own use and benefit. Isabella disapproved of the marriage – she had hoped for something better: Prince Louis's was not a resounding title, and with

Winnie's fortune she had hoped for a better family connection. But this was one matter in which her mother's wishes were of not the slightest concern to Winnie. The situation in the Camposelice household was in fact disconcertingly public knowledge – so much so that when the Duke died in August 1887, a month after Winnie had married her prince, *The World* remarked that: 'Her marriage to Prince Louis is supposed to have been the result of a desire to possess a home of her own and protection from the importunities of her mother's impecunious but enterprising husband. Now death has relieved her of the old Duke's presence, she may have occasion to regret her haste.'[8]

The only person who seems to have nourished any romantic expectations of the marriage was the bridegroom. Did Winnie assume that her reputation had gone before her and that the Prince, knowing her lesbian preferences, would realize that this was to be a *mariage blanc*? If so, she was mistaken. As the wedding day progressed it became clear that he was looking forward to a traditionally blissful wedding night. This was more than Winnie was prepared to countenance. Tradition has it that, being the first to enter the nuptial chamber, she armed herself with an umbrella and climbed on top of a large wardrobe (she herself was very small and slight). When the Prince came in he looked around him in puzzlement for his vanished bride. He soon caught sight of her brandishing the umbrella at him. 'If you touch me,' she yelled at him, 'I'll kill you!' That he never did touch her was attested in copious detail before the papal court which finally annulled the marriage after the couple separated in 1889. That year, Isabella wrote to Hawley: 'You will be surprised to hear that Winnie is suing for a separation from her husband – it seems they have bothered her so much for money that she won't stand it any longer and as he married her with false papers he is no more a Prince than I am so she is paying for her bad behaviour to me and getting punished for it – however I do not think she cares one bit about it.'[9]

It certainly seems highly unlikely that Winnie's principal concern at that moment was for her mother's feelings. She was busy consolidating the independence which marriage had at last afforded her. She, too, was determined to establish a salon, and it was to be of a very special kind – a haven for all that was newest and most adventurous in music. She had bought herself a large house with a studio on the corner of the avenue Henri-Martin and rue Cortambert, in the fashionable 16e arrondissement, and this she proceeded to decorate sumptuously, with the help of her friend Montesquiou. An organ was installed in the studio for her own use; but it was principally intended that the very best performers should play here – and play, before an invited audience, works which might only with great difficulty, if at all, have found a public hearing elsewhere. Here, too, were to be performed those works which she was now beginning to commission from her musician friends.

One of the earliest of these was a projected collaboration between Fauré and Verlaine, a song-cycle in which music and poetry would exquisitely complement each other. Fauré had already, and with great success, set to music Verlaine's *Clair de Lune*, that Watteauesque evocation of Harlequin and Columbine and the rest of the *Commedia dell'arte* troupe. Now it was suggested that composer and poet might work expressly together. Fauré was filled with enthusiasm for the project, and for the handsome fee which his young patroness proposed; he set out to find Verlaine. This was not easy, since the poet was now drifting in a state of semi-dereliction. But, after various frustrations, '*Verlaine est retrouvé*,' wrote Fauré to Winnaretta, and gave his new address: Hôpital St Antoine, Salle Bichat, Lit No. 5. His friends, wrote Fauré, had thought that the cold weather might well drive him into this refuge for derelicts, 'and they all agree that this unhappy state of affairs will serve our purpose excellently, because his imagination works best when he is in the refuge.' However, one should not hope for too much – the poet was not what once he had been. 'I hope that, in your honour, he may rise again to sublime heights,' wrote Fauré; but it was going to take more than that to reawaken Verlaine. Time and again Fauré visited him, tried to awaken his interest in possible themes, doled out a little money; but Verlaine, though always promising that, by the next time, he would have thought of a theme, could not seem to pull himself together. 'He is the most singular, odd and incomprehensible person!' mourned the composer. How could someone so wonderfully gifted be content with this perpetual shuttle between the bar and the refuge? The one was as depressing as the other, the refuge dirty, ill-lit, with visitors only allowed twice a week, the bar full of drunken wrecks.... In June 1891, however, Verlaine came up with an idea. He wrote Fauré a letter describing it. But what an idea, and what a letter!

My dear Monsieur Fauré, It is with great pleasure that I can tell you that I have hit upon an idea for our work. It should be in the comic vein, the title being *L'hôpital Watteau*. I hope it may be possible to see you soon so that I may submit to you the first sketches for this operetta which will be worthy of all the respect due both to our joint talents and to the excellent society which, let us hope, will applaud our work. Yours sincerely, P. Verlaine.[10]

Fauré had to confess himself finally defeated by the poet. Meanwhile, conscious that no work meant no money, he proposed that he should dedicate his *Cinq Mélodies de Venise* to Winnaretta, who had introduced him to that city – but under what name? To the Princesse de Scey? To Madame Singer, as she sometimes liked to be known?

His dilemma did no more than illustrate Winnaretta's own dilemma at this time, for her social position was once again very equivocal. She was not married, but neither was she a girl, nor a widow. In such circumstances it was impossible that her social standing should be enhanced. She was still young; all the advantages which had obtained before her marriage to Prince Louis (or 'Prince' Louis, as he had turned out to be) still existed; what was more, she knew a great many more people – and a great many more people knew her, and her tastes both intellectual and sexual. It would be much better if she married again.

The person most insistent on the necessity for this regularization of Winnie's social status was Montesquiou. They had met some years previously, while she was Princesse de Scey, and had become great friends. He had helped her organize some of the artistic manifestations at her studio, and invited her to his own (where, given his own tastes, she need have no fear of unwelcome molestations). She introduced him to her musical friends, such as Fauré, Chabrier, Debussy; he introduced her to his own special discoveries, such as the young Marcel Proust. Montesquiou was certain that he had exactly the right person for Winnie: Prince Edmond de Polignac, the scion of a distinguished family, cultured, musical – he was a gifted composer – unmarried at the age of fifty-nine, and notoriously homosexual.

The two had been acquainted for some years and were the best of friends; the idea, when once it was suggested, was evidently an excellent one. But could Winnaretta face the ordeal of marriage once again, even to such a charming and understanding man? M. de Polignac, for his part, would also have to put up with a good deal of gossip, should he contract such a marriage. But he appeared quite unperturbed. While he was visiting the painter Jacques Emile Blanche at his villa in Dieppe, old Madame Blanche, the painter's mother, commented cynically that this would not be the kind of wedding at which one would play Mendelssohn's wedding march. 'So the lute is going to marry the sewing-machine?' she said. Prince Edmond replied that it was more a question of the dollar marrying the sou. To prove that he was quite fit enough, even at fifty-nine, to undergo such an ordeal, he jumped over a chair with his feet together.[11] Meanwhile his relatives were trying to dissuade Winnaretta: Edmond, they said, was quite mad. But once she had decided that this was the right thing to do, nothing would dissuade her. In December 1893 the pair were married.

What had they expected? What, for that matter, had their friends expected? In no case, it is safe to say, had anyone expected what actually occurred. This had been planned as a marriage of convenience in the most cynical sense, but neither of the protagonists were cynics; and it soon became quite clear it had turned into a marriage of love – not sexual love, perhaps, but in every other respect quite unmistakably the real thing. Whenever he was away from her Edmond penned long letters to his 'Dearest Winn', his '*Bien chère et bien aimée* Winn'. The letters chattered about music, travel, the latest articles and reputations – all the interests which they so passionately shared – and all ended with the fervent desire that they might meet again soon. Never in their lives, otherwise so extremely dissimilar, had either of them been the object of a true and disinterested affection; both found the experience overwhelming. 'Mutual confidence, the certainty of affection, and the unshakable knowledge that we shall always belong to each other, these are the real blessings of life,' wrote Edmond to his '*chérie, chérie* Winn'.

It was literally a marriage of true minds. The Prince shared his wife's passion for music and for all that was newest and most adventurous in that field. Together they continued her salon in the rue Cortambert; together they entertained musical and literary notabilities such as Anna de Noailles, Abel Hermant, Marcel Proust – but no longer Robert de Montesquiou.

For Montesquiou, although he might have been expected to rejoice at the successful realization of his great plan, was on the contrary outraged. He had not expected such excess of emotion, such vulgar happiness. He had envisaged a cynical and civilized marriage of convenience and here the thing had turned into a love-match! It was intolerable. Furious beyond measure, he wrote a poem of the utmost malice entitled 'Vinaigrette' – an obvious pun on 'Winnaretta'. Winnie not only prided herself on her musicianship, but also did more than a little painting, which she had studied quite seriously as a young girl. She displayed considerable competence, and every year held a salon of her own pictures and those of some friends in her studio. 'Vinaigrette' hinted in no uncertain terms that these paintings were not Winnie's work at all:

> ... un artiste la sert
> Et lui dit où se doit placer le bleu, le vert...
> Elle signe, elle envoie au Salon, le médaille
> Est pour elle....[12]

Apart from Montesquiou, however, everyone was happy about the alliance. Winnie acquired a resounding name and social position; Edmond acquired the Monet picture of 'The Tulip Field at Harlem' for which Winnaretta, then unknown to him, had outbid him at a sale, to his intense fury; the new music acquired a solid source of patronage; the artistic beau-monde acquired a new and delightful venue. The afternoon concerts at rue Cortambert, where the Comtesse Greffulhe, the Comtesse de Noailles, the Princesse de Caraman-Chimay, assembled to hear the latest compositions, were not only intellectually satisfying but (wrote Proust, with his delight in such detail) 'were also, to use the expression of the society columnists, "supremely elegant".'[13] A ray of sunlight would illuminate the Monet, the musicians would perform, and Winnaretta would seat herself beside an open

window while Edmond, who never felt warm, would wrap himself in his cashmere shawl and his travelling-plaid. ' "What is life
but a journey," as Anaxagoras said,' he quipped. It was at these
gatherings that many of the seeds of Proust's great novel were
planted. In a long letter, when the two volumes of *Du Côté de
chez Swann* were published and *A l'Ombre des jeunes filles en
fleurs* was at the printer's, Proust asked Winnaretta's permission
to dedicate this second part of his novel to the Prince's memory.
He explained that he had hoped all five volumes would have
appeared at once, in which case – although none of the characters
bore the slightest resemblance to the Prince – some malicious
persons, notably Montesquiou, would no doubt have pointed out
that one of the characters was a *grand seigneur* interested in the
arts – 'and I seem to remember, probably wrongly, that you are
sometimes taken in by malice.' But even the most determined
malice-monger would be hard put to it, thought Proust, to find
anything to gossip about in this second part.[14] (Nevertheless,
Winnaretta refused the dedication.)

To the general run of society, no doubt it all seemed very
rarefied. 'I'm dying to get to know him better but he frightens
me so much that I shall never dare speak to him,' wrote Winnie's
young sister Belle-Blanche when she first heard of the engagement. Belle-Blanche had made a marriage entirely to her mother's
taste, allying herself with the young Duc Decazes who, though
very small, was quite respectable. But Prince Edmond does not
seem to have been in any way intimidating. When he died, in
1901, after only seven years of marriage, Winnie was overcome
with grief. When her favourite niece remembered the anniversary
of his death some years later she wrote: 'Thanks darling for
remembering the 24th! I don't talk of my sorrow any more, but
not one instant has it grown easier to bear. The one thing I had,
I lost then – and there is not a day that dawns in which I don't
say, like Brontë, "How can I face the empty world again!" '[15]

Of course there were friends to help. There was, for example,
Boni de Castellane, reputedly the only man Winnaretta ever
fancied. He wrote her long letters during his divorce proceedings,
and may have had hopes of exchanging one heiress for another,
but for her there could be no question of marrying again. Then
there was Colette, one of the common denominators of this world

– a staunch friend to both Natalie Barney and to Winnaretta. Where but in Paris could one find such an incomparable female friend as Colette? Her letters radiate that hot fascination and affection for the exact detail of life which permeate all her writings. When Winnie is ill, 'My darling Winnie, I am watching over you in spirit,' writes Colette. 'That English nanny you see from your window, that is me. That wonderful moustachio'd policeman, that's me. And that damned waiter who knocks on your door by mistake just when you're getting off to sleep to take away the tea-tray, that's me, too.' From the south of France she writes: 'To-day it is very still, slightly golden, with wasps and little spiders' threads – just the weather to make Paris cry....' She proposes a small but perfect dinner party:

We shall eat the following light and savoury menu:

> Omelette au lard
> Truffles
> A wonderful cheese
> And some fruit.
> Not much wine, but good.

Leave the truffles to me (please let me know how many guests) and of course I'll look after the cheese too. If you prefer, we could have eggs baked in cream instead of the omelette. But truffles must be tackled with a fresh mouth, which hasn't been sullied by spices....[16]

However, it seems clear that from the time of Edmond's death, Winnaretta drew the greater part of her satisfaction in life from the discovery and support of new talent, especially in the musical world. The Fauré project may have come to nothing, but there were many others that succeeded. For example, a small work which she commissioned from the young Spaniard Manuel de Falla turned out to be *El Retablo de Maese Pedro*. On 9 December 1918 he writes to tell her that he has at last found a subject 'which fulfils satisfactorily the conditions which seem to me necessary for your stage and for my work'. The subject is to be found in Chapter XXVI of the second part of *Don Quixote*, and he hopes that it will seem acceptable. The subject is accepted. But it is not until January of 1923 that he can tell her that – at last! – the piano arrangement of the new work is ready. The reason for this long delay, he explains – apart from health and other practical obstacles – 'has been the development which *I myself* had not expected ... of a piece which was begun with the intention of making it a simple *divertissement*. But as it now stands it is, perhaps, of all my works, the most fantastic (*où j'ai mis plus d'illusion*).'[17] What profound satisfaction the Maecenas must feel who opens such a letter!

Of course she was rich, and the sums which seemed so insurmountable to others meant little to her; but the rich are not always generous. Few people, however, appealed to Winnaretta in vain. Nervous letters requesting her support are followed by grateful ones acknowledging it. Vincent d'Indy wants 2000 francs to underwrite a concert by his 'Schola'; Ernest Ansermet, 30,000–50,000 francs, quickly, so that he may guarantee the requisite huge number of performers necessary for Stravinsky's *Symphony of Psalms*. This piece seems to have caused problems more than once: a letter from the composer asks for her help in financing its rehearsal and presentation by the Paris Symphony Orchestra, since they cannot afford the choirs and want to omit it from the concert programme. On a more mundane level, Colette asks for a loan to buy an apartment. When subscriptions were needed to underwrite a larger project, such as the printing and publication of a friend's deserving poems, Winnaretta was the first to be approached. Her studio was available for performances of the more *recherché* works: Stravinsky's *Renard* for example (another commission) was played there before its Diaghilev Paris première, although the dancers could not perform, since there was not enough room. In short, Winnie offered what all new artists need: a means of presenting new works to the public and financial support in the meantime.

An important aspect of these activities for her was that they perpetuated, or so it seemed to her, the memory of her father. Like all the members of his last and most respectable family she had only the haziest idea of what his life had been in the years before he met her mother, while he was (amongst other things) inventing and marketing the sewing-machine whence all the money came. Alone of the children of his old age, Winnie made a certain effort to find out about his early life. She corresponded with William Singer, her oldest half-brother (more than thirty years older than herself) and gave him a certain amount of financial support, since for various complicated reasons he had not been remembered in his father's will. Nevertheless, if we are to judge by her correspondence with Maurice Paléologue when the Fondation Singer-Polignac was being mooted, her notion of her father's activities was a long way from the truth. 'You understand,' she said to M. Paléologue at that time, 'that I owe to my father a considerable fortune. But I am sixty-one years old; I am now seriously preoccupied with the arrangements that I have to make for the future of this fortune. I have made a cult of the memory of my father and it is in him above all that I want to find the inspiration for the future of my inheritance. I need a foundation with which I can associate myself during my lifetime. Instruct me; advise me.' To which Paléologue replied that, 'in view of her own interest in the arts and her father's scientific reputation, the creation of a foundation which could foster and endow artistic and scientific projects might satisfy her generous impulses.'[18] Thus are scientific reputations posthumously created. In fact, although her father had undoubted mechanical flair, he was barely literate.

The provenance of this fortune which was to be devoted to the advancement of modern music would particularly have delighted Gertrude Stein (who knew Winnaretta: they were introduced by Picasso). Of course, the service Winnaretta performed for the new music was very like what Miss Stein was doing for the new painting. Not only did she buy every Picasso and Matisse she could afford (and Miss Stein was not rich), but she held open house so that people could come and see these paintings, which were not on view at any gallery.

Why should it have been left to these American ladies to support Europe's new artists? Miss Stein saw nothing strange in this apparent paradox. It was her opinion that Americans had a head start in these matters. 'Gertrude Stein always speaks of America as being now the oldest country in the world because by the methods of the civil war and the commercial conceptions that followed it America created the twentieth century, and since all the other countries are now either living or commencing to be living a twentieth century life, America having begun the creation of the twentieth century in the sixties of the nineteenth century is now the oldest country in the world.'[19] Americans were thus uniquely qualified to appreciate twentieth-century art while Europeans were still bogged in the mire of their cultural history.

If she was right in this assessment, then it is hard to imagine any more appropriate manifestation of this thesis than Winnie Singer, Princesse de Polignac. She, if anyone, was a truly modern millionairess. Oil, silver, even railroads, belonged as much to the nineteenth as to the twentieth century. But Winnie's father had made his fortune by mass production and the hard sell. This was a truly twentieth-century fortune; what more appropriate than that it be spent on twentieth-century art?

To travel hopefully
is better ...

If Europe was fortunate in the dollar princesses – as, on the whole, it was – then so were they fortunate in Europe. For what would their lives have been had they remained in America? What would have become of these energetic, open-minded girls, so full of snap and style and ambition? If they had gained that entrée to society so eagerly coveted by their mammas, if they had bowed to popular feeling and made all-American marriages, what then? Throughout the novels and stories of the period the same family group recurs – the dashing daughter dragging in her wake a complaisant but bewildered mother, an indulgent but uninterested father. But these mammas, too, had been dashing girls in their time. Were their daughters, then, doomed to do no more in the end than drag wistfully after *their* daughters, to pursue their own version of the social chimera? Daisy Miller may have paid for her boldness by dying of the Roman fever – but would a more interesting fate have awaited her had she gone back home to Utica?

The paradoxical fact was that, having produced the 'all-conquering American girl', the only prospects America could offer her were desiccated ones. Cut off from the real excitements of the men's world – the business world – the posturings of society made a poor outlet for those energies so carefully nurtured in youth. A Victoria Woodhull might break through the conventions, start her own stockbroking office on Wall Street, stand for President – but Victoria Woodhull was no lady: far from it. As for the energetic, intelligent and ambitious woman who was and wished to remain a lady – one need only look at Mrs Stuyvesant Fish to see what might be in store for *her*.

Mrs Fish was one of the great matriarchs of New York society in the Gilded Age. Early in the 1890s she established her position as society's *enfant terrible*, a position which she retained for the next fifteen years. Mrs Fish's was a life of barely suppressed fury. She was unrestrainedly rude whenever she felt like it ('And this is my Louis Quinze room,' proudly announced an acquaintance showing her newly decorated house. 'And what makes you think so, dear?' inquired Mrs Fish.) The outrageous and expensive antics at her parties were frequently reported in the papers, and earned her the disapproval of Mrs Vanderbilt as being 'the kind of thing that gets the rich a bad name,' adding fuel to the fires so eagerly fanned by Eugene Debs and his socialists. But the fact was – and this may have been what really infuriated Mrs Vanderbilt, although how could she say so? – that Mrs Fish expended her money, her imagination, her powers of generalship, very largely on showing society exactly what she thought of it. That tea party for dogs at which the most costly *foie gras* was served, that dinner at which an ape dressed in uniform was solemnly sat amongst the guests – what were they but enormous snooks cocked at the very society of which Mrs Fish was so established a leader, and with which she was so unspeakably bored?

In these frolics Harry Lehr was her able lieutenant. In Lehr Mrs Fish found a true kindred spirit – as cynical, as blasé, as heedless as herself, and withal as fascinated by society, as wholly unable truly to discount it. Penniless, plausible, charming, and homosexual – husbands could rest happily undisturbed by this solitary male presence among their wives and daughters in mid-week Newport, although the reason why could not of course be acknowledged. Lehr, determined to establish himself upon a sound financial footing, married the innocent Miss Elizabeth Drexel, heiress to the Drexel banking fortune. 'I know what your favourite flower is, pet, it's the marigold!' quipped Mrs Fish. On their wedding night Harry revealed to his bride, till then radiant at the thought of having captured the most fascinating man in New York, that he was repelled by women, and could never bring himself to be alone with her in private – although he would be all that was expected in the way of a gallant husband in public. And with this sad situation poor Mrs Lehr lived for many years, since not only was divorce a scandal, but she was and remained in love with Harry, and forever hoped that things might change.

To the Paris of Diaghilev's Ballets Russes, of Picasso, of Stravinsky, of Colette, of Gertrude Stein, Natalie Barney and Winnie de Polignac, came these sad ghosts. They lived in a house which had been built for Louis XIV's Grand Maréchal des Logis de la Maison du Roi, but which had fallen into neglect and was rescued and restored by Mrs Lehr.

Tall windows overlooked a trim garden with venerable trees; inside the house were fine *boiseries*, Louis Quinze furniture and marqueterie floors, busts, tapestry, and bibelots of a uniform opulence.... In our midst, silent and staring as from the world of the dead, yet garbed in a purple velvet jacket which contrasted strangely with his worn, pale face and lustreless eyes, was our host.... The Gilded Age had passed, but some of its survivors were moving like mechanical puppets through these over-polished and over-heated rooms. Even now they took their frivolities seriously, and their dinners were highly spiced with the Almanac de Gotha.[1]

Were these the rewards of belonging to the 'Four Hundred?... In lusting after dead courts these representatives of the blue blood of New York showed little understanding of the realities of that aristocracy of which their own daughters and nieces, grandsons and granddaughters now formed so indissoluble a part. Did Winnie de Polignac, Anna de Talleyrand-Périgord, ever visit them? If so, they can only have reflected on their good fortune in that their mammas were never received by these people, and thus they themselves never enclosed within this narrow orbit. As for Mr and Mrs Lehr and their friends, did they ever look past the names and see the real people who were contained within those resounding titles? Probably not; we see what we want to see, and warts held no interest for them. What, then, did they want to see? They did not really know – and that was their tragedy. They knew what was not done, but not what to do.

In this, they were quite different from the majority of their compatriots. The dollar princesses, like Isabel Archer – like almost all Americans – 'affronted their destiny'. It was their hallmark. They did not bow to arbitrary fate. They knew what they wanted and they went out to get it. In the land of opportunity the choice was there: one made one's own fate. The dollar princesses made the mark they did because they carried this philosophy into areas where it had been hitherto unheard-of. Birth, after all, was an accident, and in Europe the rest of one's life followed naturally from that accident. By comparison, how little was accidental about the lives of Maud Burke, Minnie Stevens, Mary Leiter! The choice was before them, the possibilities were there, and they – or their mammas – chose. In Europe one lives to the best of one's ability, but in America one picks a lifestyle. It was a concept already in operation in the nineteenth century, though perhaps less self-consciously so than now. The corollary, of course, is that there is more heart-searching about the results of one's choice. Being the result of conscious decision rather than cruel fate, it must turn out right. Thus the unhappiness of a Mary Leiter, during those first sad years in England, is redoubled; the determination of a Maud Burke to make the life she wants, unequalled by any Englishwoman.

It is fitting that this freedom of choice should be the characteristic legacy of the New World, since it is to just such decisiveness that the United States owes its very existence. The greatest decision of all had been taken by their grandfathers and great-grandfathers, to leave the Old World and make for the new. They chose to go – and that is to say, they chose to choose; and this – the right to choice – was the legacy they handed down. If their granddaughters chose to return, to make the voyage in the opposite direction, it was perhaps partly because they sensed that the other option most evidently available to them – to join the ranks of American high society – effectively closed the avenues of choice. The ambition of Ward McAllister and his friends had been to create something static – a fixed standard – and in this they had, up to a point, succeeded. The adventure lay all in breaking in: once inside those select circles, it was at an end. One had arrived, and where else could one wish to go? And – in the United States – what greater anomaly than that could be imagined? To reach the self-appointed top is not necessarily to achieve the greatest satisfaction. Who would not rather be a buccaneer?

Notes

1: 'We are the dollar princesses'

1 Peacock, *Famous American Belles of the Nineteenth Century*, pp. 66–7.
2 Henry James, *Pandora*, p. 115.
3 Eliot, *Heiresses and Coronets*, p. 28.
4 Ibid, p. 28.

16 Vanderbilt, *Queen of the Golden Age*, pp. 185–6.
17 Chanler, *Roman Spring*, p. 237.
18 Eliot, op. cit., p. 25.
19 McAllister, op. cit., p. 118.
20 Strange, op. cit., p. 67.
21 Vanderbilt, op. cit., p. 218.
22 Wharton, *The Buccaneers*, p. 6.

2: Artificial High Societies

1 Adams, *Letters*, p. 214, July 1871.
2 Tallant, *Mardi Gras*, pp. 188–9.
3 Seebold, *Old Louisiana Plantation Homes and Family Trees*, p. 3.
4 Stead, *If Christ Came to Chicago*, p. 101.
5 Bourget, *Outre-Mer*, p. 72.
6 Seebold, op. cit., p. 13.
7 McAllister, *Society as I have found it*, p. 50.
8 Ibid., p. 48.
9 Ibid., p. 124.
10 Irving, *Knickerbocker's History of New York*, p. 93.
11 McAllister, op. cit., p. 245.
12 Ibid., p. 160.
13 de Wolfe, *After All*, p. 18.
14 McAllister, op. cit., p. 118.
15 Strange, *Who Tells Me True*, p. 94.

3: Young Men on the Make

1 Stead, op. cit., p. 72.
2 Collier, *England and the English*, p. 155.
3 Ibid., p. 144.
4 Warwick, *Afterthoughts*, p. 46.
5 Leslie, *The Fabulous Leonard Jerome*, p. 219.
6 Letter quoted in Huber and Wilson, *Baroness Pontalba's Buildings*.
7 Balsan, *The Glitter and the Gold*, p. 7.
8 Ibid., p. 7.
9 Eliot, op. cit., p. 181.
10 Ibid., p. 185.
11 Castellane, *Confessions*, p. 95.
12 Ibid., p. 101.
13 Ibid., p. 105.
14 Ibid., p. 123.
15 Ibid., p. 123.

Notes

4: American Beauties

1 Bourget, *Outre-Mer*, p. 100.
2 Ibid., p. 85.
3 Peacock, op. cit., p. 270.
4 Ibid., p. 267.
5 Chanler, *Roman Spring*, p. 209.
6 Henry James, *Pandora*, p. 115.
7 Bourget, op. cit., p. 86.
8 Ibid., p. 86.
9 Veblen, *Theory of the Leisure Class*, p. 89.
10 Henry James, preface to the New York edition of *Daisy Miller* p. x.
11 Bourget, op. cit., p. 99.
12 Letter to her father, quoted Nicolson, *Mary Curzon*, p. 86.
13 Wharton, *A Backward Glance*, p. 62.
14 Vanderbilt, op. cit., p. 30.
15 Tallant, op. cit., p. 135.
16 Frances Trollope, *Domestic Manners of the Americans*.
17 Henry James, *A London Life*, London, 1889.
18 *Town Topics*, 31 March 1906.
19 Collier, op. cit., p. 9.
20 Adams, *The Education of Henry Adams*, p. 195.
21 Introduction to *Titled Americans*, 1890.

5: Getting Married

1 Wharton, *The Buccaneers*
2 Stead's speech to the people of Chicago, 'Who are the Disreputables?' quoted in Stead, op. cit., p. 107.
3 Wyndham, *Life and Letters* – from Melton Mowbray, 22 February 1913.
4 Quoted Eliot, op. cit., p. 31.
5 *New York Tribune*, 29 March 1888.
6 Strange, op. cit., pp. 70–1.
7 Ibid., pp. 9–11.
8 Ibid., pp. 9–11.

9 Balsan, op. cit., pp. 47–8.
10 Consuelo's testimony before the Rota, quoted in Vanderbilt, op. cit., p. 45.
11 Balsan, op. cit., pp. 47–8.
12 Leslie, *Jennie*, p. 54. The affair is dealt with at length in this book.
13 Ibid., p. 137.
14 Morton Frewen, who married Jennie Churchill's sister Clara. Quoted Leslie, *Jennie*, p. 136.
15 Balsan, op. cit., p. 51.
16 Leslie, *Jennie*, p. 35.
17 Ibid., p. 36.
18 Ibid., p. 35.
19 Balsan, op. cit., p. 52.
20 Evidence before the Rota, quoted Vanderbilt, op. cit., p. 45.
21 Balsan, op. cit., p. 53.
22 Ibid., p. 56.
23 Corelli, *Free Opinions*, 'The American Bounder', p. 141.
24 Ibid., p. 142.
25 *Town Topics*, 14 Feb 1885.
26 All quotations in this account are taken from Eliot, op. cit., pp. 87–9.
27 Lewis, *Edith Wharton*, p. 42.
28 Ibid., p. 45. Mr Lewis discusses this incident at length, and all quotations relating to it are taken from this source.
29 Vanderbilt, op. cit., pp. 187–8.
30 Nicolson, op. cit., p. 55.
31 Ibid., p. 55.
32 Ibid., pp. 56–7.
33 Leslie, *Jennie*, p. 47.
34 Ibid., p. 81.

6: Great Expectations–France

1 Wharton, *The Custom of the Country*, p. 489.
2 Castellane, op. cit., pp. 12–13.
3 Fiske, *Off-Hand Portraits of Prominent New-Yorkers*.
4 Letters in the possession of Mr Frank Regas, New Orleans.

Notes

5 Fiske, op. cit.
6 *Commercial Advertiser*, 3 December 1892.
7 Balsan, op. cit., p. 37.
8 Ibid., p. 38.
9 *Town Topics*, 31 January 1885.
10 Clermont-Tonnerre, *Memoirs*, I, p. 222.
11 Castellane, op. cit., p. 92.
12 Clermont-Tonnerre, *Memoirs*, II, p. 74.
13 Castellane, op. cit., p. 94.
14 Ibid., p. 129.
15 Ibid., p. 131.
16 Wharton, *French Ways and Their Meaning*, pp. 100–14.
17 Castellane, op. cit., p. 277.
18 Ibid., p. 143.
19 Clermont-Tonnerre, II, pp. 79–80.
20 Castellane, op. cit., p. 149.
21 Clermont-Tonnerre, I, p. 222.
22 *Chicago Daily Tribune*, 3 February 1906.
23 Ibid., 3 February 1906.
24 Letters quoted in the Castellane divorce case, reported in *Chicago Sunday Tribune*, 4 November 1906.
25 Castellane, op. cit., p. 213.
26 Wharton, *French Ways and Their Meaning*, p. 128.
27 Clermont-Tonnerre, II, p. 79.
28 Castellane, op. cit., p. 165.
29 *Chicago Sunday Tribune*, 4 February 1906.
30 *Chicago Daily Tribune*, 8 November 1906.
31 Clermont-Tonnerre, II, p. 79.
32 George Painter, *Marcel Proust*, II, pp. 104–5.
33 Clermont-Tonnerre, II, p. 80.

7: Great Expectations – England

1 Clermont-Tonnerre, II, p. 82.
2 Balsan, op. cit., pp. 76–7.
3 Letters in the possession of Lady Alexandra Metcalfe, kindly made available to the author

from his notes by Nigel Nicolson.
4 Collier, op. cit., pp. 374–5.
5 Balsan, op. cit., p. 71.
6 Ibid., p. 71.
7 Letters in possession of Lady Alexandra Metcalfe.
8 Balsan, op. cit., pp. 106–7.
9 Collier, op. cit., p. 374.
10 Adams, *Letters*, p. 99.
11 Collier, op. cit., p. 5.
12 Wyndham, *Letters*.
13 Letter in Astor Archive, Reading University.
14 Ibid.
15 Balsan, op. cit., pp. 125–6.
16 Ibid., p. 174.
17 Nicolson, op. cit., p. 93.
18 All quotations from Mary's letters not otherwise acknowledged are taken from notes kindly loaned to the author by Nigel Nicolson made of letters in the possession of Lady Alexandra Metcalfe.
19 Nicolson, op. cit., p. 85.
20 Clermont-Tonnerre, II, p. 64.
21 Balsan, op. cit., p. 143.
22 Wharton, *A Backward Glance*, p. 271.
23 Ibid., p. 262.
24 These details are taken from an article by Victoria Glendinning which she kindly made available to the author.
25 Balsan, op. cit., p. 125.
26 Painter, II, pp. 322–3.
27 Stein, *The Autobiography of Alice B. Toklas*, p. 73.
28 Channon, *Chips*, 13 December 1943.

8: Setting the pace: society

1 Lloyd George, November 1917, quoted by Asquith, *Diaries 1915–1918*.

2 Leslie, *The Jerome Connection*, p. 67.
3 Introduction to *Titled Americans*, 1895.
4 Asquith, op. cit., p. 354.
5 From George Moore, *Memoirs of my Dead Life*, quoted by Rupert Hart-Davis in his introduction to Moore's *Letters*.
6 Moore, *Letters*, p. 34 (Oct. 1904).
7 Camplin, *The Rise of the Plutocrats*, pp. 103–4.
8 Fielding, *Emerald and Nancy*, p. 1.
9 Ibid., p. 149.
10 Hart-Davis, introduction to Moore's *Letters*, p. 10.
11 Moore, *Memoirs of my Dead Life*, quoted by Hart-Davis in the introduction to Moore's *Letters*.
12 Fielding, op. cit., p. 6.
13 Cunard, *GM: Memories of George Moore*, p. 20.
14 Moore, *Memoirs of my Dead Life*, quoted by Hart-Davis in the introduction to Moore's *Letters*.
15 Cunard, op. cit., p. 38.
16 Fielding, op. cit., p. 86.
17 Ibid., p. 97.
18 Ibid., p. 86.
19 Asquith, op. cit., p. 335.
20 Ibid., p. 335.
21 Nancy Cunard, op. cit., p. 39.
22 Sitwell, *Great Morning*, p. 252.
23 Channon, op. cit., December 1942.
24 Fielding, op. cit., p. 32.
25 Sitwell, op. cit., p. 252.
26 Acton, *Memoirs of an Aesthete*, p. 220.
27 Sitwell, op. cit., p. 251.
28 Cunard, op. cit., p. 113.
29 Fielding, op. cit., p. 100.
30 Ibid.
31 Channon, op. cit., p. 421, 2 Feb 1948.
32 Ibid., 23 Sept 1942.
33 Ibid., introduction, p. 4; 31 May 1927.
34 Ibid., 14 May 1935.
35 Ibid., 10 June 1939.
36 Fielding, op. cit., p. 120.
37 Channon, op. cit., 11 and 12 June 1936.
38 Ibid., 23 June 1940.

9: Setting the pace: politics

1 Walter Elliot, quoted by Christopher Sykes, *Nancy*, p. 247.
2 Balsan, op. cit., p. 205.
3 Sykes, op. cit., p. 379.
4 Quoted by Michael Astor, *Tribal Feeling*.
5 Ibid., p. 21.
6 Sykes, op. cit., pp. 81–2, quoting from Nancy Astor's unpublished autobiographical draft now in the Astor Archive, Reading University.
7 Ibid., pp. 138–9.
8 Nicolson, op. cit., p. 145.
9 Ibid., p. 142.
10 Ibid., p. 156.
11 Article written for the *Sunday Times*, 1956; now in Astor Archive, Reading University.
12 Balsan, op. cit., p. 216.
13 Ibid., pp. 227–8.
14 Letter in Astor Archive, Reading University.
15 Letters in Astor Archive, Reading University.
16 Article for *Sunday Times*, 1956, now in Astor Archive, Reading University.
17 Election speech, 1919; from press cuttings in the Astor Archive, Reading University.
18 Sykes, op. cit., pp. 195–6.
19 Letters in Astor Archive, Reading University.
20 Sykes, op. cit., p. 199.
21 Ibid., p. 305.

22 Quoted Sykes, op. cit., pp. 246–7.
23 Letter in Astor Archive, Reading University.
24 Balsan, op. cit., p. 204.

10: Setting the pace: culture

1 Acton, op. cit., p. 221.
2 Ibid., p. 149.
3 Morrill Cody, quoted in Wickes, *The Amazon of Letters*, p. 165.
4 Stein, op. cit., p. 94.
5 Wickes, op. cit., p. 166.
6 Ibid., p. 106.
7 Letter in possession of the Singer Co., New York.
8 Brandon, *Singer and the Sewing Machine*, pp. 213–14.
9 Letter in possession of the Singer Co., New York.
10 Correspondence in the possession of M. Alain Ollivier.

11 de Cossart, *The Food of Love*, p. 42.
12 'Vinaigrette', in *Quarante Bergères*, by Montesquiou, quoted by de Cossart in *Apollo*, August 1975.
13 'Le Salon de la Princesse Edmond de Polignac', by Horatio, *Figaro*, 6 September 1903.
14 Letter in the possession of M. Alain Ollivier.
15 Letter in the possession of M. Alain Ollivier.
16 Letter in possession of M. Alain Ollivier.
17 Letter in possession of M. Alain Ollivier.
18 de Cossart, op. cit., p. 173.
19 Stein, op. cit., p. 105.

11: To travel hopefully is better ...

1 Acton, op. cit., pp. 171–2.

Bibliography

ACTON, HAROLD, *Memoirs of an Aesthete*, London, Methuen & Co., 1948, reprinted 1970.

ADAMS, HENRY, *The Education of Henry Adams*, Boston and New York, Houghton Mifflin, 1918.

ADAMS, HENRY, *Letters of Henry Adams*, ed. Worthington Chauncey Ford, Cambridge, Mass., Riverside Press; London, Constable & Co., 1930.

ARTHUR, STANLEY CLISBY, *Old Families of Louisiana*, Baton Rouge, Claitor's Publishing Division, 1971.

ASQUITH, LADY CYNTHIA, *Diaries 1915–1918*, London, Hutchinson, 1968.

ASTOR, MICHAEL, *Tribal Feeling*, London, John Murray, 1963.

BALSAN, CONSUELO VANDERBILT, *The Glitter and the Gold*, New York, Harper and Row, 1952.

BOURGET, PAUL, *Outre-Mer*, London, T. Fisher Unwin, 1895.

BRANDON, RUTH, *Singer and the Sewing Machine*, London, Barrie and Jenkins, New York, J. B. Lippincott Co, 1977.

BURNLEY, JAMES, *Millionaires and Kings of Enterprise*, London and Philadelphia, 1901.

CAMPLIN, JAMIE, *The Rise of the Plutocrats*, London, Constable & Co., 1978.

CASTELLANE, BONI DE, *Confessions*, London, 1925.

CHANLER, MARGARET TERRY, *Roman Spring*, New York, Little Brown, 1934.

CHANNON, HENRY, *Chips: The Diaries of Sir Henry Channon*, ed. Robert Rhodes James, London, Weidenfeld and Nicolson, 1967.

CLERMONT-TONNERRE, DUCHESSE ELISABETH DE, *Memoirs*, I *Pomp and Circumstance*, II *Years of Plenty*, London and New York, Jonathan Cape, 1929 and 1932.

COLLIER, PRICE, *England and the English*, London, Duckworth, 1909.

Bibliography

CORELLI, MARIE, *Free Opinions*, London, Constable, 1905.

COSSART, MICHAEL DE, *The Food of Love – Princesse Edmond de Polignac (1865–1943) and her salon*, London, Hamish Hamilton, 1978.

CUNARD, NANCY, *GM:Memories of George Moore*, London, Rupert Hart-Davis, 1956.

ELIOT, ELIZABETH, *Heiresses and Coronets: the story of Lovely Ladies and Noble Men*, New York, McDonnell, Obolensky, 1959.

EMERSON, R. W., *Essays and English Traits*, ed. Howard Mumford Jones, Cambridge, Mass., Belknap Press of Harvard U.P.

FIELDING, DAPHNE, *Emerald and Nancy*, London, Eyre and Spottis-woode, 1968.

FISKE, STEPHEN, *Off-Hand Portraits of Prominent New Yorkers*, New York, Lockwood & Sons, 1884.

HOBHOUSE, JANET, *Everybody who was Anybody – the biography of Gertrude Stein*, London, Weidenfeld and Nicolson, 1975.

HUBER, LEONARD, V., and WILSON, SAMUEL, JR, *Baroness Pontalba's Buildings and the remarkable woman who built them*, New Orleans, Louisiana, 1964.

IRVING, WASHINGTON, *History of New York from the Beginning of the World to the End of the British Dynasty, by Diedrich Knicker-bocker*, edition published 1900, New York, G. P. Putnam and Sons.

JAMES, HENRY, *Daisy Miller, Pandora, The Patagonia and other tales*, New York Edition of Henry James, vol. XVIII, London, Mac-millan Co.; New York, Scribners, 1909.

LESLIE, ANITA, *The Fabulous Leonard Jerome*, London, Hutchinson, 1954.

LESLIE, ANITA, *Jennie*, London, Hutchinson, 1969.

LESLIE, SEYMOUR, *The Jerome Connection*, London, John Murray, 1964.

LEWIS, R. W. B., *Edith Wharton – a biography*, New York, Harper and Row, 1975.

MCALLISTER, WARD, *Society as I have found it*, New York, Cassell Publishing Co., 1890.

MOORE, GEORGE, *Letters to Lady Cunard 1895–1933*, London, Rupert Hart-Davis, 1957.

NICOLSON, NIGEL, *Mary Curzon*, London, Weidenfeld and Nicolson, 1977.

PAINTER, GEORGE, *Marcel Proust*, London, Chatto & Windus, Vol. I, 1959, Vol. II, 1965.

PEACOCK, VIRGINIA TATNALL, *Famous American Belles of the Nine-teenth Century*, Philadelphia and London, Lippincott, 1901.

SACKVILLE-WEST, V., *The Edwardians*, London, Hogarth Press, 1930.

Bibliography

SEEBOLD, HERMAN DE BACHELLÉ, *Old Louisiana Plantation Homes and Family Trees*, Louisiana, privately printed, 1944.

SITWELL, OSBERT, *Great Morning*, London, Macmillan, 1948.

SMALLEY, G. W., *Anglo-American Memories*, London, Duckworth, 1911; second series, London, Duckworth, 1912.

STEAD, W. T., *If Christ Came to Chicago*, London, Review of Reviews, 1894.

STEIN, GERTRUDE, *The Autobiography of Alice B. Toklas*, London, John Lane, 1935.

'STRANGE, MICHAEL' (Blanche Oelrichs), *Who Tells Me True*, New York, Scribners, 1940.

SYKES, CHRISTOPHER, *Nancy: Life of Lady Astor*, London, William Collins Sons and Co., 1972.

TALLANT, ROBERT, *Mardi Gras*, New York, Doubleday, 1948.

Titled Americans: A list of American ladies who have married foreigners of rank, annually revised, issued quarterly. Illustrated with armorial bearings. New York, 1890–1915.

TROLLOPE, FRANCES, *Domestic Manners of the Americans*, reprinted from fifth (1839) edition, London, Geo. Routledge and Sons, 1927.

VANDERBILT, CORNELIUS, JR, *Farewell to Fifth Avenue*, London, Gollancz; New York, Simon and Schuster, 1935.

VANDERBILT, CORNELIUS, JR, *Queen of the Golden Age*, New York, McGraw-Hill, 1956.

VANDERBILT, GLORIA and THELMA, LADY FURNESS, *Double Exposure*, London, Frederick Muller, 1959.

VEBLEN, THORSTEIN, *The Theory of the Leisure Class*, New York, Macmillan, 1899; London, Unwin Books, 1970.

WARWICK, FRANCES, COUNTESS OF, *Afterthoughts*, London, Cassell & Co., 1931.

WHARTON, EDITH, *French Ways and their Meaning*, London, Macmillan, 1919.

WHARTON, EDITH, *A Backward Glance*, New York, 1934; London, Constable and Co. Ltd., 1972.

WHARTON, EDITH, *The Buccaneers*, New York and London, D. Appleton–Century Co., 1938.

WHARTON, EDITH, *The Custom of the Country*, New York and London, D. Appleton–Century Co., 1913.

WICKES, GEORGE, *The Amazon of Letters*, London, W.H. Allen, 1977.

WOLFE, ELSIE DE, *After All*, London, Heinemann, 1970.

WYNDHAM, GEORGE, *Life and Letters*, ed. J. W. MacKail and Guy Wyndham; 2 vols, London, 1935.

ZELDIN, THEODORE, *France 1848–1945*, I, *Ambition, Love and Politics*, Oxford University Press, 1973.

Index

Index

Index

Index

Index

Index